CW00822588

THE PROMISE OF
WOMEN'S BOXING

The Promise of Women's Boxing

A Momentous New Era for the Sweet Science

Malissa Smith

Foreword by
Claressa Shields

ROWMAN & LITTLEFIELD
Lanham • Boulder • New York • London

Published by Rowman & Littlefield
An imprint of The Rowman & Littlefield Publishing Group, Inc.
4501 Forbes Boulevard, Suite 200, Lanham, Maryland 20706
www.rowman.com

86-90 Paul Street, London EC2A 4NE, United Kingdom

British Library Cataloguing in Publication Information Available

Library of Congress Cataloging-in-Publication Data
Names: Smith, Malissa, author.
Title: The promise of women's boxing : a momentous new era for the sweet science / Malissa
    Smith ; foreword by Claressa Shields.
Description: Lanham, MD : Rowman & Littlefield, [2024] | Includes bibliographical references
    and index. | Summary: "The Promise of Women's Boxing details the exciting period from the
    first ever inclusion of women's boxing in the 2012 Olympics through the true 'million-dollar
    baby' women's super-fights of 2022 and beyond. Rich in content, the stories that emerge focus
    on boxing stars, important battles, and the challenges women in boxing still face today"—
    Provided by publisher.
Identifiers: LCCN 2023059042 (print) | LCCN 2023059043 (ebook) | ISBN 9781538177716
    (cloth) | ISBN 9781538177723 (epub)
Subjects: LCSH: Women boxers. | Boxing for women.
Classification: LCC GV1136.3 .S56 2024 (print) | LCC GV1136.3 (ebook) | DDC
    796.83082—dc23/eng/20240123
LC record available at https://lccn.loc.gov/2023059042
LC ebook record available at https://lccn.loc.gov/2023059043

For Jed and Izzi—my rocks, my heart, my everything.

CONTENTS

Contents

Foreword

Claressa Shields

I will never forget walking out of the Olympic stadium in Rio de Janeiro back in August 2016 with a second gold medal around my neck. I had just made history with back-to-back gold medals, exactly what I had come to do, but there was no obvious path forward in women's boxing. I'd accomplished everything I had wanted to do in the amateurs and it would be a long four years until the next Olympics. The pros didn't look so promising, either. Sure, there had been some great fighters like Ann Wolfe, Laila Ali, Christy Martin, and Jacqui Frazier-Lyde, but it had been ten years since any women's fights were on television. The sport had gone dormant. Current female world champions told me they were getting $5,000–$10,000 for purses, and that was for title fights.

I was asking myself the question that this book sets out to answer: what *is* the promise of women's boxing?

That night as I returned to my room at the Olympic Village, I got a text from Heather Hardy, who had just fought Shelly Vincent in Brooklyn and had won. "Congratulations on your victory," she said. "You are doing so much for women's boxing." And then she let me know that her fight, the same day as my second gold medal, also made history. "We were broadcast on the NBC Sports Network!" I took it as a sign. "If she can do it," I thought to myself, "then I can, too."

A few months later, I was ready to sign my first pro contract. I was visiting with Andre Dirrell, the pro boxer from my hometown in Flint. He told me, "Claressa, I've been around boxing for twenty plus years. I know you have these big aspirations, but you're not going to make a million dollars in boxing. You're not going to be able to fight on TV like the men do." And this is somebody who's not a hater of me. In fact, he's a mentor and more like an uncle to me. "It's just not going to happen, even with you being as great as you are." I know he wanted to protect me. I remember looking at him before I signed my contract and I said, "Andre, we will remember this moment."

My first fight was that November with Roc Nation. I fought against Franchon Crews-Dezurn and made $50,000 for my first pro victory. Things went fast from there. When my manager, Mark Taffet, told me my third fight would be the main event on Showtime, I thought it was a hoax. But the day before the fight I was still the main event and I was like, "Wow, it's really happening."

Fast-forward ten years. I got my rematch with the only boxer who I have lost to in the amateurs, Savannah Marshall. We headlined the O2 Arena in London to a sold-out crowd. I got my million-dollar purse.

But even after a sell-out fight in London, I continued to get push-back from networks in the United States. "Your fans can't fill venues at home," they said. Well, this past spring twelve thousand people showed up at Little Caesar's Arena in Detroit to watch me fight. They came from all over Michigan and the Midwest. We even had some UK fans in the house. Then they said, "That was great but you can't sell pay-per-view." But I already had; in March 2021, I was the first female boxer to head-line a pay-per-view fight card since Laila Ali fought Jacqui Frazier-Lyde, twenty years before.

I work my ass off to stay in first place. I want to have more accom-plishments than everybody. If I could go back to the Olympics I would, just to keep breaking records. I want to be undeniable. This is part of my strategy.

The other part of my strategy—and this is just as important—is the promotion part. I work really hard at it. When upcoming boxers ask me how to become visible in this sport, I tell them what I've been doing the past few years.

First, I went on a boxing tour. If any of the greats were fighting, I was there, often on my own dime. I was determined to show my face, talk to fans, take pictures, and be in that atmosphere. I wanted my presence in those rooms to say, "I'm just as accomplished as these male fighters. I belong here."

As a result of this, I grew my fan base to nearly a million followers. Some of these followers will love your story and they will be the ones flying out to a fight. Embrace the haters. Some haters are going to pay money to fly out to see you get your ass kicked. A big following like that makes it harder for the networks to say you can't sell tickets.

Even when you've got the recognition that I have, it's still challenging to control the narrative about you. When I learned that some of my fans were afraid of me, I started showing more vulnerable sides of me. I share my victories and I share my fears and challenges. I want people to know I am a beast but I am not a monster. I'm also well-spoken and pretty and smart. And yes, I am an ambitious woman.

To the girls who are coming up behind me, you don't have to be anything like me. You can be the complete opposite. If you want to be a female boxer who's mean as hell, embrace it. If you want to be really feminine, embrace that. There is room for all of us.

Boxing has grown so much in the past ten years. Girls are getting stronger and faster. Today there are so many great fighters with great stories, and you will read about their challenges and triumphs in the pages to come. There's Katie Taylor who dressed like a boy to train in Ireland, Amanda Serrano, Franchon Cruz-Dezurn, Mikaela Mayer, Seniesa Estrada, Alicia Baumgartner, Ebanie Bridges, Natasha Jonas, Chantelle Cameron, Caroline Dubois, Savannah Marshall, and so many others. And then there are people behind the scenes like Christie Halbert who I will forever be grateful to for her role in helping women get a shot at the Olympics. Every movement needs a historian. Malissa Smith has chronicled our stories, our love of the sport, and our fight for equality in her first book and now in this one you are holding.

We have fulfilled many promises—and yet there are more to be filled: more fairness, more equity, more opportunities to showcase our greatness. We need three-minute rounds, like they do in the amateurs. Amanda Serrano's recent unification three-minute, twelve-rounder bout was another first and we need to build on that momentum.

We could do a lot more if we were more of a community. I would love to see us go to each other's fights and bring our fans to each other's attention. All of us who are boxing now had someone open a door for us. We need to do the same for the next generation of girls so they get to express themselves in the ring like we have.

The next ten years will probably see my retirement. Before that happens, I would love to see a girl who fights better than me. I look forward to the comparisons to me. I will say, "Cool. I'm glad that y'all look at her in such a light because that's important that we carry on like that." And when that time comes, it will bring me a lot of joy to give her my blessing.

ACKNOWLEDGMENTS

My journey through boxing has had a long arc. I have been a fan since childhood, finally getting up the nerve to learn the rudiments of the sport under the tutelage of several very forgiving trainers at Brooklyn's Gleason's Gym beginning in the late 1990s. It is there that I began to meet women who boxed in the amateurs and as professionals. I followed along in their careers, observing Melissa Hernandez and Belinda Laracuente going through their paces, along with such champions as Alicia Ashley, Sonya Lamonakis, Heather Hardy, Ronica Jeffries, Melissa St. Vil, and Alicia Napoleon, among the many others who passed through Gleason's.

Those observations and relationships led me to my academic interest in women's boxing as I pursued a master's degree in liberal studies. With that in hand, I had the deep honor to write *A History of Women's Boxing*, the first comprehensive history of the sport *The Ring* magazine dubbed "The Bible of Women's Boxing."

Since its publication, I have become an advocate for women's boxing. I have formal relationships with the International Women's Boxing Hall of Fame, *The Ring*'s women's ratings team, and the International Boxing Hall of Fame, all of which have been enormously gratifying and have given me the opportunity to deepen my commitment to the sport. I also write frequently about women's boxing and appear with regularity on podcasts based in the United States as well as the United Kingdom. Through all these endeavors, I feel enormously humbled by women who box and look upon my small part in amplifying their stories as a labor of love and one I feel proud to support.

The great thing is that I have never been alone in these pursuits—and must note as a first order of business my enormous indebtedness to Christen Karniski, Executive Acquisitions Editor, Sports and Recreation, at Rowman & Littlefield. She was my absolute rock seeing me through my first published work, *A History of Women's Boxing.* Writing a book for the first time through was enormously challenging—as can be imagined. Without Christen's patience, gentle prodding, and superb editing skills, I would never have gotten through it.

I also have Christen to thank for pushing me to write this second book, *The Promise of Women's Boxing.* She quite rightly recognized that the growth the sport has seen since the introduction of women's boxing at the 2012 London Games deserved an in-depth examination. I am grateful to her for offering me the opportunity to write it—and for her continued patience, prodding, and recognition that I suffer from run-on sentence syndrome! All of the members of her team have been enormously helpful, especially Cameron Hipps and Samantha Delwarte, and I could not have completed this project without their support.

I want to also acknowledge my debt of gratitude to two-time gold medalist and three-time undisputed boxer Claressa Shields for her generosity in agreeing to write the foreword. She has shared her personal commitment to the sport, and her message of unity is an important one. As with most things in boxing, she was not alone in her endeavors, and I want to particularly thank Sue Jaye Johnson for her wonderful assistance with the foreword.

My rocks and stalwarts in my boxing world are perhaps too numerous to mention, but as a start, with most humble appreciation, I would be nowhere in my advocacy work for women's boxing without these dear people: Sue Fox, Amy Green, Terri Moss, Wanda Countiss, Eddie Montalvo, Jimmy Finn, Bruce Silverglade, Mark Jones, Thomas Gerbasi, David A. Avila, Andrea Smith, Suzy McMeeking, Sasha Jones, Dr. Sarah Crews, Dr. Cathy Van Ingen, Blanca Gutiérrez, Diego Morilla, Yesica Palmeti, Irene Desserti, Lupi Beagle, Sue Jaye Johnson, Sarah Deming, Eddie Goldman, Chris Baldwin, Jill Diamond, Alicia Ashley, Marq Piocos, Sheila Oviedo, Christopher Benedict, Marian Trimiar, Jill Morley, Bonnie Mann, my Gleason's Gym trainers Lennox Blackmoore and Don

Saxby, and the late boxing journalist Michael O'Neill, whose commitment to women in the sport was unparalleled.

No book is ever written alone, and for support of my writing efforts, I would be nowhere without Izzi Stevenson, Jed Stevenson, Kirk B. Smith, Tamar Smith, Achim Nowak, Patti Claflin, Nadia Jaber, Vincenta Papas, and fellow Dollbaby writing retreat members, Terri-Lynne DeFino, Diana Muñoz Stewart, Cal Primer, Karin Gastriech, Erin Turbitt, Rebecca Mullen, Sara Silver Cohen, Mary Daly, Kelly Ramsdell, Stephanie Averill Benboe, Jennifer Weise, and Nancy Caronia. I'd be remiss if I did not mention the fabulous Cobble Hill Brooklyn location of the One Girl Cookies café and owners Dawn Casale and Dave Crofton, whose comfortable seating, perfect Wi-Fi, smooth running power, and yummy treats kept me going for many a writing afternoon.

I am also indebted to the boxers, promoters, managers, and other denizens of the boxing world who were so incredibly generous of their time and without whom this book could never have been written to include: Mark Taffet, Claressa Shields, Sue Jaye Johnson, Sue Fox, Lou DiBella, Jill Diamond, Diego Morillo, Yesica Palmetta, Irene Deserti, Yuriko Miyata Nishiwaki, Heather Hardy, Sonya Lamonakis, Corey Erdman, Terri Harper, Andrew "Stefy Bull" Bulcroft, Sue Fox, Kath Woodward, Sarah Crews, Blanca Gutiérrez, Thomas Gerbasi, Ed Brophy, Brooke Millbrook, Melissa McMorrow, Shelly Vincent, and Christy Martin.

This book also would not be complete without the generous support of photographers who have so kindly agreed to allow me to use their work: Mary Ann Owen, Jim Diamond Photographer, Terrell Groggins/My Art My Rules, and Rakeem Noble.

With all the help I have received, I must be very clear in noting that the content is my own, including the selections of topics and the perspectives I have presented. I have worked hard to include a representative overview of the period covered in the book. That has meant that I have focused on boxing stories and historical points along the way that I felt added to a greater understanding of women's boxing. I recognize that there are people and events that I have not included, particularly boxers who have turned professional in the last couple of years such as Caroline

Dubois, Sandy Ryan, and 2020 British gold medalist Lauren Price. My intent has assuredly not been to slight anyone; rather, I have done my best to encompass the whole to include the challenges many women continue to face. Checking the veracity and accuracy has also been an important feature of the work, and any errors are my own.

Most of all, this book could not exist without the incredible women of the ring whose remarkable skills, heart, and love of their sport makes all things possible.

ACRONYMS AND ABBREVIATIONS

AAU   American Amateur Association
AIBA   International Amateur Boxing Association (through 2020,
            see IBA)
BBBC   British Boxing Board of Control
BWAA   Boxing Writers Association of American
GBU   Global Boxing Union
IBA   International Boxing Association (replaced AIBA in 2020)
IBC   International Boxing Council
IBF   International Boxing Federation
IBHOF   International Boxing Hall of Fame
IBO   International Boxing Organisation
IBU   Irish Boxing Union
IFBA   International Female Boxing Association
IWBA   International Women's Boxing Association
IWBF   International Women's Boxing Federation
IWBHF   International Women's Boxing Hall of Fame
IWPHA   International Women's Professional Boxing Association
JWBC   Japan Women's Boxing Commission
LCC   London County Council
MMA   Mixed Martial Arts
NAC   Nevada Athletic Commission
NBA   National Boxing Association
NWA   National Wrestling Association
NYSAC   New York State Athletic Commission
PAL   Police Athletic League
Team GB   Team Great Britain

TKO	Technical Knock Out
UFC	Ultimate Fighting Championship
USABA	USA Boxing Association
WBAN	Women's Boxing Archive Network
WBA	World Boxing Association
WBC	World Boxing Council
WBF	World Boxing Federation
WBO	World Boxing Organization
WIBA	Women's International Boxing Association
WIBF	Women's International Boxing Federation
WIBO	Women's International Boxing Organization

Introduction

With her undisputed lightweight title belts on the line, the 2012 lightweight Olympic gold medalist, Katie Taylor, entered the main arena at Madison Square Garden to the slow-moving song, "Awake My Soul." In counterpoint to the loud, undulating crowd of eager, cheering fans, she took in the moment as her opponent, the seven-weight class champion, Amanda Serrano, continued to dance around the ring in expectant excitement.

The first boxing super-fight of the era, headlined by two women in Madison Square Garden's arena, lived up to its hype and then some on the magical night of April 30, 2022. The two contestants fought the battle of their lives in front of a sold-out crowd. As reported by the DAZN Boxing streaming service, it also had 1.5 million viewers, purportedly the largest number of viewers in history for a women's boxing event until that time.

Barely six months later, Claressa Shields, the two-time middleweight Olympic gold medalist in the London 2012 Games and Rio 2016 Games, started her ring walk at London's O2 Arena. She performed a hip-hop dance number in red, white, and blue boxing shorts, an homage to Apollo Creed, the fictional character of the *Rocky* franchise of films. Smiling broadly, she expertly executed her moves backed by two dancers. In the ring, her opponent, Savannah Marshall, a 12–0 professional fighter who had the distinction of being the only person ever to have defeated Shields, back in 2012 when they competed as amateurs at the women's world tournament, moved coolly about the ring.

Shields and Marshall were fighting at the head of an unprecedented all-female eleven-fight card in front of the sold-out crowd of twenty thousand adoring fans. Broadcast worldwide on Britain's Sky Sports to over 150 countries and in the United States on the ESPN+ streaming service, the promoter for the event, BOXXER announced an astounding two million plus viewers.

The Taylor–Serrano and Marshall–Shields cards are in a direct lineage to women's boxing's first ever inclusion in the Olympics at the London Games of 2012. In the games, women demonstrated an elite level of skills on par with their male counterparts in a sport that had otherwise excluded them from amateur athletic competition as little as ten years before in some nations. As a demarcation point, however, that standard of excellence was a gauntlet in the long, three-century arc of women's boxing history. A history fraught with highs and lows, periods of absences and flurries of participation and interest, and always imbued with the heart and great promise of the women who fought.

Women have been boxing as prize fighters since the 1720s. They most famously contested the sport in London at Figg's Amphitheater also known as the Boarded House, near the old Oxford Road and at Hockley in the Hole in Clerkenwell Green, a stalwart of sport and gaming in Georgian England. To the roars, cheers, and jeers of the crowds, fighters such as the so-called City Championess, Elizabeth Wilkinson Stokes; Hannah Hyfield; Ann Field; and Mary Welch, among others fought for upward of three-guinea prize money while holding half a crown in each hand: ". . . the first woman that drops the money to lose the battle."[1]

Very little of these stories of bravery and gumption come down to us today. As noted by historian Christopher Thrasher, "We forgot Wilkinson not because of her failures, but because of ours. We sacrificed truthful recollection on the altar of cultural expediency."[2]

In other words, as the sport has evolved and grown, boxing is and for long stretches has remained a gendered male-only sport, with the evidence of continuous female participation forgotten from one era to the next. Each such resurgence has therefore become a seeming first across the span of three hundred years of women contesting in the sport.

Still, through historical works such as Pierce Egan's *Boxiana: or, Sketches of ancient and modern pugilism,* published in 1830, the fact of women contesting in the sport has been passed on, as have numerous references in books, songs, and pamphlets, and through the press. In our more modern era, that has also meant the popular culture vehicles of magazines, film, and television, and finally contemporaneously, online streaming services, and social media.

FIRST GREAT WAVE: VICTORIAN LADIES TAKE UP THE GLOVES

The first wave of women's boxing in the United States was inspired by the thirst for entertainment found in Variety Theater. This progenitor of Vaudeville consisted of several shows a day filled with acts from singers to dramatic readings by famous people of the day, to animal acts and exhibitions of physical culture. This latter category began to show such feats as pedestrianism (running a mile on stage in under eight minutes to win a prize), weightlifting, and novel presentations of sword fighting as the first part of an act that featured boxing in the finale—an homage of sorts to the first British prize fighting contests in the early 1700s that were contested with cudgels and fists.

One such act seemingly legitimized the idea of female fisti-cuffs: Madame and Monsieur D'Omer, from France (although likely a pair of British performers). They were first seen at New York's Park Theater in 1874. While their show initially relied on a "death-defying sword act to enthusiastic crowds,"[3] the next part of their show featured Msr. D'Omer shooting an arrow through his wife's head. It was Mlle. D'Omer's skill as a boxer, however, that attracted even greater attention from the audience. As a press account in the *New York Clipper* stated, "This portion of their entertainment has no objectionable features, and enables ladies to gain an insight into the manner in which professional 'mills' are conducted without having their sensibilities shocked."[4]

At return engagements, the pair refined their act to feature boxing and began to bill Mlle. D'Omer as "The Lady Athlete and only Female Boxer in the World." A *New York Sun* review of their offering in February 1876 exemplified the acceptance of her prowess, noting, "her position in sparring is graceful, and every blow is given with judgement"; moreover, she "pummeled the Monsieur so scientifically and effectually that he, panting for breath bowed to the audience saying: "That's my first defeat in a while!"[5]

The D'Omer act no doubt inspired the bon vivant owner of Harry Hill's Variety Theater to make a fateful decision. A notorious destination, it joined the infamous night life on the Bowery in New York City's mid-1800s with offerings that spanned from dancing girls to African American minstrel shows, and importantly became a venue for sparring matches to entertain both its highbrow and lowbrow customers.

Ever the impresario, Harry Hill's sparring shows proved particularly popular and ushered in an era of actual prize fights on his premises beginning in the 1870s. They also afforded him the chance to expand his boxing empire, and with a showman's touch for what the crowds would clamor for, he staged the first acknowledged boxing match between two women in America (although there had been earlier ones).

We cannot know what was going through the minds of Nell Saunders and Rose Harland when they famously took up the gloves on the fateful afternoon of March 17, 1876, for their "main-event" three-round bout. They had, however, been given a modicum of training, a few weeks at least, and witnesses stated they appeared excited by the prospect. Varying reports also noted the winner was offered a prize of $200 and the loser, a silver-plated butter dish.

The pair had also reportedly acquitted themselves with "science," which added to the legitimacy of the fight. The *New York Herald* noted that the two women "display[ed] considerably more science than some of the male novices that infrequently box before the public."[6] They also reported that Saunders was given the nod for the butter dish, though the *New York Times*[7] noted that she had won $200 in cash, with Harland receiving a $10 bill from one of the customers.

The true winner was women's fisticuffs, as the fight portended the start of an entire era of boxing beginning with Harry Hill's nightly entertainments, which even featured African American female fight nights. As soon as the following year, Rose Harland along with other alumna of Harry Hill's began to perform in venues along the entertainment circuits, and by the early 1880s, the highly popular female pugilism shows were performed as far away as California.

Harry Hill also teamed up with Richard K. Fox, who'd bought the infamous *National Police Gazette* in 1876. Renowned for its lurid headlines and their accompanying prurient etchings, Hill and Fox together began to promote both men's and women's boxing. Such female pugilists as Hattie Stewart, the "female John L. Sullivan" and champion woman heavyweight; Hattie Lewis, the first female world boxing champion; and Libby Kelly, noted as the first female champion boxer were among those touted in the *Police Gazette* as important figures in boxing in the 1880s.

The notoriety also helped fuel the popularity of female pugilism on Variety Theater stages worldwide. The boxing shows spread as far afield as the British stage and in such places as Canada and Australia, as well as inroads toward the end of the 1890s into Continental Europe. The popularity led to the development of boxing fitness programs across the United States becoming acceptable, if controversial, with one entrepreneur going so far as to create pneumatic gloves that made sparring "safer" for women. The brutality of boxing, however, could not be denied, especially in the era of bare-knuckle performances, and while the sport remained an element of popular culture, as controversial as it was for men, it was even more so for women.

The waning of the Victorian era saw a renewed interest in the expression of physical culture for men and women, of which boxing, while at its periphery, did play a part. This fin-de-siècle sea change as represented by the return of the Olympic Games in 1896 was both a clarion call to the Greco-Roman ideals of physicality and an expression of the "new man" and "new woman" that had captivated the age.

In many ways, boxing optimized the renewed pursuit of physicality as one of rugged individualism and the personification of physical strength, even for women. And while the sport did not appear in the first two Olympic Games, men and women performed in exhibition boxing events at the St. Louis Exhibition and Games of 1904.

For women, this also meant less restrictive clothing, an atmosphere of relative freedom as women rode their bicycles with abandon, and a progressive attitude toward women's pursuits including physical culture. In America, it was an era of female journalism, with the likes of Nelly Bly; so-called "Gibson" girls, who pursued careers in business; and even spectatorship at boxing events, most famously the March 1897 "Gentle-man" Jim Corbett versus Robert Fitzsimmons prizefight, held in Carson City, Nevada, and at subsequent film showings of the fight a couple of months later.

In the United Kingdom, the resurgence of the popularity of boxing created a star of sorts in Polly Fairclough (later Polly Burns), who became a fixture at fairgrounds boxing events that toured England. Much as on the American variety theater stages, members of the audience were invited to fight four rounds for the chance to win cash prizes and the bragging rights for having defeated Fairclough. She was also variously hailed as the lady boxer champion of the world with a roster of winning championship bouts. While actual championship bouts were apocryphal at best, her continued notoriety till her death in 1959 proved an alluring detail of history that came into public consciousness from time to time, despite the seeming absence of women's boxing stories as being worthy of news coverage or consideration.

THE NEW CENTURY

Abounding in electric lights and the hopeful brilliance of a new century, American women had a right to feel optimistic about their place in the world. For the women of the ring, however, the optimism generated by putting on an exhibition at the St. Louis Exhibition of 1904 was short-lived. Women's boxing was not added to the roster of sports for the 1908 Olympic Games while men's boxing was, and closer to home in the United States, women continued to be excluded from amateur boxing under the auspices of the American Amateur Association (AAU).[8]

There was also a decided "sea change" in attitude toward women in sports, as the progressive spirt that saw women participate in a variety of individual and team athletic pursuits was dampened by innuendo both explicit and implicit. Aside from notions that women were getting too much freedom to the detriment of their duties as wives and mothers, the discourse was also tinged with notions that such sports promoted unhealthy sexual freedoms and inwardness—a euphemism for lesbianism.

Women's boxing, however, persisted with such figures as Texas Mamie, Ellen Devine, Flora Ryan, and Goldie O'Rourke, an English championess fighting in the early 1900s to some notoriety, and with continued press coverage. In this period, as well, the United States was undergoing what one reporter referred to as the "jiu-jitsu craze." Deemed as fitness and self-defense, it was seemingly a more acceptable form of physical culture than boxing and had pride of place in early film newsreels and exhibitions. Not to be outdone, Texas Mamie herself was reported to have begun teaching self-defense as part of the noble art of boxing in New York City.

The depth of the participation of women in the sport can also be garnered from the April 1912 newspaper coverage of a boxing match in Michigan. Myrtle Havers, nineteen of Flint, Michigan, fought in what was billed as the girl's championship of Michigan knocking out Mabel Williams, twenty-two, of Grand Rapids, renowned as the best female boxer in the state for several years. They were reported to have fought with "eight-ounce gloves and under straight Marquis of Queensbury rules."[9]

While there is not a lot on record, per se, of Michigan's women's boxing history or how such bouts were managed, the newspaper coverage that was picked up across the nation reveals how boxing had become a sport women practiced competitively—and given its ready acceptance in the press, it is fair to surmise that there were other pockets of this type of competition across the United States.

Boxing for women did have a decidedly international cast. With World War I dawning, the Lady Boxers troop gained good notices, with such fighters as Newcastle's Nicol Brady and a Belgian boxing talent, Alice Fleury. The French boxing star, Mlle. Marthe Carpentier, appeared with the troop as well. She otherwise garnered notoriety in the world press, not all of it positive, when she knocked out an English fighter named Mrs. Lucie Warner in the fourth round at a Paris venue.[10] With that touch of infamy on her side, an attempt was made to put on a female card in Paris the following month only to be dashed by H. Hennion, the prefect of police, "on the ground it would foster brutality among women."[11]

Despite public denunciations of female pugilism, during World War I, women were considered an acceptable "replacement" talent for male

7

boxers following their calls of duty at the front, with one newspaper going so far as to advertise for female boxers.[12]

Women also began to make inroads in the sport outside of the ring as exuberant cheering fans at boxing shows, with headlines proclaiming the phenomenon with one newspaper publishing an article in 1914 under the banner, "Prize Fighting Becoming a Favorite Pastime for Women."[13]

Riding the popularity of early self-defense and the notion that with a war on, women were on their own, such self-styled boxers and physical fitness experts as Vera Roehm began to have a place in promulgating the idea that boxing skills were an ideal way for women to defend themselves. Roehm famously worked on a short entitled *The Womanly Art of Self-Defense*. The film, listed as a two-reel educational film, was distributed in 1917 by Paramount-Bray and was disseminated widely.

The business side of the sport saw female participation as well. Famously, Elizabeth Tucker, a Cherokee woman, became a boxing manager and trainer for her twin pugilist brother, Lonnie Tucker, a featherweight, as well as her younger brother, Frank Tucker. She herself gained notoriety in a series of articles she penned in 1917 and was billed as "the only woman boxing manager in the world."[14]

THE INTERWAR YEARS

The upheaval and trauma of the World War I and its loosened boundaries for gender were hard to put back into the bottle, so to speak. Hemlines went up just as women's hair was chopped short into fashionable bobs. Women smoked and drank, legally and otherwise, and took to wearing pants as a fashion statement. They also became fixtures at ringsides as exemplified by Mae West, who patronized the fights on a regular basis after she moved to Hollywood in the early 1930s.

Writers from Djuna Barnes to Ernest Hemingway penned journalistic pieces on women at the fights—with Barnes teasing out the phenomenon as riding the wave of further feminine emancipation from the strictures of the prewar world, including the notion of women overtly ogling half-naked men in the ring. Even the Manassa Mauler himself, heavyweight champion Jack Dempsey, supported women as audience members and felt it would be good for the sport.

Dempsey also supported women who boxed, stating, "Women are beginning—as they should—to take up boxing seriously as they take up swimming, riding and other athletics. It is all the working out of the theory that a sound body and a sound mind travel together."[15]

As boxing fitness and boxing as self-defense for women gained traction again, it also began to appear in films. The 1927 silent film *Rough House Rosie*, starring Clara Bow, was a case in point. She played a showgirl who is set upon by a masher boyfriend and socks him in the jaw. Bow also had a nightclub number where she and her fellow dancers wear boxing gloves and is also seen at ringside, supporting her new boxer boyfriend. The screenplay had been based on a short story by Nunnally Johnson that appeared in the *Saturday Evening Post*. The film itself is lost, but the plucky character of Rosie remains on the existing fragments of film. The German film *The Fighting Lady*, also produced in 1927, provided a more serious treatment of the subject, with the main character taking up boxing after being mugged in the park. Her boyfriend feels threatened by her ability to take care of herself, and after an argument, she storms out and takes a walk in the same park. A would-be mugger comes upon her, but she lays him out flat with three swift blows. Her boyfriend, who had surreptitiously followed her, comes upon the scene. He takes pride in her abilities and helps her drag the mugger to the police, basking in the subsequent newspaper headlines.

Women also continued to box. American fighters such as Jeanne Lamar (also Jeanne La Mar), Mae Devoreaux, Vera Roehm, Princess Pat Henry (married to the boxer Prince Henry), Kiddy McCue (of St. Paul), Laura Bennett, and Gertrude Allison had a place in the intersection of boxing and fitness. They were joined by Annie Newton and France's Mlle. Gonraud.

The African American entertainers Emma Chambers Maitland and Aurelia Wheeldin billed themselves as champion boxers during the 1920s and 1930s on the Variety Theater circuit in the United States and Europe. In 1928, an article entitled "Wields Wicked Left" published in the black-owned newspaper the *Pittsburgh Courier* stated, "Maitland was heading to Cuba to box and that she had just returned from a 'successful ring siege in Mexico.'"

The article went on to state, "The powerful left hand of Miss Maitland has helped her win bouts."[16]

As a coda to Maitland's efforts, the pair also famously put on an exhibition match at the New York Golden Gloves in April 1934, a much-lauded event.

The remaining footprints of female boxing as a serious pursuit that crossed continents are faint, but there are traces, whether as fighters or in roles that supported the sport. Belle Martell owns pride of place as California's first female ring announcer, amateur fight promoter, and timekeeper. A revered figure in the Los Angeles area, she was to become the state's (and very likely the United States') first licensed female referee. Unfortunately, her appearances in her latter role were not without controversy. After only a few weeks as a referee, she was effectively removed from her position when the state of California Athletic Commission issued Rule 256, stating, "No license will be granted to members of the female sex to referee, second or manage in the ring when other performers are of the opposite sex." Given there were no licensed female boxers, she had the title but no opportunity to practice her well-honed skills.[17]

Still, women were persevering in the sport on a variety of fronts in popular culture. As America entered World War II, images of Wonder Woman punching Nazis were a feature in panels from the popular comic published bimonthly during the war.[18]

The first Dixie Dugan comic book published in 1942 features her in a boxing ring knocking back a boxer with a left jab. The caption reads, "Wow! Too bad that ain't Hitler's chin!"[19]

Such images and constructs recalled the greater acceptance of women "performing" men's roles during World War I, including in boxing. And despite the setbacks experienced by Belle Martell in her pioneering efforts in the ring, women such as Pennsylvania's Helen Zivic (the wife of fighter Fritzie Zivic); Juanita Yeargain, the "First Lady of Boxing" in Topeka, Kansas; and California's Aileen Eaton were entering the field as boxing promoters with some success.[20] And, of course, women continued to box in whatever spaces they could find.

WOMEN, BOXING, AND THE ERAS OF CHANGE

If the war years had taught women anything, it was that they were on their own despite whatever entreaties they heard to the contrary. And if 1950s America heralded an era of compliant young wives and mothers who would willingly isolate themselves in suburban tract housing in pursuit of the American dream, the reality was something quite different.

Yes, there were red scares and the rising existential fear of the atomic age, but these concerns were accompanied with the rise of social justice and independence movements all over the world. Whether in the rise of the Labour Party in the United Kingdom; Communist and Socialist parties across Europe; independence movements across Asia, Africa, and South America; or America's rising civil rights consciousness, the upheaval of the second world war had planted seeds of profound change.

As the 1950s unfolded, however, attempts to enforce the strictures of gender "normative" behaviors were in evidence. Women in America and the UK who'd found meaningful work and a sense of empowerment during the war found those positions stripped away to make room for the "boys" who'd been decommissioned from the military after the war. For the wives, daughters, and sisters of these returning men, this meant being relegated back to "pink" jobs in offices or service work, if they could find work at all, along with the appeals to stay at home to raise their babies.

For the young single women, who'd lived through the Great Depression and were honed by war, their "normal" was something slightly different. No Jazz Age awaited them, but it was an era when women pushed against the strictures that confined them. The ultimate push against the boundaries of the gender binary was boxing itself. Long a bastion of hypermasculinity, women made remarkable progress by the end of the 1970s when professional women's boxing in America became a fact of life.

The most tenacious woman to fight in this early period was Barbara Buttrick. At 4'11" tall, the self-proclaimed "Mighty Atom of the Ring" and alternatively "Battling Barbara" became a phenomenon in the United Kingdom when she came down from her home in Yorkshire to London to take up the sport. Buttrick became an aficionado of boxing after reading an article about the famous fairground's boxer, Polly Fairclough

(Polly Burns). Inspired by what she read, she decided there and then to become a boxer and began training herself in her backyard.

Turning eighteen, Buttrick headed to London in early 1948 to begin training at Micky Woods's Mayfair Gymnasium. Under the tutelage of her trainer (and eventual husband), Len Smith, Buttrick's hard work and growing skill came to the attention of the gym's owner. Woods, in turn, signed her as a "tough girl" and launched a media campaign that brought her notoriety and positive press from as far away as Australia. Buttrick's prominence also spurred on other women, including Cath Thomas, who had the temerity to put on an exhibition bout at a venue outside of Sydney, Australia, to the consternation of local authorities who banned her from "giving public performances in New South Wales."[21]

Buttrick herself was banned from putting on an exhibition bout with a male boxer by the British Board of Boxing Control (BBBC). In the best tradition of the "show must go on," Buttrick alighted on the stage at the "main event" and performed solo on a series of apparatuses, ending the evening in a glow of green light as she shadowboxed—an homage of sorts to the women who'd performed similar acts on stages all around the world.

Unable to move the BBBC to reverse its ban of female boxing, starting in 1949 Buttrick signed on with a succession of traveling fairgrounds boxing tent shows that played the countryside across England and in 1952 across France. As with her boxing heroine, Polly Fairclough, Buttrick boxed all comers, male or female, in her catchment weight, and even had some "official" bouts (though unlicensed) with other women who had actual boxing skills.

In the United States, a small pocket of women began to box in the same period. Wrestling had become popular, and the public's appetite for the sport included an acceptance of female battles and even mixed male and female tag teams. The wrestling cards left open opportunities to "sneak" in a female boxing bout—often between two wrestlers, but also nonwrestlers. The popularity of these shows provided space for such fights on the circuit of small-town venues where such shows played. Boxers such as Jo Ann Hagen from South Bend, Indiana, who was trained and managed by Johnny Nate, a former Golden Gloves champion who developed a stable of female fighters, were prominent. Other fighters included Pat Emerick, Phyllis Kugler, and Audrey Burrows.

Through the early 1950s, women fought and won praise for their skills and tenacity. Buttrick herself came to America following her sojourn across France, and both boxed and wrestled to keep in the game. By 1954, Buttrick had begun to make a name for herself, and won the opportunity to battle Jo Ann Hagen in Calgary, Canada. At 5'7", Hagen towered over Buttrick and easily won; however, Buttrick's come-forward style and excellent defensive skills left her unmarred. Most notably, the fight was the first female bout to be broadcast from coast to coast on Canadian radio and garnered impressive notices in the press.

While still often one step ahead of sheriff's deputies who shut down venues, and with the AAU still vehemently opposed to including women in their amateur ranks, these intrepid fighters continued to press the boundaries of acceptance.

Hagen and Kugler for their part made public appearances at local promotional events and both were guests on the nationally broadcast *Steve Allen Show* ahead of their showdown bout in late 1956. The following year, Buttrick and Kugler became the first women to be professionally licensed in the state of Texas by the Commission of Labor. They fought in San Antonio, a boxing town, and Buttrick was singled out in the press for her "sharp left jab and grim determination as she forced the fight with her outclassed opponent. . . ."[22]

Despite terrific notices, the fight card was poorly attended, and the second show that had been promised was canceled due to the sudden imposition of a weight class discrepancy between the two fighters. Buttrick was considerably lighter, but despite her having soundly won, the fight was canceled, and it would seem no other professional bouts between two women were held in Texas for many years to come.

The early 1960s seemed to have even less apparent women's boxing activity than the early 1950s, though women such as Aileen Eaton and Belle Martell continued to find success as fight promoters. Wrestling remained active and popular especially on the small venue circuit, and whereas boxing cards featuring women became harder to find, boxing special features were added to wrestling cards. Wrestlers such as Jean

Antone and Kay Noble, known wrestling rivals, also famously boxed on cards beginning with their first boxing in January 1965—which led to a third-round victory knockout for Noble.

A fight in October of the same in 1965 was covered under the headline of "'Boxing' Fem Rasslers Shine," and went on to describe how Antone went down in the third round from a knockout.[23]

Other fighters on this circuit included wrestlers Betty Niccoli and Rhonda Jean, but as for nonwrestling boxers, the South Bend fighters had all stopped boxing and there were few fights that garnered enough information to be reported in the press in this era.

While women in boxing may have been dormant, the period saw a renewed effort to question the status quo in the United States for prohibitions against women earning a living as professional wrestlers and boxers, spurred on by the burgeoning second wave feminism that was gaining momentum in the late 1960s. President Lyndon B. Johnson's signature "on Executive Order 11375 in the fall of 1967, expanding a 1965 order that prohibited sex-based discrimination in federal employment and by contractors working for the federal government" was all crucial to these efforts.[24] The net effect of the act was to create a climate of equal employment, and while it did not pertain to state athletic commissions, per se, the sea change in federal statutes began to filter down to state and municipal organizations.

The wrestler and sometime boxer Betty Niccoli, for one, challenged New York State's law prohibiting the licensing of female practitioners in October 1970. Widely reported in the press, the record on the review of her case by the Commission has been lost, but the ban on women's wrestling was eventually overturned in the spring of 1972.[25] The ban on professional women's boxing licensure, however, remained in place in New York State until Cathy "Cat" Davis successfully sued to overturn rule number 205.15 in 1977. Davis, along with Jackie Tonawanda Garrett (who'd initially challenged the state's licensing rules for professional licensing in 1974 and won a court case in 1975) and Marian "Lady Tyger" Trimiar, became the first three licensed female professional boxers in New York State.

Caroline Svendsen met with better success when she applied for a license to box from the Nevada State Athletic Commission (NAC) in July 1975. Svendsen was quickly granted a license and once her opponent, Connie Costello, was approved, they were granted the right to fight a four-round exhibition bout—acceding to the NAC's last-minute jitters about hosting the first legally sanctioned bout in Nevada. With everything set, a new issue arose when Costello, watching Svendsen spar during fight week, pulled out allegedly because she felt Svendsen was too good for her. Whatever the reason, a new fighter, Jean Lange, an erstwhile boxer and wrestler, agreed to the bout—which she lost by KO in the first round, in front of a sizable crowd of twelve hundred people.[26]

The first "trickle" of professionally licensed female boxers may have seemed a bit slow to the women who clamored to box, but by 1979 the popularity of the sport saw a plethora of all-women's bout cards in California and Nevada, along with occasional televised contests. On one such card, held in February 1979, Marian "Lady Tyger" Trimiar fought Carlotta Lee at the head of a six-bout card in Hawthorne, California. Cora Webber, Zebra Girl Tucker, and Toni Lear Rodriguez, among others, were on the undercard, all of whom were true pioneers in the sport. At the vanguard of women's boxing, these fighters and others became champions for newly formed sanctioning bodies such as the Women's World Boxing Association (WWBA). Other important fighters of the era were Yvonne Barkley (older sister of former champion Iran Barkley), Gwen Gemini, Sue Carlson, Sue TL Fox, Theresa Kibby, Lavonne Ludian, the Canadian fighter Brit Van Buskirk, and Dora Webber (Cora's twin sister).

Boxing does have its controversies, and the sport's first "golden girl"—Cathy "Cat" Collins, who'd even been the first woman to grace the cover of boxing's premiere magazine, *The Ring*—was at the epicenter of it. Newspaper reporter Jack Newfield had penned an article in 1978 claiming that Collins and her manager, Sal Algieri, had padded her record "using phony names for fights" and paying fighters to take a dive.[27] Collins's career was to suffer, and she eventually left boxing entirely, even though she'd been the subject of a 1979 documentary on Public Television.

Replete with their own controversies, when it came to amateur boxing, the AAU was still a hard "no" to allowing women to participate in amateur contests. This meant the women who wanted to fight had only one vehicle—taking the skills they learned in the gym straight into the professional arena. As a result, the press and others often grabbed a hold of the less prepared as a reason to belittle all women who boxed.

One way to close out the era was the image of the singer and actress Barbra Streisand sporting boxing gloves for her film *The Main Event*. In her unlikely comedic star turn, she played a boxing manager for her fighter, Ryan O'Neill. Sure, it was played for laughs. But it did make a statement about how far women had come vis-à-vis perceptions of their place in the exclusive male-only domain of boxing.

FROM TOUGH WOMAN CONTESTS TO PAY-PER-VIEW

The era of the 1980s and 1990s saw huge changes in the sport. Women who boxed were making inroads in the sport, and as the 1980s began, there were over twenty-five licensed boxers in the state of California alone. Promoters who were meeting success were also looking beyond California and Nevada. Vern Stevenson, who'd met with some success and was at the head of the WWBA, looked to Miami as a new locale. He was assisted by Barbara Buttrick, who though retired from fighting for nearly twenty years, was eager to jump in to help grow the sport. Their eagerness, however, was not met with the kind of success they'd hoped for as women's fighting opportunities sputtered across the 1980s.

The fact of women in boxing rings, however, did have an allure, and at least one impresario had a gleam in his eye: Arthur Dore. Under the moniker of first *Toughman* and then *Toughwoman* contests, Dore offered men and women the opportunity to box for 3 two-minute rounds in heavily padded gloves. The only requirement was that the fighters had had five or less amateur fights, and for women, that they had trained for a minimum of a month before their fight date. The contests proved very popular, leading not only to opportunities to fight additional tournaments, but for the women who'd gotten their first taste of the sport, a stepping stone to becoming professional fighters—the most famous of whom was Christy Martin.

The specter of women fighting in the ring also led boxing clubs that had traditionally catered to men to open opportunities for women to train. Gleason's Gym in New York City, which had only one changing room, closed the gym three nights a week so they could exclusively offer women classes. It proved to be so popular, it helped them over their economic "hump," and when the gym moved from its digs near Madison Square Garden to DUMBO, Brooklyn, co-owner Bruce Silverglade ensured they'd have both men's and women's changing rooms.

The challenges for women in boxing, however, continued: low pay, limited opportunities on fight cards, lack of sanctioning bodies, hazing from the press, and the continued freeze out of amateur boxing, which made it harder to hone the skills necessary to safely compete.

Marian "Lady Tyger" Trimiar, a pioneer who'd first started to campaign for the sport in 1974, was particularly vocal. By 1987, Trimiar was fed up with paydays in the hundreds, the lack of opportunities, and the ridiculousness of things like breast protectors and other impediments to the game imposed by state and local commissions. Her next step was an age-old tactic in labor disputes: she went on a hunger strike, along with fighters Del Pettis and Joan Metallo.

Picketing at the April 6, 1987, Sugar Ray Leonard–Marvin Hagler fight, they hoped to draw attention to the plight of women in the sport and shame promoter Bob Arum. Their cause was lost in the excitement of Leonard's win, but it did not deter the women, nor Trimiar, who carried on alone with the intention of picketing in front of Don King's offices in New York City. Eventually ending her hunger strike, she stated, "Women should be not treated as weirdos to box. People say women have to be lesbians or crazy to box. That's not true and it's very unfair. They don't say that about men."[28]

A fighter who pushed against such denigrating comments was Christy Salters, later to become known worldwide as Christy Martin. Braving the ring on a dare in 1986, she entered a *Toughwoman* contest in her native West Virginia. She went on to win six contests before turning professional in 1989. Under the tutelage of her soon-to-be husband, Jim Martin, she began to campaign in the sport in September 1989 in local shows in and around Tennessee, West Virginia, and other venues in the

South and as far north as Michigan. There was no shortage of opponents as women tenaciously entered the sport. This included fellow *Tough-woman* veteran Andrea DeShong, and by 1993, Martin had amassed a winning record to include a plethora of wins by knockout. Coming to the attention of Don King—who'd given a promise to Lady Tyger Trimiar to promote women back during her hunger strike—he was immediately hooked by the prospective female fighter with skills, knockout power, and enough savvy to have already promoted herself in her signature pink color.

That same year, 1993, and across the country in Bellingham, Washington, a sixteen-year-old Jennifer McCleery, fighting under the name Dallas Malloy (named for her favorite character in the film *On The Waterfront*, Terry Malloy), along with her parents, sued to be allowed to box other women in the amateurs. Challenging the rules that prevented women from participating in amateur boxing programs as competitors, "U.S. District Court Judge Barbara Rothstein issued an injunction" that, effectively, ended the nearly century-long prohibition against women competing in sanctioned amateur boxing programs in the United States.[29]

In Ireland, an Irish boxer named Diedre Gogarty was drawn to the sweet science watching her boxing hero featherweight champion, Barry McGuigan, in the mid-1980s. Inspired by McGuigan, Gogarty managed to squirrel a bag into a closet in her nice and tidy middle-class home (her parents were dentists) and worked out in secret.

As Gogarty put it, "I grew up with very proper parents who didn't believe young ladies did things like that. So I kept it a secret basically for a few years. But then when I saw Sugar Ray Leonard fight Marvin Hagler, I decided I couldn't keep it a secret any longer. So I went to the local boxing club."[30]

Once at the gym, everyone assumed she was there to ogle the boys, but her steely-eyed gaze was fixed on boxing techniques, and as she watched, she learned. At some point the coach at the gym begrudgingly let her train a bit, entering an exhibition kickboxing bout in 1991 as her only vehicle to compete. She'd also already come up against the Irish Athletic Boxing Association (IABA), whose continual hard "no" to license women to box would take several more years to soften.

Undeterred and with the determination of a champion, she went to England first. Gogarty managed to find a few underground fights (women's boxing was still illegal there as well) against women such as Sue Atkins, who were just as determined to beat the ban, before finding her way to Louisiana in 1993 and trainer Beau Williford. He was less than enthused at first, but after agreeing to train and manage her, she returned the favor with impressive outings at fight venues across the United States. This included a women's boxing title fight with Barbara Buttrick's nascent, Women's International Boxing Federation (WIBF) sanctioning organization in November 1993. She lost her lightweight battle to fighter Stacy Prestage but was in the growing mix of fighters to include Laura Serrano, who was leading the fight for women to fight in Mexico, and Regina Halmich who was single-handedly creating the momentum for women's boxing in her native Germany.

Christy Martin was making an even bigger splash in American boxing. Under the umbrella of Don King's promotion machine, she contested on major fight cards beginning in 1994. She was also finding a growing and deepening well of opponents in venues across the United States—some experienced, some less so, but each with a dream of boxing professionally on the big stage.

One such event made unparalleled history and set the course of women's boxing into a new era of the sport.

The night was March 16, 1996, marking Mike Tyson's opportunity to return to the ranks of heavyweight championships against WBC champion Frank Bruno, who'd held the title since the prior September. The pay-per-view (PPV) card had a total of five championship bouts at the MGM Grand, a premier setting for boxing matches of this caliber. At the bottom of the card were only two non-title fights, a welterweight bout, and a six-rounder between Christy Martin and Deidre Gogarty.

Given the enormity of the card, the venue was packed with fans even for the preliminaries. Some knew who Christy Martin was, and perhaps an even smaller handful had an awareness of Deirdre Gogarty. What most fans weren't prepared for, however, was a skilled end-to-end slug-fest between two highly accomplished women of the ring. By the end, Martin was triumphant, with a unanimous decision on the cards, blood streaming from her nose, and Gogarty somewhat dejected, feeling as if she'd not given her best effort despite having survived the onslaught of Martin's relentless punching with her own fierce countering.

But Gogarty was no pushover, as Martin put it: "[S]he hit me with a good, straight counter right hand to the face, and it broke my nose. It gave me a nosebleed that my cut man was never able to stop. Later one sportswriter said it was the most valuable nosebleed in history."[31]

Martin's bloody face gave way to a whirlwind in the days after the bout, leading to an almost universal acknowledgment that women could not only box but provide a caliber of fighting that was worth the price of admission. With the press attention and a coveted cover photo of Christy Martin on the April 15, 1996, issue of *Sports Illustrated* magazine under the title *The Lady Is A Champ*, women's boxing had seemingly arrived.

Boxing Daughters and the Long Road to Olympic Glory

When Laila Ali, the daughter of the iconic heavyweight champion of the world, Muhammed Ali, first stepped into the boxing ring on October 8, 1999, a new era in boxing began. Here was the daughter of arguably the most famous boxer in history, bringing new meaning to the concept of a boxing family.

She was inspired by none other than Christy Martin, and picking up the gauntlet laid down by her father, as she was to state later, "it was in my blood."[32]

Ali's boxing debut occurred during an explosion of women in the ring with the likes of Mia St. John, Lucia Rijker, Sumaya Anani, Tracy Byrd, Great Britain's Jane Couch—who took the BBBC to court and won the right for women to box in the United Kingdom, and Kathy Collins, to name a few, making names for themselves in fight venues across the United States.

Another improbable boxing daughter entering the ring was Jacqui Frazier-Lyde, a thirty-eight-year-old attorney and the pride and joy of her father, Joe Frazier, whose three-fight trilogy against Muhammad Ali was among the greatest heavyweight battles in the history of the sport. Frazier-Lyde proudly made her boxing debut in February 2000, and with that, the Ali–Frazier rivalry was reborn—in the form of the two daughters. By June 2001, the will—and, importantly, the money—was in place to put on Ali–Frazier IV at the famed Turning Stone Resort & Casino in Verona, New York, a stone's throw from Canastota, and held in a tent on the grounds of the Casino on Boxing Hall of Fame weekend.

Ali–Frazier IV was the first time a women's boxing bout headlined a PPV event. Writing in her 2002 book, *Reach!*, Laila Ali noted, "Journalists came from all over the world" and the reach of the reporting was global. She added she was "determined to demonstrate my fighting prowess in front of the largest audience I'd ever drawn."[33]

The eight-round, main-event fight turned into an all-out war with the two women battering each other through all eight, hard-fought rounds. Laila Ali was given the nod with a split decision. In speaking after the fight, Frazier-Lyde said, "We made a contribution to the sport . . . and to me that's winning."

Ali conceding that she'd won by split-decision said, "It was a good fight. I have to give Jacqui her props. She fought hard. I should have boxed more. But I'm glad that I won fighting her fight."[34]

While sports writers conceded that both fighters put on an entertaining show, the consensus was the bout was more suitable for an under-card—and was in the general keeping of continuing dismissiveness for women in the ring, despite the inroads and improvements in fighting ability on display.

The "freak show" element, however, kept being called out as other daughters such as Freeda George Foreman (George Foreman), J'Marie Moore (Archie Moore), and Irichelle Duran (Roberto Duran) entered the ring to mixed results and lousy press overall. Mia St. John, who'd entered the boxing scene in the late 1990s, also made a splash around the same time, appearing on the cover of *Playboy* magazine with a broad smile and two red boxing gloves covering her bare chest. The representations of the sport as nothing more than side-show carnival acts otherwise dismissed the serious intentions of female boxing practitioners and their efforts to improve the skill level and concomitant entertainment value of the bouts.

THE RISE OF AMATEUR BOXING

On a parallel track, amateur women's boxing in the United States continued to develop. Women participated in all levels of amateur contests (where available), even and including local, regional, and national Golden Gloves tournaments. The United States was not alone in sanctioning amateur boxing, and by 2001 some thirty countries were offering opportunities to box in amateur contests.

The development of boxing programs in the United States and around the world caught the attention of AIBA, the international amateur boxing organization. So much so, the first AIBA Women's World Boxing Championships were held in Scranton, Pennsylvania, from November 27–December 2, 2001, another important milestone in the history of the sport.

Such fighters as India's Mary Kom, America's Devonne Canady, Sweden's Frida Wallberg, and French boxer Myriam Lamare were among the 125 athletes who came to Scranton from thirty countries to compete and win medals in an extraordinary showing for a sport that was still illegal in many places. The caliber of fighting also led AIBA to host a second Women's World Boxing Championship the following October in Antalya, Turkey—this time with 185 entrants from thirty-five countries.[35]

The next championship tournament was not held until late September 2005 in Podolsk, Russia. It saw a decrease in entrants and the number of countries represented but was notable for contesting across thirteen weight classes and represented the first tournament entry for Ireland's Katie Taylor. While the future Olympian and current European women's champion was eliminated in the second round, it did mark her debut with AIBA.

The success of the first two tournaments and the anticipated level of play at the 2005 third AIBA Women's World Championship contributed to the organization's decision to submit a proposal to include women's boxing in the 2008 Beijing Olympic Games. In an executive session shortly thereafter in late October, the IOC rejected the request to include the sport in the games. Kelly Fairweather, the IOC sports director at the time, explained that "this decision was purely taken on a technical basis as recommended by the Programme Commission." He went on to state, "[w]e look forward to seeing progress in women's boxing over the next few years."[36]

Not to be denied, AIBA took seriously "an invitation to resubmit for inclusion in the 2012 London Games," and recommitted to that position under the new leadership of Dr. Ching-Kuo Wu in November 2006. A fourth women's world championship was also held, coinciding with the leadership change. Held in New Delhi, India, the tournament saw 174 boxers from thirty-three countries. The excitement was also palpable as the women strove to further the high-stakes goal of Olympic inclusion. The 2006 tournament also saw a return of Katie Taylor, who won gold, as well as a bronze medal for new entrant and future Olympian Marlen Esparza, representing the United States.[37]

The following year, in 2007, AIBA also put on two special exhibition bouts in Chicago, Illinois, for the benefit of IOC. The exhibition showcased two pairings highlighted by Katie Taylor fighting an opponent at lightweight and Marlen Esparza and her opponent at flyweight. After that success, AIBA further demonstrated its commitment to women in the sport by establishing a women's commission, issuing new rules to closer align men's and women's boxing, and setting up a new junior championship division.

The Women's World Championship set for Ningbo City, China, in November 2008, however, was the pivotal event to "sell" women's inclusion in the 2012 London Games. With a total of 237 boxers from forty-two countries competing across thirteen weight categories, the fighters represented five continents, and demonstrated fighting prowess with the debuts of future Olympians such as Great Britain's Nicola Adams and Natasha Jonas, the United States' Quanitta "Queen" Underwood, and China's Ren Cancan and Dong Chen.

The caliber of boxing and the enthusiasm of the national organizations spurred the AIBA executive committee to unanimously agree to formally submit a proposal to include women's boxing in the 2012 London Games. With their submission in February 2009, AIBA proposed four weight categories and forty women. AIBA further revised their proposal in June 2009 to three weight categories with thirty-six women. While only offering flyweight, lightweight, and middleweight categories for women would be a hardship for women fighting across the other weight categories, AIBA's calculus was to get in the Games first, and worry about adding weight classes and participants later.

Meeting in Berlin, Germany, in August, the IOC's executive board met and voted to include women's boxing in the 2012 London Games. "I think it's a very important and symbolic message from the IOC to the world," Dr. Wu was quoted as saying, while the *New York Times* opined, "[O]ne of the sturdiest gender barriers in the Olympics came crashing down."[38]

In furtherance of amateur women's boxing, AIBA held the 2010 Women's World Boxing Championships in Barbados from September 9–18. It saw an explosion in participants, jumping to 257 entrants from a total of sixty-six individual federations from across the globe. It also set the stage for federations to begin the process of developing Olympic trials for their home entrants ahead of the international qualifying event, which was slated to be held during the seventh AIBA Women's World Boxing Championships to be held in Qinhuangdao, China, in May 2012.

"No" Is Not an Acceptable Answer

The excitement of the run-up to the Olympics, did not, however, put women's professional boxing on hold, in any sense. American champion boxers such as Ann Wolfe, Alicia Ashley, and Holly Holm, and fighters from across the globe, including Canada's Jelena Mrdjenovich, French boxers Myriam Lamare and Anne Sophie Mathis, Argentinian greats Yesica Bopp and Marcela Elian Acuña, Mexican legends Mariana "Barbie" Juárez and Jackie Nava, and Norway's Cecilia Braekhus, to name several, were the leading edge of remarkable professionals who in picking up the gloves were proving that women were not only consummate denizens of the ring, but remarkable elite athletes who were committed to growing the sport.

In the United States, Laila Ali continued to be the face of women's boxing even though she retired from the sport in 2007. Her crossover appeal kept the idea of women contesting in the ring alive. The name recognition did not, however, lead to continued institutional support of the sport. Quite to the contrary, even as boxing became more popular worldwide, and the skill level of its contestants begin to rival their male counterparts, support for the sport seemingly collapsed in the United States. Women did, however, continue to contest in boxing—some even on cards that were broadcast—but whereas women were routinely broadcast on American fight cards in 2003, by 2009, they were no longer included on ESPN or Showtime boxing cards.

Bucking the trend in the United States, DiBella Entertainment, for one, began to feature women on their local shows. Under the Broadway Boxing moniker, women were placed on the undercard starting in 2006. Shown locally on cable television, the fights were very popular. The crowd-pleasing showings, coupled with an ability to sell lots of tickets, led DiBella's organization to add a female bout to some of their broadcast fight cards beginning in 2011. With headliners such as middleweight champion Sergio Martinez and HBO Boxing as a broadcast partner, even without being shown on the main broadcast, women were appreciative of being given any opportunity at all, as they were essentially invisible to mainstream boxing media.

The promise of the Olympics, however, was an enduring one, and the excitement of the Olympic Trials in the United States in February 2012 was the culmination of over one hundred years of wishing and hoping for a return to the Games.

Held at the Northern Quest resort in Spokane, Washington, twenty-four women competed for the three coveted spots. The three champions chosen included the sixteen-year-old Claressa Shields, a boxing phenomenon from Flint, Michigan, for the middleweight spot who would be seventeen in March, and thus able to qualify for a berth. Quanitta "Queen" Underwood, a USA Boxing national champion at lightweight, won that coveted spot, and Marlen Esparza, the USA Boxing national champion at flyweight, took home that honor.

The team of Esparza, Underwood, and Shields was crowned as the historic first team of female boxing Olympians and was set for the final qualifying event in May 2012 to be held as part of the AIBA Women's World Boxing Championships in Qinhuangdao, China. With a record-breaking seventy-seven nations sending 343 athletes to the competition, even without the Olympic qualifying contests, the event proved that women's boxing had taken hold from Vietnam to Bolivia, Nigeria to Hungary, and back again, demonstrating the global reach and strength of the sport.

A total of sixteen countries qualified twenty-five athletes for the Games at the event, while a further eleven athletes would be assigned by a complex quota system and rulings from a tripartite commission. Claressa Shields had suffered her only loss to Savannah Marshall from the United Kingdom, but given that Shields was ranked in the top two she was awarded an Olympic berth. Marlen Esparza was also eliminated from medal contention but like Shields was in the coveted top two spot. Queen Underwood had lost as well at the championships but had to wait till a ruling was handed down despite her number two position in the Americas. Finally informed in June that she would represent the United States in its first women's boxing team, the trio became media darlings ahead of the Games set to start in London at the end of July.

The 2012 London Games themselves allowed the female participants to demonstrate extraordinary skills in front of the sold-out crowds at the ExCel Arena, where it was said the noise level was not only deafening but record-breaking. In all, twelve women were crowned with Olympic medals, including the gold medal winners: Nicola Adams, flyweight; Katie Taylor, lightweight; and Claressa Shields, gold. Marlen Esparza took home bronze for the United States. Queen Underwood had been eliminated in her fight against the Natasha Jonas from the United Kingdom, heartbroken at her loss.

As a sort of coda to the extraordinary sight of women contesting at the Olympics, Barbara Buttrick, "the mighty atom of the ring" and Great Britain's first postwar female boxer, said, "When I was around, I would never have dreamed women boxers would ever get into the Olympics. But now they've got that credibility, and that will bring a lot more girls into it because they'll feel more comfortable going into a gym."[39]

Her words proved prophetic as the women continued to explode onto the boxing scene with the skills, desire, and drive that continue to push at the boundaries of the sport.

PART I

2012–2016

THE INCLUSION OF WOMEN'S BOXING IN THE 2012 LONDON GAMES WAS a thunderbolt for the sport. Here was the long sought-after legitimacy of a promise fulfilled—one made in 1904 when women first exhibited the sport. The excited fans cheered so loudly the decibel levels at London's ExCel Exhibition Centre peaked well into the red as the newly minted gold medal boxing stars Nicola Adams, Katie Taylor, and Claressa Shields demonstrated their prowess in the ring. If there had been a sense that the shiny gold objects would impact the professional side of the sport, however, that did not materialize, at least not in the immediate aftermath of the Games. All three gold medal winners chose to remain in the amateurs, viewing that the time was not right to trade in the accolades and surety of a blossoming amateur circuit for the uncertainties of professional boxing. While the new Olympic stars remained in the amateurs through the 2016 Rio Games, such professional champions as Cecilia Braekhus (Norway), Alicia Ashley (United States), Melissa Hernandez (United States), Jelena Mrdjenovich (Canada), Erica Anabella Farias (Argentina), and Zulina Muñoz (Mexico) continued to propel the sport with their boxing excellence. Their prowess inspired yet more fighters, including Heather Hardy (United States) and Amanda Serrano (United States), whose efforts would propel them both to push the boundaries of women's participation on televised cards and in the burgeoning era of a new appreciation of the sport. The period rounded out with the Rio 2016 Games, which saw Claressa Shields repeat her gold medal win—the first American boxer, male or female, to do so. As a bookend for the start of the period, it also coincided with the first major streaming event for a professional women's boxing match by NBC Sports showing the bout between Heather Hardy and Shelley Vincent for the WBC international featherweight title.

CHAPTER ONE

The Morning After

WITH THE EXCITEMENT OF THE FIRST EVER INCLUSION OF WOMEN IN the Olympic Games over and done with, what happened next? In the United States, it meant a greater rush to push for expanded opportunities for girls to participate in amateur programs. There was also some growth in amateur programs aimed at bringing girls and women into the sport, rounding out the era with the Olympics of 2016 in Rio, which saw the United Kingdom's Nicola Adams and the United States' Claressa Shields repeat their gold medal wins. For Shields, there was the added accolade of being the first American boxer, male or female, to win back-to-back gold, and proved to be a wonderful bookend for the period.

WINNING GOLD, WINNING BRONZE
The first order of business in the United States after the triumph of women's boxing's first showing in the Olympic Games was to push forward the notion that its inclusion would solidify legitimacy and a brighter future.

What was most remarkable was by their very presence at the Olympics, USA Boxing's Olympic team of Esparza, Underwood, and Shields had begun to inspire a new generation of girls entering the sport. In the immediate aftermath of the Olympics, The Beautiful Brawlers II all-female show was held at the Pacifica Lodge in California. As noted by the show's promoter, Blanca Gutiérrez, there had already been "a surge in females wanting to get ready for the next Olympics . . . in Rio in 2016."[1]

For the girls who had watched their older boxing sisters fight on the Olympic platform, those Olympic dreams seemed to portend a golden era for their sport. After all, with two women's boxing Olympic medals, a gold and a bronze, the only boxing medals brought home from London by the USA Boxing team, female or male—one would have thought there would have been a triumphant acknowledgment at the very least, plus some promotional deals for the returning boxing elite.

As it was, Marlen Esparza had promotional opportunities in place prior to the Games with the Coca-Cola Company and Cover Girl. Little was forthcoming, however, for Claressa Shields or for Queen Underwood, who had been eliminated in the first round of the Games.

Yes, there were multiple media interviews. Most notably, Shields appeared on Comedy Central's *The Colbert Report*. She came across as affable, funny, and enthusiastic during her five-minute segment. Shields also successfully parried with Colbert, telling him, "I love hitting people" when asked why she boxed—drawing laughs from the studio audience and charming responses from Colbert.[2]

During her swing through New York City for *The Colbert Report*, she also appeared on BET's *106 & Park* show, alongside Olympian and gold medal winner Angelo Taylor. Shields proved to be a winning personality, proudly lauding the fact that she was from Flint, Michigan.

Closer to home, Shields immediately invested in paying it forward in her community by offering such things as free boxing clinics to children. Asked about why she was so keen on training kids, she answered, "I hope that when I'm able to teach them about boxing, I'm able to teach them about what to do in life, too . . . I had a few downfalls and a few situations when I didn't think I could do it anymore but I just kept going."[3]

She also talked about her investment in the future at the presentation of the Philadelphia-based 2012 Liberty Award ceremony honoring boxing legend Muhammad Ali.

"I'm a positive person," Shields said. "There are a lot of people who look up to me. . . . As far as giving back to my home community, it's just something I want to do."[4]

Shields had the honor of standing with boxing champion Laila Ali as she gave the award to her father along with Susan Francia, the two-time gold medalist in rowing.[5]

Capitalizing further on her new status, and as a native daughter of Michigan, Shields threw out the ceremonial first pitch ahead of a double-header between the Detroit Tigers and Minnesota Twins at Comerica Park in Detroit, on September 23, 2012 (a feat she would repeat after winning her second gold medal in 2016, and several times after that). She also landed on a few other stages, appearing on the red carpet at the *BET Honors* show, for one, but there were no substantive endorsement offers or opportunities.

As a USA Boxing champion, Shields received a $1,000 monthly stipend to cover her boxing expenses. She also accepted a sizable cash bonus from the U.S. Olympic Committee, along with others on the USA national team who won gold.[6] She did not, however, appear all aglow in smiles, in a USA team jacket festooned with her glistening gold medal on the proverbial Wheaties box. Furthermore, in returning to Flint, Shields lived pretty much as she had lived before, including finishing up her last year at Flint Northwestern High School with the graduating class of 2013 in between events, and boxing training, albeit with a film crew continuing to follow her around assembling footage for a documentary.

For Shields, a seventeen-year-old who had won an extraordinary victory, the constant drumbeat of not having also come into immediate promotional deals weighed heavily. She had met her goals, but the insistence by others that there be an immediate cash award and recognition alongside other gold medal–winning athletes caused her to doubt her own feelings.

Shields did, however, have a strong sense of who she was, and taking pride in all she had achieved, continued to box, winning her first tournament after the Olympics in October at the Seagate Convention Center in Toledo, Ohio. Shields also won the middleweight crown at the 2012 USA PAL Championship for the second year in a row, this time defeating the reigning USA Boxing National Women's light heavy champion, Franchon Crews-Dezurn.[7] Shields fought three more bouts as an elite boxer in early 2013 against Canadian amateur champions Mary

Spencer and Ariane Fortin in two non-championship bouts, along with Canadian newcomer Alison Greey in a special salute to boxing Olympians held in Flint.

Shields's next amateur contests, in 2013, came with considerable consternation as, due to a rule change by AIBA, all eighteen- and nineteen-year-olds were mandated to compete in the youth division. Shields, who had turned eighteen in March, would be required to contest in the youth division until she turned nineteen the following spring and could once again compete in the elite division. Her status as the reigning Olympic gold medalist notwithstanding, Shields led the USA Boxing team of Junior and Youth boxing athletes at the Women's Junior/Youth World Championships held at the Albena resort in Bulgaria. Her coach, Jason Crutchfield, was able to accompany the team as well, and capably managed her to victory and the championship title.[8]

With the achievement of her Olympic gold medal, and the intention to compete again in the upcoming 2016 Rio Games, Shields held on to her desire to have a place in the world. As part of that arc, Shields began to reveal much of her own story, while also continuing to allow herself to be shadowed by Peabody Award–winning journalist and producer Sue Jaye Johnson, and filmmakers Zackary Canepari and Drea Cooper. Assembling over four hundred hours of footage, the filmmakers eventually assembled an award-winning, eighty-nine-minute documentary feature entitled *T-Rex: Her Fight for Gold*, which premiered at the 2015 South by Southwest Film Festival held in Austin, Texas.

The triumph of her Olympic moment and those that followed, however, paled in comparison to how she had won at life. Having survived horrific sexual abuse, neglect, the incarceration of her father, and the eventual death of her beloved grandmother, the Olympian who was learning to give voice to those who were voiceless had herself been without speech as a young child—remarkable achievements that those around her knew were unique to her and the shining star she truly was.

FINDING A PATH FORWARD

When Marlen Esparza returned home to Houston, Texas, after her bronze medal win at the 2012 London Games, she stated her life was never the same. She was recognized in supermarkets, on the sidewalks, and was sought after for events. Along with other Latino Olympians, she was honored at the Thirteenth Annual American Latino Media Arts (ALMA) Awards show, which aired on September 21 on the NBC network.

With bronze around her neck, Esparza immediately began exploring the development of a clothing line. The twenty-two-year-old Olympian was also cast not only as "relentless in the ring," but as "beautiful, girly and charming with a winning personality." Her new manager went on to say, "We'll introduce Marlen to Hollywood and develop her fashion and beauty business for a robust career and business outside the ring."[9]

She also picked up another endorsement opportunity with McDonald's. Having boxed since the age of twelve, by the age of sixteen it was a full-time endeavor alongside her schooling. She also viewed it as a way to "make money to support my family just so money would not have to be an issue, but I never thought I would do that through boxing. Boxing is just what I love to do."

By March 2013, Esparza had expanded her promotional opportunities to include Nike and Procter & Gamble, among others, with the goal of starting college (much as Shields did in the fall of 2013 when she started at Olivet College). Esparza had further noted, "Your actions, no matter what you do, [are] a reflection of the sport and you must represent yourself with pride. On the road to success, we must think about our impact on the world [and] of how people will view you today and in the future."[10]

Esparza, who had flirted with the idea of leaving boxing in the immediate aftermath of the Olympics, was back in the ring in April 2013, winning the 2013 USA National Championship final at flyweight over challenger (and future Olympian) Ginny Fuchs. She also scored big with wins in Puerto La Cruz, Venezuela, alongside USA Boxing teammate and fellow Olympian, Queen Underwood.

The two other gold medal winners, Great Britain's Nicola Adams (flyweight) and Ireland's Katie Taylor (lightweight), had fared very differently. For Adams, who'd won the first women's Olympic gold medal in boxing history, she had the double joy of winning it at home at the London Games. The immediate aftermath was electrifying, as she became a genuine heroine and was appointed a Member of the Most Excellent Order (MBE) on the list published at the end of 2012 for her services to boxing.[11] With this honor, she followed in the footsteps of the pioneer boxer Jane Couch, who had been awarded an MBE in 2007 for her services to sport—which included winning the right for women to fight professionally in the UK.[12]

In Ireland, Taylor, who'd already enjoyed the status as a national treasure, the gold medal solidified her place as an icon. The populace of her hometown of Bray had cheered her performances in an empty field on a giant screen standing alongside visitors from as far away as Limerick in the west of Ireland. Her gold medal win, as exemplified by the exuberance of her hometown crowd, put the nation into a frenzy of pride.

Having been given the honor of being the Irish Olympic team's flag bearer, she had, in the words of Ireland's president, Michael D. Higgins, "lifted the spirits of a nation." Meanwhile, Ireland's prime minister, Enda Kenny, homed in on Katie Taylor as "a force of nature whose pioneering spirit and boxing brilliance have seen her realise her personal dream of winning Olympic gold."[13]

At year's end, having been feted since her Olympic triumph, she was honored with the coveted "Sportswoman of the Year" award by *The Irish Times*/Irish Sports Council, and having chosen to remain in the amateurs, continued in her winning ways throughout 2013, including two homecoming bouts in Bray.

Even for non-Olympian amateur boxers, in the United States, there was some movement for recognition. The 2012 USA Boxing National Super-Light Champion and 2013 National Golden Gloves Light Champion, Mikaela Mayer, appeared in a new Dr. Pepper spot, part of their national "One of a Kind" advertising campaign. As Mayer put it at the time, "Olympic-style boxing isn't a household sport, so anything we can do to help educate people about it is great for the sport."[14]

For these newly minted icons of the sport, the aftermaths were decidedly different in terms of acceptance and opportunity. One thing that was the same, however, was their judgment that the time was not yet ripe for turning professional and pouring their hopes and dreams into their efforts to win places at the 2016 Rio Games.

Beginning the Road to Rio

With Olympic women's boxing solidly in place, USA Boxing needed to ensure the next class of Olympians would be ready to contest at the 2016 Olympic Games in Rio de Janeiro, Brazil.

In 2013, the USA Boxing National Championship event in April included the youth, senior, and elite divisions. Other tournaments giving women opportunities to contest at the elite level were the Women's National Golden Gloves held in July, and the National Pal Championships held in early October. From the perspective of the USA Boxing team of elite athletes who were supported in international competition, the winners of the coveted Elite National Championships tournament held in April 2013 would be given the nod and the support from the Olympic Center in Colorado.

For the elite national team members, this meant opportunities to compete at the women's continental championships with Olympians Marlen Esparza (fly) and Queen Underwood (light) winning at their Olympic weights. With Claressa Shields out of competition because of AIBA's rules change, Franchon Crews-Dezurn attempted to win the tournament at middleweight, but was defeated by Yeneiber Guillen from the Dominican Republic.

Crews-Dezurn had been a stalwart of USA Boxing's national championship since winning her first middleweight crown in 2005. She also began gaining her international experience in 2006 when she won gold at the Pan American Games, and was national middle weight championships in 2011, 2012, and 2013.

With some slight changes to the timing of 2014 championship tournaments, the USA/Canada Duel held in March 2014 saw Esparza and Underwood winning at their Olympic weights, along with Franchon Crews-Dezurn at middleweight, who took a decision over the Canadian champion, Mary Spencer. Later in the summer, Claressa Shields, having turned nineteen in March, was back on the USA Boxing elite team—giving the 2012 Olympic squad of Esparza, Underwood, and Shields another chance to dominate with gold medal wins.

The 2014 Elite World Championships held in Jeju City, South Korea, tested the mettle of the 2012 Olympic team, with both Marlen Esparza and Claressa Shields winning world titles in their respective weight classes. Underwood did not fare as well at lightweight, experiencing a loss to a Bulgarian fighter, Svetlana Staneva, in the preliminary round, that was eventually won by the reigning Olympian, Katie Taylor.

With her win at the Elite World Championships, Claressa Shields was also named the "Outstanding Boxer of the Tournament," a singular honor for the American Olympian. As if that wasn't enough, at the banquet held in celebration of the tournament, Shields was also named the 2014 Elite Woman Boxer of the Year.

Speaking about her fighter of the year award to ESPN's Aimee Berg, Shields said, "I'm just so humbled. It healed my heart. I felt all the pain from losing my only match (in 2012) go away. I was overjoyed."

With filming completed on her documentary, *T-Rex*, the premiere of the film was set for the South by Southwest Film Festival in March 2015. Her life at home in Flint, however, was beset with family issues surrounding her decision to raise her cousin's baby as her own. The legal matters surrounding her adoption of the baby became acrimonious, however, making it impossible for Shields to move forward.

While that road closed, her Olympic dream of repeating her gold medal win in Rio still loomed large for her. Shields had also split with her longtime coach, Justin Crutchfield, several months earlier, noting, "It was kind of mutual, I guess. At first, I was very heartbroken. He's like my second father. He always looked at me like I was a kid. At 18, though, I wanted to have my own car, my own apartment; I wanted to do things for myself."

She'd also wanted a boyfriend and to enjoy life a little, but as she said, "We could never come to fair grounds about the whole dating thing."[15]

With all of that in mind, Shields made the move from her home in Flint to the Olympic Training Center in Colorado Springs to focus anew on preparing for the 2016 Rio Games.

A Sea of Stories

In the run-up to Rio 2016, the only significant international tournament for American Olympic hopefuls in 2015 was the Pan American Games qualifier ahead of the Pan American Games held in Toronto, Canada. In the year's National Championships, Mikaela Mayer had prevailed at lightweight, with Queen Underwood having gone up to the super lightweight category, while Esparza and Shields and retained the pride of place as USA National Champions.

Mayer lost in the preliminary round of the Pan American qualifier at lightweight, while both Esparza and Shields were able to prevail. At the Pan American Games, Marlen Esparza lost in the final to the Canadian champion, Mandy Bujold, while Claressa Shields emerged victorious over the Argentinian middleweight, Lucia Noelia Perez, to capture gold.

For the elite boxers of USA Boxing, the next big hurdle was the final Olympic Trials tournament set for Memphis, Tennessee, on October 26 through November 1, 2015. The competition had a total of four competitors for each of three Olympic weight classes: flyweight, lightweight, and middleweight.

Reigning Olympic bronze medalist Marlen Esparza admitted that when she did not bring home gold in 2012, she "just didn't feel right." "About four or five months before nationals came around again in 2013, I had to make a decision: start training full time and get back into it 100%, or let someone take my spot."

Agreeing with fellow teammates Christina Cruz and Franchon Crews-Dezurn that the flyweight division is among the most competitive at the trials, Esparza felt there was a target on her back. She was in the unique position of having endorsements, longevity as a national champion, and a drawer full of international titles and trophies. She'd also expressed doubts along the way. As Esparza put, "To be honest, people aren't so happy for me this time around."

Speaking about Esparza, Franchon Crews-Dezurn said, "It's a gift and a curse, because when we first started we didn't have the Olympics, you know what I mean? We didn't know anything but just fighting, and you get older and it comes with more responsibility. . . . Especially

Marlen and her situation, being a world figure now in boxing. It's just like she just deals with things I couldn't relate to."[16]

Unique among the USA Boxing–sanctioned tournaments, the twenty-four participants in the Olympic Trials had an opportunity to fight for a second time before facing elimination from the trials across three preliminary rounds, two challenger rounds for fighters with one loss, and the finals. The second-chance opportunities added both to the tensions and drama of the tournament.

For the day one results, and as expected, Olympic gold medalist Claressa Shields easily defeated her first-round opponent, Naomi Graham, 3–0. They also saw 2012 bronze medalist Marlen Esparza gain a 3–0 win over Melanie Costa. In the lightweight division, current USA lightweight champion Mikaela Mayer won a split decision, 2–1, over Stalacia Leggett, and the number two seeded fighter, the always tough Tiara Brown, defeated Amelia Moore decisively by the score of 3–0, setting up a possible showdown for the lightweight crown.

In a sea of stories as to how and why women box, Stalacia Leggett, who had passed the California bar in 2014, concurrently followed her dream to box. A former high school gymnast, Leggett had won the right to participate in the Olympic Trials final, after successfully competing in the first preliminary Trials competition held in June 2015. A practicing attorney in California, she eventually left boxing to become a deputy district attorney in Los Angeles County.

Shields's challenger Naomi Graham also came to the Olympic Trials with a story. As a serving U.S. Army soldier, Graham was given the opportunity to join the army's World Class Athlete program early in 2015. Graham had been inspired to box by her sister, Rachel Clark, a professional in the sport from 2008 to 2011. Having struggled through her early adulthood with a stint of homelessness and couch surfing, Graham's decision to sign up for military service in 2013 gave her the impetus to turn her life around—and to finally give her dream of boxing a firm footing. In speaking about her boxing, Graham said, "The military teaches you to be adaptable in any situation, and I believe I take that into the ring. . . . Because any style I see, I immediately adapt as soon as I see something that needs to be adjusted."[17]

Esparza's precompetition worries included three main competitors for her Olympic spot. Alex Love, a tough, scrappy fighter from the U.S. Army team, had a close, 2–1, loss to Virginia (Ginny) Fuchs, who matched Love for her come-forward, winner-takes-all style, but in a southpaw package. She'd also narrowly lost in the 2012 Trials and had spent the ensuing years perfecting her skills and abilities. Perpetual New York Golden Gloves winner Christina Cruz, who'd dropped down in weight to the 112-pound category to contest for an Olympic berth, also won in her fight, while Jamie Mitchell lost a 3–0 decision.

The day two results were equally exciting. Teammates and old foes Marlen Esparza and Christina Cruz battled for supremacy in the flyweight division in a close contest that still broke 3–0 to Esparza. Other winners included Alex Love, who remained in the contest by DQ (disqualification) when opponent Jamie Mitchell came in overweight—and with her prior loss was knocked out of the competition.

Both Tiara Brown and Mikaela Mayer won as well. Brown fought a decisive 3–0 win over Rianna Rios, while Mayer fought hard against an onslaught from Jajaira Gonzalez to take the 2–1 split decision. That left Brown and Mayer to fight each other in third-round action.

In the middleweight division, Claressa Shields fought a tough, hard fight against Tika Hemingway with haymakers that boxing writer and former Golden Gloves champion Sarah Deming, who live-tweeted the event, described as coming "all the way from Flint" to take the unanimous win. Raquel Miller defeated Franchon Crews-Dezurn in a split decision, but as this was Crews-Dezurn's first loss in the contest, she maintained her berth in the third round.[18]

The third night of Olympic Trials action saw flyweight boxer Virginia Fuchs, lightweight Mikaela Mayer, and middleweight Claressa Shields each clinch a berth in the upcoming Olympic Trials finals on Saturday night. All three have been undefeated in the tournament to date, earning them the right for a corner in the finals and two days off.

Virginia Fuchs had sealed her final berth by defeating Olympic bronze medalist Marlen Esparza, 2–1, in a tough, tough battle. This was their fourth meeting at the championship level—with Fuchs victorious for the first time. Speaking of her win, Fuchs said, "I stopped her from getting in her rhythm. I got my space and I used my jab. My jab was the key. It feels amazing. It feels so good because this is what I've been working for. For the past four years, this is what I've been working on. This is what I came here to accomplish."

At lightweight, Mikaela Mayer came up a 3–0 winner in her fifth meeting against number two seeded Tiara Brown. Of her win, Mayer said, "She was coming toward me and that allowed me to use my boxing skills which is what I'm good at. That 1-2-3 was landing every time."

Claressa Shields pulled out a flawless technical performance to seal her place in the finals by defeating the veteran Raquel Miller. Shields said, "She was really patient and backed up a lot of the fight. She came forward some but I landed the cleaner, harder shots. She landed a few right hands but I kept going forward and kept landing jabs. I landed a lot of jabs."[19]

SECOND CHANCES FOR THE RIGHT TO BE AN OLYMPIAN

In accordance with the rules of the double elimination tournament, the following two nights were to be set aside for two sets of challenger bouts to choose the other finalist for final competitions. With her loss, 2012 Olympian Marlen Esparza was in the unenviable position of needing to battle out the second-chance fights to win a chance to be the opponent in the finals—a second meeting with Ginny Fuchs.

At middleweight, Franchon Crews-Dezurn remained in the contest by handing Naomi Graham her second loss—setting up a fight with Tika Hemingway for her first challenge bout, with the winner taking on Raquel Miller for the right to fight Shields in the finals.

The first of the three contenders for challenger action was flyweight Christina Cruz. At thirty-two years of age, Cruz won the right for a second shot at doing battle after losing to 2012 Olympic bronze medalist Marlen Esparza but it was not enough to gain a berth in the final. Cruz was able to persevere by decision against Giovanna Comacho, 3–0.

Lightweight boxer Jajaira Gonzalez, the eighteen-year-old who pushed hard in her battle against Mikaela Mayer in the second round only to fall in defeat, used pressure and aggression to defeat Rianna Rios, 3–0. Gonzalez won the right to face Tiara Brown in what promised to be a terrific battle of wills between these two talented boxers, with the winner to face Mayer in the finals.

Tika Hemingway narrowly defeated the veteran Franchon Crews-Dezurn, 2–1, for the right to continue to challenge at middleweight. Both fighters had competed in the Olympic Trials in 2012. Hemingway used aggression to finally muscle through to take the contest, though Crews-Dezurn pushed to gain the momentum throughout the bout. Hemingway's win set up her battle against Raquel Miller in the challenger contest for the right to fight Claressa Shields in the final.

Coming into the final challenger night, each of the fighters had endured a loss. Each fighter stared down their opponent facing their own potential to lose their Olympic dreams. As the final challenger night unfolded, each battle for the right to fight in the finals was hard fought and, in some cases, fraught with history as veterans who had encountered each other before in the squared circle knew it was all down to what would happen in their four rounds of action.

For the reigning Olympic flyweight bronze medalist, Marlen Esparza, it meant redemption and being on track for what seemed inevitable at the beginning of the week before she was stopped cold by Virginia Fuchs. In defeating Christina Cruz, a fighter's fighter who fought a brilliant outsider's game with angles and heart, Esparza was now pumped up to rewrite the script with Fuchs and come away with what must have felt like her rightful place.

In the lightweight division, the eighteen-year-old, punches-in-bunches phenom, Jajaira Gonzalez, who had fought Mikaela Mayer to a 2–1 split decision in their battle, came away victorious over 2014 World Championship bronze medalist, and three-time USA Boxing National Champion, Tiara Brown. Gonzalez, a Junior and Youth World Champion, used aggression and pressure to counter Brown's veteran technical ring savvy in carving out the 3–0 decision.

Former champion Tika Hemingway, contesting for a berth in the finals against reigning Olympic gold medalist Claressa Shields, garnered a sense of inevitability in her win over Raquel Miller, even though the battle was closely contested with a lot of back and forth in momentum and opportunities to be exploited. No matter who fought Hemingway, there would always be costs facing the hard-hitting puncher whose physicality in the ring set traps for her opponents—and while she'd lost once to Shields in the Olympic Trials, her boxer's heart insisted she fight hard for a chance to win Olympic glory.

On the night of the finals, the excitement was palpable if filled with the tension of the athletes—though, as noted by Sarah Deming, "Compared to the historic 2012 Trials in Spokane, this was a low-rent affair, overshadowed by a bigger men's tournament and largely ignored by media."[20]

The flyweight bout was first, with contender Virginia Fuchs winning her bout through her relentless technical execution and determination. With her beautiful jab laying down the foundation, and her longer reach, Fuchs wove in and out to smother Esparza's output and frustrate the veteran Olympian. In the end, Fuchs won by a 2–1 margin, unseating the 2012 bronze medalist Marlen Esparza.

"I got my space and got my rhythm," Fuchs said of her efforts. "I didn't let her get her rhythm. I knew by the end of the second round and the whole third round, 'I got this.'"[21]

Fuchs, who'd struggled most of her life with obsessive-compulsive disorder, had in her triumph represented a particularly gratifying beacon of hope for others who lived with the affliction.

As the reigning Olympic gold medalist in the middleweight division, Claressa Shields exuded confidence and ease as she effortlessly fended off her challenger. Tika Hemingway had loudly proclaimed that she'd take it from her, but Shields had other plans and outboxed Hemingway with an impressive 3–0 performance. With the win, Shields achieved another history-first milestone as the United States' only two-time female boxing Olympian.

As for the lightweight upstart, eighteen-year-old Jajaira Gonzales pushed the envelope in her win over Mikaela Mayer to hand Mayer her first loss—and the need for a box-off to determine who would join Fuchs and Shields as the third member of the team.

Coming into the box-off, Mayer brought strong technical abilities, and with her longer reach the ability to box "tall," whereas Gonzalez brought aggression, pressure, and fast hands that seemed relentless in their bout for supremacy and would be the test for Mayer in the rematch. Moreover, for all her youth, Gonzales had already won an impressive array of international titles and readily matched Mayer's competitive fire.

Michaela Mayer's coach, Al Mitchell, put it this way: "Jajaira beats you down. She throws so many punches and she don't mind getting hit, and she roughhouse. It reminds me of the old days in Philly, and I love that."[22]

The hours in between the two bouts were nonetheless fretful and difficult. Mayer said that lying in bed before the final face-off with Gonzales, she'd had to work through her feelings: "You feel sorry for yourself for a second then you just have to pull yourself out."

Mayer also said that when it came to her fight plan, she "had to pick up the movement and pick up the boxing skills. I couldn't stand in front of her."

As the fight ensued, Mayer fought with greater aggression and used her four-inch height advantage to "make her miss."

In the end, Mayer said, "It was the third round where I started to pick up my movement and I said, 'Let me remember to just have fun with this, use my boxing skills and frustrate her.' . . . "

That proved to be a winning combination, with Gonzalez admitting, "that she was 'a bit more tired' than she had been" the previous evening.[23]

As the tournament closed, it had to be remembered that the twenty-four women who came to Memphis to fight for a place at the Olympics each brought considerable drive, determination, and skills as boxers. It was no easy feat to compete at the level of Olympians across any sport, and harder still for women. Yet seemingly it was hardest of all for female boxers, who not only had to seek out opportunities for support during their four-year odyssey for a place on the team but had to endure the slights and prejudices of a wider public that was indifferent at best to their cause and had little understanding of their efforts in the ring.

USA BOXING'S RIO 2016 OLYMPIANS

With the team set, USA Boxing's new head coach, Ireland's Billy Walsh, exemplified the commitment of the organization. His confidence was heightened by USA Boxing's willingness to put the effort into upgrading the boxing facilities at Colorado's Olympic Center in preparing for the upcoming Olympic Games. He also took steps to meet with the individual coaches working with the fighters to integrate the training and other unique factors that went into the relationship between an individual fighter and their trainer.

Walsh also knew the next hurdle was to prepare his team for the upcoming Olympic qualifiers: the continental Olympic qualifier to be held in March 2016 in Buenos Aires, and the final qualifier at the women's world championships slated for May 2016 in Kazakhstan.

The first hurdle in Buenos Aires toward solidifying a place at the 2016 Games was in winning gold at the qualifiers. The reigning 2012 Olympic gold medalist, Claressa Shields, sealed her 2016 Olympic hopes when she defeated Canada's Ariane Fortin-Brochu with a decisive, unanimous, 3–0 win. Shields, who'd suffered a minor wardrobe mishap just prior to the bout, noted, "I feel like the stuff that happened before the ring [with her uniform] kind of affected me in the first round. I didn't start out the way I wanted to, using my jab. I wanted to go out there and use my power," Shields said. "I feel good now. I'm glad that it's done with, and I can look forward to the World Championships [in May]. I'll have tougher and taller opponents, so I look forward to that."

Mikaela Mayer also triumphed when she defeated the Mexican champion Victoria Torres. Having already defeated Torres the month before as part of the World Series of Boxing event, Mayer felt confident—but still ensured that she maintained the focus she needed to land cleanly and decisively while holding Torres at bay.

Prior to the Torres fight, Mayer had to box a nemesis in Puerto Rican boxer Kiria Tapia. As Mayer put it, "Revenge is sweeter when I had to fight her for two qualifying fights. The first was for the Pan Am Games."

"The game plan going in was to make sure that I fake a lot because you don't know when she's going to punch . . . and not pulling back again but slowing down the movement and stepping to her with the right hand. Now I focus on my next opponent and I don't even know who it is because Bill [Walsh] wouldn't let me look at my bracket from the beginning. I see why now because I had the toughest bracket. I had to fight all the top girls and I dealt with it one fight at a time so it worked really well for me."[24]

In the end, Mayer was victorious and came away with the gold medal win and a berth in at the Rio Games.

Mayer's journey to her Olympic place on the USA Boxing team had taken her a full six years from coming a close second to Queen Underwood in the 2012 Trials, to her win in Buenos Aires—a triumph that carried particular poignancy after such a long journey.

In the aftermath of her win, Mayer said, "I just can't believe that after all these years and steps that this was the final step and now it's over. I'm going. . . . Now, next is the Olympics."[25]

Ginny Fuchs, who'd also been on a six-year journey, fared less well in the semifinal round of the qualifier when she suffered a loss to the Colombian boxing champion, Ingrit Valencia. Even with the loss, Fuchs did not leave Buenos Aires empty-handed and brought home a bronze medal. What she was not assured, however, was the opportunity to compete at the 2016 Rio Games. For that, Fuchs would have to qualify for the Olympics during the Women's World Championships in Astana, Kazakhstan.

Happiest of all, however, may have been Claressa Shields, who had turned twenty-one during the Olympic qualifier. She was also returning to the United States having accomplished another major milestone in her life, as the first American female boxer to gain a place in back-to-back Olympics, and to the debut showing of the documentary *T-Rex* in theatrical release at the Detroit film theater in Michigan.

The showing of the film near Flint, while a homecoming of sorts, was also an opportunity to measure the growth and maturity of the driven young woman's incredible journey to the pinnacle of amateur sports with so much more to accomplish. She'd left home the previous May to live at the Olympic Center to focus on her continued opportunities for growth in the sport and the world beyond. Back in Flint, to view the film that chronicled her efforts to win her first gold medal in the maelstrom of family, boxing, and the stories that compelled her seventeen-year-old self, was an opportunity to see the woman she had become.

Speaking of her life in Flint in the years after her first Olympics, the reflection point was deeply personal. "It was hard for me back home, emotionally and mentally," she said. "It was getting hard to train and stay focused. I was losing sight of what is important. That's my boxing career. I was always stressed out. I was always sad. I was missing training."

Ten months after having moved to the Olympic Center in Colorado, she was relieved at the idea that she could be in a place where "They take care of bills. . . . They cook for you. You get free massages. You are really taken care of. You are a priority there."

As stunning as it may have sounded, it was perhaps the first time in her life when she could relax and not have to stress about what so many take for granted. She also noted, "There is so much motivation all around. You don't want to lay around. You want to train because everybody has that same goal, going to the Olympics."

Shields had also started to assemble a circle of trusted advisers with whom she could work. This had led to her first endorsements, and a successful negotiation with Universal Studios to create a feature-length biopic about her life. The focus, however, remained boxing, and her place in it.[26]

With the women's Olympic boxing team nearly set, there was one more hurdle to solidify spots in all three Olympic weights at the 2016 Rio Games: Ginny Fuchs had to earn her place at the 2016 AIBA Women's World Championships in Astana.

USA Boxing brought a total of ten champions across all weight classes, including the three Olympic weights to the championships, with high hopes for medaling and sealing the flyweight place on the 2016 Rio women's boxing team. Since both Shields and Mayer had won their place at the Games, their competition game plans were to win gold for the right to be called world champions. Fuchs had the added pressure of not only winning a medal, but the need to be in the top four placement to win her place at Rio.

With a red jersey signifying the Red Corner, Fuchs came out to fight in the seventh bout of the first day's afternoon session—facing an old foe in the Blue Corner, Brazilian fighter Graziele Jesus De Sousa. In an auspicious showing, Fuchs dominated across the four rounds in a duplicate of her last outing with De Sousa in Argentina, winning the bout as decisively with a 3–0 score.

Unfortunately for Fuchs, her second outing against the Azerbaijani fighter, Anna Alimardanova, was less successful. Fuchs lost a majority decision, with two judges scoring the bout 39–38 with a third scoring the bout 38–38. In the immediate aftermath of the bout, Fuchs tweeted out, "Thanks for the support, my Olympic dream isn't over. Losses fuel determination I have (for) myself, Team USA (and) America."[27]

In a moment of reflection about her loss, Fuchs felt she had "messed up by looking too far ahead." She added, "I was not focusing on the moment. And actually, that's what my OCD [obsessive-compulsive disorder] stems from. I'm always so focused and worried about how am I going to be clean enough, blah, blah, blah, instead of just focusing on enjoying the moment. That's the biggest thing I took from not getting to box at Rio."[28]

Based on the Olympic qualification rules, Fuchs's only other opportunity would be if either Canadian boxer Mandy Bujold or Colombian fighter Ingrit Valencia landed in the top four, since both had already qualified for Rio. In the end, however, neither fighter hit the podium, which meant Fuchs would not be making the trip to Rio.

Other stories at the Championships included Marlen Esparza's reinvention at light flyweight, noting, "I'm not done. This is not over," and a further positive post on social media, stating, "Let's do this." Through her grueling battles, Esparza was able to win a bronze medal, and a certain amount of vindication as she alighted the podium.[29]

Mikaela Mayer was also eliminated in the preliminary rounds—though, given her berth, she was assured it did not impact her Olympic standing.

In all, under the new leadership of head coach Billy Walsh and his staff of trainers, American women were able to gain a record-setting five medals at the World Championships, led by Claressa Shields, who emerged with a gold medal at middleweight for the second time in her career. The other medalists were heavyweight Shadasia Green, who won the only silver medal for the team, and two more bronze medals for women's light heavyweight, Franchon Crews-Dezurn, and Christina Cruz, fighting at bantamweight.

The team medal output was second only to host country Kazakhstan and China, with six medals apiece at the Championships.

BUMPS ON THE ROAD TO RIO

If women's boxing had been mostly ignored at the Olympic Trials in 2015, in the run-up to the Olympics, the media, beyond boxing's diehard supporters, began to catch on.

As early as June, Claressa Shields was being touted as a woman to watch at the 2016 Rio Games as she attempted to be the first American to win back-to-back gold medals. Shields was also slated to appear in *ESPN The Magazine*'s "Body Issue," alongside such sports luminaries as NBA star Dwayne Wade; five-time Olympic diver Greg Louganis; Olympic volleyball medalist April Ross; and the first transgender athlete to appear, Chris Mosier. The only other female boxing champion to have appeared in the "Body Issue" was Marlen Esparza in 2013.

All was not always rosy, however, for Shields and head coach Billy Walsh. As Shields put it, "He came and just forced the whole Ireland culture, the whole Ireland style of boxing on us, and I was just like, 'I don't wanna box like Katie Taylor.' Like, I love the way she boxes, but that's not what I prefer. I was thinking: 'What I do works. Now, I'm willing to learn whatever it is you want to teach me, but I'm only going to use what I feel is beneficial to my style.'

"It was not working out. I was living at the Olympic training center and there were times when I said, 'Look, I'm gonna move back home. If we don't fix this, I'm leaving!' And then, finally, I think he saw that I was really about what I was talking about; he saw that I was for real, that I really believed and knew that I could win the Olympics again; that I was a hard worker and that I pushed myself . . . ."[30]

Billy Walsh also admitted to some rocky moments.

"Oh, we clashed heads quite a bit in the first few months. . . . I had to explain to her I wasn't trying to change her," Walsh said. "What I said to her was: 'What you did in London won't be good enough in Rio. Everybody has been watching you, studying you, getting better to beat you. We've got to keep ahead of the posse. So the tools I'm giving you are to make you better, so you can fight any girl at any distance in any situation."[31]

As the months passed, Shields and Walsh were able to find a détente of sorts that built to a close bond.

Shields put it this way:

> I'm happy that he taught us some of the things that he did. For example, the culture that he brought over from Ireland where everybody on the team becomes friends despite our differences, despite us fighting each other before—that was him. He brought that 'we're all friends' type of culture; he brought activities that we did together daily or weekly, and it definitely made us closer as a team . . . [and] I'm thankful for Coach Billy Walsh . . . I did learn some things from him: I know how to do a check-hook like Katie Taylor if I ever need to do one.[32]

Walsh had also laid out his plans as a long-term strategy for individual fighters and the team. "I said, ' . . . I'm going to be here until 2020. You're going to be here for a few months. I've got to implement the program. I want you a part of it, but here are my rules and regulations. This is what we need to be doing.' So [Claressa Shields] went home, had a good think about it, came back in, and we started all over again."

In the run-up to the Games, Walsh also took point as women's head coach, adding Kay Koroma as men's associate coach and Augie Sanchez as men's assistant coach. Walsh was also implementing his thoughts on improving coaching across the boards to ensure a long-term investment in amateur boxing for women and men.

"You teach one boxer, you teach one boxer," he says. "You teach one coach, you teach a hundred boxers. We need a better education system around the country."[33]

As Walsh had told Shields, his investment in the team was long term, but what he hoped for was an opportunity for the Olympic squad to medal through the incremental improvements he'd already implemented.

AT THE 2016 RIO GAMES

Women's boxing at the Olympic Games in Rio consisted of the same three weight classes as the 2012 London Games: flyweight, lightweight, and middleweight. A total of thirty-six women had won spots to compete, consisting of twelve competitors for each weight category. One significant change was to be the scoring system with the addition of a professional-style 10-point must system. Once scored, the final scores of each of the five judges would be "reduced" to a single number with fights announced as 3–0 (unanimous), 2–1 (split), or 2–0 (split draw), though only three of the five judges' scores would be counted at the end of each round. Already in effect in prior AIBA tournaments, there was still some question as to how it would play in the Olympics.

Another significant change only affected men's boxing and caused considerable controversy. For the first time since the 1984 Olympics, men would compete without headgear. IOC spokesperson Mark Adams said: "AIBA provided medical and technical data that showed the number of concussions is lower without headgear. They have done a lot of research in the last three years. The rule will go ahead for Rio."

AIBA's belief was the competitions would be more exciting without headgear. Women in the ring, however, would continue to be required to wear theirs "due to a relative lack of data on head injuries in the comparatively young sport of female boxing."[34]

AIBA had made the rule change in June 2013 with an effective date to coincide with the 2016 Olympic Games—based on their research that claimed removal of headgear would reduce concussive risk, a find that was immediately ridiculed but left to stand. With the headgear rule, however, the minimum age for male fighters in the Olympics was raised to nineteen.

An even more controversial change was AIBA's decision to allow male boxing professionals to compete in the Rio Games—allowing a total of twenty-six places at the July qualifying event. While a few professional boxers admitted to being intrigued by the idea, which had first been floated in February 2016, most were firmly against it. The World Boxing Council's president, Mauricio Sulaimán, took particular exception, stating it would be "harmful and dangerous."

With the passage of the rule by 95 percent of the Federations, WBC took a strong stance against the rules change and stated, in part, "The WBC has taken a stance and decided that any WBC champion and top-fifteen rated in our rankings is forbidden to participate until clear guidelines and safety measures are in place. If they do they will be banned from the WBC for two years."[35]

Following in the footsteps of the WBC, the IBF noted any IBF title holders would be stripped of their titles, and non-title holders removed from their rankings for a period of one year.

In announcing the position, Daryl Peoples, the IBF president, stated, "Making this decision was not difficult for us. We felt it was important for the IBF to get involved and take a stance against professional boxers competing against amateurs due to safety concerns, as part of our commitment to this sport is to promote the health and well-being of the boxers."[36]

Given the short time span between the announcement and the start of the men's qualifying tournament, the likelihood of participation by professional boxers was low. The rules change would also allow professional women's boxers to compete, but given the places were already set, it was mute until the 2020 Tokyo Games.

Rules changes aside, the most troubling of controversies was reported by *The Guardian*'s Owen Gibson just days before the men's boxing events were to commence on August 6. In an article that ran on August 1, Gibson wrote that judges and referees were alleged to be influencing the draws and bouts for the upcoming Games. He noted, "One senior figure said there was 'no doubt' some of the judges and referees in Rio 'will be corrupted.'" He alleged a group of referees get together before major championships to decide "how to score certain bouts."

The allegations had also plagued the 2008 and 2012 Games, but they had become more sophisticated since that time to include the use of hand signals and head movements to indicate which corner to reward with the win in each round. Such corruption was alleged to give preferential treatment "to reward countries prepared to pay to host AIBA championships."

In response to queries, AIBA stated in part: "[O]ur role is to ensure a fair and transparent competition and that the thousands of spectators and millions of fans enjoy an amazing tournament with 13 great and undisputed gold medalists. We reiterate that, unless tangible proof is put forward, not just rumors, we cannot further comment on these allegations."[37]

In early July, as the team readied for their trip to Rio, USA Boxing announced that Ginny Fuchs would come to Rio as captain of the team. A popular choice, it was felt she would provide "support to all of her teammates on the U.S. Boxing Squad and consistently [lead] their team warm-ups with her own unique flair."[38]

It was also a way for her to join her fellow Olympians, and even if she was not able to compete, her steadiness and capacity to mentor her teammates was an important ingredient for the hoped-for success of the American Olympic squad at the Games.

Shortly after the announcement as the team was preparing to embark to Rio, Mayer, perhaps summing up the feelings of all the boxers on the team, said, "I've always believed I'd be here, but I also knew that the chances of being here were going to be slim. This was my dream before I knew it was possible."[39]

Shields was particularly relaxed and happy going into the Games. As a returning gold medalist, she was drawing attention from the media. And to aid in the promotion of her participation in the Games, PBS's *Independent Lens* series was premiering a broadcast of *T-Rex: Her Fight for Gold*, on August 2, just days before the start of the Games.

The start of the women's boxing preliminary rounds was set for August 12, beginning with the flyweight and lightweight preliminary competitions. All three reigning gold medalists had qualified to defend their titles to include the UK's Nicola Adams (fly), Ireland's Katie Taylor (light), and American Claressa Shields (middle).

In her first outing at the lightweight preliminaries, Mayer had taken on the American-born Jennifer Chieng, representing the Federated States of Micronesia. Chieng had won her place in the Games with a Tripartite Commission place, a qualification process specifically for National Olympic Committees (NOCs) with less than eight athletes. Mayer was able to dominate the fight with a 3–0 score, though the much shorter

Chieng showed heart and skill even as she took hard shots to the body and the head from Mayer as the rounds wore on.

Reigning Olympians Adams, Taylor, and Shields each had a "bye" in the preliminary rounds, which meant their first competitions would be in the quarterfinals.

The first fight of the morning for the lightweight quarterfinals session was held on Monday, August 15, between Katie Taylor and the Finnish fighter, Mira Potkonen. The contest went to Potkonen with a 2–1 final total based on the 39–37, 38–38, 37–39 judges' scores. Taylor clearly won the first round, with an amped-up Potkonen taking the second. Taylor also seemed to take the third round with a closely fought accounting in the fourth. With the heartbreaking loss, Taylor was not only knocked out of the competition, but out of medal contention.

Across the five judges' score cards, Taylor had won the contest, but most notably, in keeping with the Olympic scoring system, the computer randomly dropped two of the five tallies. In Taylor's case, the two judges dropped just happened to have scored the bout in Taylor's favor.[40] Not much was made of it at the time; however, there was additional controversy a day or so later when Irish Olympic teammate Michael Conlan lost his quarterfinal bout on the score cards along with explosive cries of foul.

Mikaela Mayer's quarterfinal bout was the first fight of the evening session. Wearing the colors of the Blue corner, Mayer's opponent was the Russian fighter, Anastasiia Beliakova. A surprise was the chorus of boos mixed in with the cheers as the fighters were announced, and again throughout the fight. A close, competitive battle, in the end the final score was 2–0 to Beliakova, based on 39–37 by two judges and 38–38 by the third.

Speaking about Mayer's loss, coach Billy Walsh said, "To be honest, I've just had a look at the judging. It was crazy. Are they looking at the same bloody fight or what? Her performance was excellent, she gave everything she had. . . . I thought she did enough to win it."

Mayer's disappointment was palpable. "It was a close fight so it makes it even more disappointing,"[41] she said, adding, "It's frustrating to lose when the fight is so close . . . because you know that maybe one or two more combinations could have won it."[42]

"I thought I might have pulled it off at the end but . . . I also know this is boxing. If you let a fight get that close, you don't know who they are going to give it to."[43]

One thing for certain, Mayer was determined to remain in boxing.

Of the reigning gold medalists, only Claressa Shields (United States) and Nicola Adams (United Kingdom) remained.

Nicola Adams faced the Ukrainian boxer, Tetyana Kob, in the flyweight quarterfinals held on August 16. Adams fought well to take the fight with a unanimous 3–0 final score.

For Shields's quarterfinals bout on August 17, she faced the Russian middleweight Yaroslava Yakushina. In their last outing at the 2014 AIBA Women's World Championships, Shields had defeated her by unanimous decision to take the gold medal. With no apparent boos from the crowd, the popular Shields began to contest with a tight defense and controlled offence, with punches in bunches as openings appeared. Yakushina fought gamely but did not have a lot of answers for Shields's ring supremacy. As a result, she handily won a 3–0 unanimous decision.

The semifinal flyweight was held the following afternoon on August 18. Nicola Adams was set to a rematch with the southpaw Cancan Ren. In their first outing at the Olympics, Adams defeated Ren to take the gold medal at the 2012 London Games. With so much on the line for Adams, if she was nervous, she did not show it as she executed her gameplan with precision even when Ren reached in to hold, with Adams bombarding Ren in the clinches whenever possible. Keeping her composure throughout, even with Ren up on all three cards on the first round, the joy and relaxation that Adams displayed, whether on the front foot or the back foot, brought her the unanimous 3–0 win in the final score of the bout.

If Shields had hoped to face Great Britain's Savannah Marshall in the semifinals or finals, those hopes had been dashed when Marshall lost to Nouchka Fontijn of the Netherlands in the quarterfinals.

Shields's opponent in the semifinals was the middleweight from Kazakhstan, Dariga Shakimova, whose losses in earlier competitions had been to such fighters as Franchon Crews-Dezurn and Savannah Marshall. Shields threw with accuracy and quickness, while slipping Shakimova's output. Following Walsh's instructions to the letter, Shields worked on such things as feinting her left followed by her powerful overhand right, while continuing to display total control of the action. Through four rounds, Shields won a decisive 3–0 unanimous victory, having put on a virtual boxing clinic.

The flyweight final was listed as the first fight of the afternoon session on August 20. Nicola Adams's opponent was French boxer Sarah Ourahmoune. Having defeated her in their four previous outings, Adams was confident coming into the ring and continued to use her extensive repertoire of boxing techniques to capture the gold medal with a unanimous 3–0 win.

On the podium with her second gold medal hanging from her slender frame, Nicola Adams became the first British boxer to win back-to-back gold medals since middleweight Harry Mallin achieved that honor in 1920 and 1924. With her win, she would also forever be enshrined as the first female boxer to achieve that status in the Olympics.

Sunday, August 21, 2016, was a make-or-break day for women's boxing history in the United States as Shields entered the ring to resounding cheers to face her opponent, Dutch middleweight Nouchka Fontijn. Shields had defeated Fontijn the previous May at the 2016 AIBA Women's World Championships final with a decisive win to capture the gold medal title. At twenty-eight, Fontijn had begun her amateur career in 2013 with an excellent record of achievement. Coming into the ring, Fontijn had a two-inch reach advantage, but only came into the finals with two mixed-decision wins.

Relaxed and loose, Shields used her speed and, heeding to coach Billy Walsh, set up shots. Fluid and with gorgeous head movement and defensive posturing, Shields continuously slipped Fontijn's shots, giving new meaning to the adage *make 'em miss, make 'em pay* each time Shields countered with a flurry of shots of her own.

With the fight over, Shields could barely contain herself as she waited expectantly for the referee to raise her hand. Once announced as the winner, she beamed as she took a moment, having just won her second gold medal. After a beat, she thanked the crowd as she walked toward the apron of the ring before turning and performing a cartwheel on her way back to her corner. On the floor of the arena, she held an American flag high, running around the ring before draping it around herself while making her way toward the exit.

With her achievement, Shields became the first American boxer—male or female—to win back-to-back gold medals. Asked what's next for herself after winning gold two times, Shields breathlessly responded, "I don't know, I don't know what's next," proclaiming, "oh, thank you Jesus," as she threw her flag-laden hand in the air.[44]

To another interviewer and with a bit more composure, Shields proclaimed, "I want to let it be known that I'm not just a great female boxer, but I'm one of the great[est] boxers to ever live."[45]

Both Nicola Adams and Claressa Shields had achieved extraordinary heights for women's boxing with their back-to-back gold medal wins. Lightweight boxer Estelle Mossely won her gold medal, only the second for the weight category in Olympic history, by a 2–1 split decision over Junhua Yin of China—placing her as one of the top three elite amateur female boxers in the world.

What those momentous wins would mean over time was an unknown, as was the question of whether Shields and Adams, along with Taylor, Mayer, and others of the 2016 class of Olympians, would remain in the amateurs. The challenge was a great one, as women's professional boxing coming out of the Games was uneven at best for opportunity, pay equity, promotion, and even the chance to be seen on boxing media.

Despite the greatness that had been achieved, there was also ongoing drama at the Olympics themselves.

On August 17, it had been revealed that AIBA had "removed some judges and referees after controversy over fight decisions and the new professional style scoring system."

The next day, a top boxing executive with AIBA was "reassigned with immediate effect in the wake of corruption claims and concerns over judging decisions."[46]

Asked about the scoring problems, Billy Walsh called out the inequities, saying, "The judging has been atrocious." He added: "The last time

I saw it as bad was in Seoul in 1988 when Roy Jones got robbed in the final."[47] It should be noted he did not bring up Mayer's loss.

The corruption at the heart of the scandal would play itself out over the months and years to come, but it could not take away what had been achieved by the women who contested in the sport with great skill, courage, determination, and effort.

And while the three female 2016 Team USA Olympians had made no decisions as to whether they would continue as amateurs, the commitment made by Billy Walsh to USA Boxing's elite amateur program was palpable and helped set the stage for the Olympians of 2020.

CHAPTER TWO

The Challenges of Being "Old Gang" Women of the Ring

THE TRIUMPH OF WOMEN IN THE OLYMPICS CAST A LONG SHADOW ON "old gang" female professional boxers with little or no amateur backgrounds. These fighters had been pushing for the elevation of the sport during the long, lean years of little if any media exposure in places like the United States and the United Kingdom, along with the difficulties of unearthing promotional opportunities.

The American boxer Melissa Hernandez exemplified the dilemma: She won the WBC female featherweight title over Canada's Jelena Mrdjenovich by unanimous decision at the Shaw Conference Center, in Edmonton, on September 14, 2012, but it wasn't televised in the United States and barely covered, even in the American boxing press. The following March, when Hernandez defended her title against Mrdjenovich, she lost the belt on points following a stoppage due to a headbutt in the second round. It was similarly barely reported on. This lack of coverage put enormous pressure on the growth of women's professional endeavors in the sport, but the women persevered, leveraging social media to bring the case directly to boxing fans and the boxing elite.

Fighters such as Amanda Serrano (United States) and Heather Hardy (United States), who had not risen to the level of winning major titles, were fighting for little money and little exposure at the time of the Olympics. Serrano's ticket seemed to be her technical brilliance, and for Hardy, a drive and an activism that pushed the boundaries the instant she was given the opportunity to fight. Both saw success in their push for acceptance and recognition, fighting on major cards, and breaking through the seeming media blackout by appearing live on streaming services and television, beginning with Serrano's six-round unanimous decision win over Fatuma Zarika on CBS Sports in May 2015. At the same time, such promoters as Lou DiBella's *DiBella Entertainment* began to sign more fighters with the belief that there was a future in such opportunities. Through it all, the women of the ring persevered to push through the inequities.

THE "PRO" LIFE

Way back in 1974, boxer Marian "Lady Tyger" Trimiar told an interviewer why she was pushing to become a licensed professional fighter. What she talked about was her desire to be an Olympic boxer. As early as 1974, she sparred with male boxers in an attempt "to convince officials there should be a ladies division in the Olympics."[1]

She was never able to realize that dream, but she did help propel the sport forward as a pioneer boxer in the late 1970s and early 1980s. That spirit of pushing for opportunity was never quite realized, leading her to stage a very public hunger strike in April 1987 to bring recognition to the financial, promotional, and working conditions of professional female boxers.

Fast-forward to 2012, and much had changed.

Women were in the Olympics.

The June 2001 Ali–Frasier IV bout card between Laila Ali and Jacqui Frazier-Lyde demonstrated that women could headline pay-per-view fight cards, and by 2005 internationally recognized sanctioning bodies such as the World Boxing Council had started to bestow women's world championship titles. Female fighters in the sport were also reaching heights of mainstream popularity in places like Argentina and Mexico, but in the United States, much had also remained the same. The paydays were virtually nonexistent, mainstream boxing media were no longer broadcasting female bouts, and women were stuck with poor promotion and ill treatment in the form of lousy venues, minimal opportunities, and an indifference at best from boxing media with a few notable exceptions.

Tensions also existed within combat sports. Mixed martial arts (MMA) was making inroads into the limited national dollars available for such shows in the United States, with boxing beginning to lose out. The MMA shows, while more brutal and with less "science," proved very popular and accessible as an entry point, with a lot of gory gladiatorial grappling inside the dystopian cages.

The bouts were also bloodier, fast paced, and provided audiences with a lot of instantaneous gratification as a stand-in for hand-to-hand martial combat. Showtime's *Strikeforce* broadcasts routinely included women's bouts beginning with such fighters as Miesha Tate and Rhonda Rousey. Rousey had already won notoriety as a bronze medalist in judo at the 2008 Beijing Olympic Games. With her win, she had become the first American, female or male, to medal in the sport since its inclusion at the 1992 Barcelona Games.

Competing in MMA, Rousey won her first title on a *Strikeforce* card when she challenged Tate in 2012. Ultimate Fighting Championship (UFC) president Dana White saw something in Rousey, and signed her to compete for a title at the UFC 157 show set for the following February.

For women in boxing in the United States, the notoriety and inclusion of their sisters in MMA on national broadcasts was another hopeful sign their time under the camera lights might come sooner rather than later. Coupled with the implicit promise of the Olympics, the women of boxing remained as determined as ever, finding whatever routes they could to success.

Boxer Heather "The Heat" Hardy was a seeming case in point. Her debut professional fight on August 2, 2012, occurred just a few days before the first bouts in the 2012 London Games. The former 2011 USA Boxing national lightweight champion had lost her repeat bid in March 2012 in the quarter finals to Tiara Brown.

Having reached the age of thirty, and with a lackluster 3–3 amateur record that closed her out of any remote chance to compete for a berth in the Olympics, Hardy was still in love with boxing, which pushed her to continue to train until something turned up.

Hardy had begun her career in kickboxing. A single mother, having survived an abusive marriage and a rape, Hardy's commitment to combat sports was a lifeline for her. Feeling unsatisfied with the options open to her in kickboxing, Hardy switched to boxing, finding a home in the storied Gleason's Gym in the DUMBO neighborhood of Brooklyn, New York.

There was something about the smell of a real boxing gym, imbued with decades of dreams and the champions who had come before. These included such female legends in the sport as the reigning WBC world super bantam champion, Alicia "Slick" Ashley, with whom Hardy had started to train. Ashley had won the coveted WBC green belt by unanimous decision. She'd been the main event in a fight promoted by Joe DeGuardia's Star Boxing at the Hunts Point Produce Market in the Bronx against American Christina Ruiz in July 2011—representing an old-gang quirky model of the state of women's boxing in the pre-Olympics years.

Early in the summer of 2012, boxing promoter Lou DiBella approached Hardy to have her pro debut on an upcoming Broadway Boxing card to be held at the legendary Roseland Ballroom.

Hardy jumped at the chance, gleefully telling an interviewer, "It was a quick decision. Do you wanna have a fight? All right. Within three weeks of putting gloves on my hands, I had my first fight."[2]

DiBella had been adding women to his fight cards since as early as 2006 under the aegis of his company, DiBella Entertainment, showcasing talented female fighters. He'd started his company after leaving his role at HBO, where he'd been vice president of programming and the force behind such ventures as the highly popular *Boxing After Dark* series. The first woman boxer he featured was Maureen "The Real Million Dollar Baby" Shea (super feather). After a few years he featured Keisher "The Boxing Diva" McLeod-Wells (flyweight) and Sonya "The Scholar" Lamonakis (heavy), who even appeared on the undercard of an HBO fight broadcast from Foxwoods Casino in 2011, and again in 2012 shortly after the Olympics.

Asked why he had begun to put women on his shows, DiBella said, "Because I saw how hard those women were working and how much they deserved an opportunity to showcase their talent, because they weren't doing it for the money . . . because there was no money, back when I first started televising."[3]

As DiBella's newest find, Heather Hardy was given a four-round showcase against Mikayla Nebel who, though 0–2 coming into the ring, felt it was an even fight because her first two opponents had gone on to win titles.

In the first round, it appeared that Nebel was on to something after landing Hardy on the deck with a straight right in their fast-paced opening round. Hardy continued to eat punches but started dishing out hard shots of her own through the end of the frame. As one commentator on the local-market broadcast cable show put it, "Heather Hardy . . . welcome to boxing."[4]

Having sold a lot of tickets to include a crowd of supporters from her neighborhood of Gerritsen Beach, Brooklyn, Hardy was spurred on in the second round. She was also fired up by having been knocked down, demonstrating her will to win by picking up the pace and throwing nonstop as she continuously backed Nebel toward the ropes. Hardy threw a lot of combinations, including hard shots to the body and relentlessly pushed herself forward with a growing momentum for the three remaining rounds, creating even more excitement along the way from the supportive crowd.

Bowing to all four corners of the ring at the conclusion of the bout, Hardy had proved her mettle, gaining the unanimous decision, 38–37, from all three judges, and the respect of Lou DiBella, who went on to sign Hardy to a multifight promotional deal, the first woman he had formally signed to a contract.

If the Olympics were to have made a difference, in January 2013, Hardy felt the struggles and inequities of being a professional female boxer remained unchanged. "I do not see that it has made a difference in the professional sense," she said. "I am still making considerably less than my male counterparts and doing the exact same job."[5]

Shelley "Shelito's Way" Vincent was another fighter who started boxing professionally in the same period after a brief amateur career (2–2) that included winning the USA Women's National Golden Gloves 2011 bantamweight title.

Fighting out of Rhode Island, Vincent's debut had been in October 2011, and by January 2013, she'd run up a quick 6–0 record at super bantamweight, including having a place on the undercard of a nationally broadcast show at Foxwoods. Like Hardy, she had a large, vocal following, and routinely sold out her block of tickets plus some more. Ahead of her January 2013 outing at the Mohegan Sun, where she hoped at least to get a mention on the NBC broadcast, she was uncertain if the implicit promise of more opportunity after the Olympics had been met. In response to a written interview question on the topic, she wrote:

> I'm not sure . . . but it needs to happen. . . . MMA does so much for their women. . . . People will tune in. . . . An[d] I myself sell more th[a]n any male in this area. . . . And Every time I do better. . . . People do want to see it. . . . Plus women are so exciting to watch. . . . We go so hard trying to prove we belong here. . . . I have people that fly in from other states when I fight and I don't even know them. . . . All we can do is cross our fingers and hope we can get some time. . . . I think it will happen though.[6]

In the run-up to the Olympics, Maureen Shea had already found the opportunities in the United States were proving elusive. The half-Irish, half-Mexican boxer from the Bronx first came to notoriety as Hillary Swank's sparring partner for the Oscar-winning film, *Million Dollar Baby*. Shea had also fought on major cards at Madison Square Garden after her early fights with DiBella. By 2011, Shea started fighting bouts in Mexico, winning a WBC interim world feather title, and continuing to contest—and win—in a series of fights in and around Tijuana through 2013. She also began promoting fights through her Pandora Promotions company, including a non-title eight-round, main-event bout between Alicia Ashley and Crystal Hoy held at Brooklyn's Masonic Temple in 2011. Despite improvements to her record of achievement, she was unable to fight again for a title until she won the International Boxing Association (IBA) world super bantam in 2014, at a venue in Oxnard, California.

The following year Shea, then thirty-four years of age, was matched against the twenty-one-year-old Mexican IBF female world super bantam champion, Yuliahn Luna, at The Forum in Ingram, California. The co–main event fight was promoted by boxer Shane Mosely and had the distinction of being the first women's bout to be broadcast on PPV since Laila Ali won the WBC world super middle title in June 2005 on a card featuring Mike Tyson's last professional fight—a ten-year drought in women's PPV action.

In a press release promoting the fight card, Mosely said, "It's an embarrassment to boxing that UFC and MMA show more respect to their woman fighters than the boxing world does, and it's about time we caught up. I just hope the community gets behind me in this decision by buying the PPV and coming out to support at the Forum live."[7]

The Shea–Luna matchup proved to be an all-action bout with both fighters displaying flashes of boxing prowess and acumen. The scores, however, were widely varied, 97–93 (Luna), 98–92 (Shea), 95–95, and when the final numbers were tallied the bout was ruled a split-decision draw. All three judges had clearly been undecided as to whether to reward Shea for her aggressiveness or Luna for her boxing accuracy. The net result was Luna held on to her IBF belt, and Shea returned to fighting out of Mexico later in the year.

Sonya Lamonakis, who was a middle school teacher in Queens, New York, public schools, relished her professional boxing opportunities with Lou DiBella. She fought on DiBella Entertainment cards through 2012. She also famously lost her first bout against Mexican American fighter Martha Salazar fighting a six-round, three-minute-round bout in California, with unanimous decision of 60–54 by all three judges.

Back on the East Coast, she had drawn a strong following and was renowned for her ability to sell tickets, in the same way as Hardy and Vincent. Lamonakis had further chances to contest for titles the following year in 2014, winning the inaugural IBO world heavy title against Carlette Ewell, the former 2008 WIBA world heavy champion.

Keisher McLeod-Wells also continued to fight on Lou DiBella cards through 2013 and went on to win the WIBA world fly title in 2014, retiring from the sport in 2016 after losing a WBC world light fly title shot to Ibeth Zamora Silva.

McLeod-Wells was able to leverage her DiBella Entertainment stint to appear on the world's first all-female boxing reality TV series, *Todas Contra Mexico* (All Against Mexico) in March 2011. The premise of the show was to pit eight Mexican female boxers against eight "international" fighters, including McLeod-Wells. Set in Chiapas, Mexico, and loosely based on ESPN's 2008 series, *The Contender*, the show was filmed over a four-week period and hosted by Maureen Shea.

In an interview at the time, Shea said, "This is a big moment for female boxing. For a long time, the public ignored female boxing but there has been a shift in recent years in the perception of the sport. Women in boxing are gaining more respect with the way they are being portrayed, and the sport is gaining in popularity among females due to the women's empowerment movement. After this show, the world will have to take notice of female boxing."[8]

As part of the promotion for the show, McLeod-Wells appeared in a feature piece in the *New York Times*, noting that for a championship title shot, earnings were low: "Maybe $8,000, $10,000." She added, "It's pennies compared to a man. I think that's why we fight harder, because we do this for the love of the sport. There's no money really to be made."[9]

As if echoing Lou DiBella, the monetary aspects of the sport remained an open wound for women trying to earn a living solely on their boxing and is why women were intrigued by the opportunities that might open after their appearance on the *Todas Contra Mexico* show. Unfortunately, it did not prove as helpful as the fighters might have hoped.

Other international team fighters included, among others, American-born Filipina fighter, Crystal Hoy; El Paso, Texas–based fighter, Jennifer Han; Bolivian boxer and the chosen team captain, Jennifer Salinas; Peruvian fighter Linda Laura Lecca; and Polish fighter, Karolina Owczarz. While the show was broadcast in Mexico, it gained no further traction in the United States, and records of the bouts are hard to come by.

To round out the period, Hardy and Vincent met in a WBC women's international feather title bout at the Ford Amphitheater in Coney Island on August 21, 2016—the same day Claressa Shields was slated to defend her gold medal status at the 2016 Rio Games.

Hardy and Vincent had been in a rivalry for East Coast supremacy at featherweight, and with Vincent now promoted by DiBella Entertainment, the date had been set for a showdown between the two equally matched opponents with Hardy at 17–0 (4-KOs) and Vincent at 18–0 (1-KO). In the parlance of boxing, somebody's "O" had to go in the ten-round battle that would very likely go the distance.

The fight was on a Premier Boxing Champion's (PBC) fight card with Errol Spence Jr. battling Leonard Bundu in the main event. What made the evening unique is the Hardy–Vincent showdown was slated to be broadcast on the United States' NBC Sports Network, the first time PBC broadcast a women's boxing fight, albeit broadcast online and not on cable.

The Amphitheater itself was electric with anticipation. The crowd sold out thanks to the loyal fans of Hardy and Vincent, who filled the outside venue on a late Tuesday afternoon and sat tight through the preliminaries and the Spencer main-event fight waiting for Hardy–Vincent to begin. They did not mind the heat and humidity of the summer evening or the signature flash thunderstorm.

Easily the fight of the night, the closely fought contest proved to be a momentous battle, bringing Hardy the majority-decision win and the WBC championship belt with scores that may not have been entirely reflective of the fight itself: 95–95, 99–91, 97–93. The fight, however, represented women in the ring in the most favorable of lights with terrific action and a frenzied crowd supporting both fighters through the contest.

Overcome with emotion, Hardy was aware of what the moment represented. Thanking her opponent, Shelly Vincent, she said, "This bout is not possible without her. She is an incredible opponent, it was a great fight, and I thank her for the chance we both gave all women tonight."

Thanking Lou DiBella, Al Hayman, and NBC for the opportunity, she was asked what the fight meant for women's boxing. "I hope it makes people know that we're out here, there's so many of us . . . there is a sea of female talent," and taking a beat she said, "Tonight we had Claressa Shields become the very first, ever, Olympic American boxer . . . to be two-time Gold medalist."

With that sentiment, she made it clear that the linkages between the twinned paths for women in the sport both as amateurs and as professionals, regardless of the path, was built on the hard work, sacrifice, talent, and excellence in execution that would continue to elevate the sport.

OLD GANG CHAMPIONS: MELISSA HERNANDEZ, LAYLA MCCARTER, JELENA MRDJENOVICH

Melissa "Huracan Shark" Hernandez was a Puerto Rican fighter who grew up in the Bronx. As an amateur, she had won the 2004 National PAL women's elite championship at lightweight by stoppage by the referee. She turned pro in 2005, and famously fought in a Global Boxing Union championship bout in Las Vegas that had been contracted by opponent Layla McCarter for twelve three-minute rounds. Held as the main event at the Orleans Hotel & Casino on February 14, 2007, Hernandez lost the bout in the eighth round, but won by split decision in an 8, three-minute round rematch two months later at the same venue.

Hernandez was an established fighter with a 17–3–3 record when she entered the ring to fight an equally brilliant Canadian fighter, Jelena Mrdjenovich, with a 28–8–1 record a month after the 2012 London Games. Their first outing had been the year before in an eight-round non-title battle. Hernandez was then the interim WIBA lightweight champion, with a lot of confidence and swagger in the ring—taking the bout by split decision for the win.

With a lot on the line for their rematch, including Mrdjenovich's WBC world feather title, Hernandez put on a sizable show for the Canadian audience and those who were able to view the broadcast. Billed at Mrdjenovich–Hernandez II, Hernandez dazzled the crowd on her ring walk, dancing, and shimmying, and sporting a Mrdjenovich T-shirt.

The defending champion, Mrdjenovich, from Edmonton, Canada, enjoyed enormous popularity and support, and routinely had her battles shown on Canadian broadcast outlets. She was also looked upon as a trailblazer in Canadian women's boxing and with a strong right hand and

KO power, whether at feather or lightweight, was considered by her peers in the sport to be a boxer's boxer.

By the time of her bout with Hernandez in 2012, Mrdjenovich had been a multiple title winner, including the first WBC super featherweight title, which she won in 2005 and held until her loss to fellow Canadian Olivia Gerula in 2009.

Cast as the main event, both fighters were poised to give the sold-out Shaw Center and the coast-to-coast fans on Canada's Sports Net an exciting battle. The bout included open scoring with interim scores announced at the end of the fourth and seventh rounds.

Hernandez began the fight at southpaw but was able to seamlessly switch to her orthodox stance while dancing around the ring. As the fight enfolded, Mrdjenovich attempted to keep her jab going and to fight at distance. She also maintained a high guard and threw straight rights and left hooks to complement her jab. Across the fight, Hernandez was just a bit quicker to the punch, though with Mrdjenovich maintaining her high guard, she was not particularly hurt. What she was unable to do was execute clean punching. Hernandez became very adept at tying her up, and managing the distance, she was also aggressive on the front foot despite Mrdjenovich's four-inch height advantage and longer reach. Maintaining the advantage across the bout in a hard-fought contest, and never really allowing Mrdjenovich to take the momentum, Hernandez became the new WBC title holder with a unanimous decision, 98–92, 97–93, 98–92.

Shouting, "I wanted the T-shirt," Melissa Hernandez, with the belt being wrapped around her body and sporting her new, WBC-emblazoned shirt, said, "Jelena is the best at 126 in the world. I told everybody she is a beast, and she is a beast!"

Continuing as the interviewer peppered her with questions about her game plan, Hernandez said, "The whole thing with Jelena is, she hits incredibly hard, so, yeah, you've got to get the hell out of there. You know what it is, Jelena is a beast, and the game plan was to stay there with her. Jelena had me hurt six times in the fight, but if I were to coast that's when she was going to catch me."

Smiling broadly at the camera, Hernandez called for Mrdjenovich to come to ring.

Equally humbled by the gesture, she walked a broad arc around the ring to join Hernandez, and said, "Thanks Edmonton, you guys are a hell of a crowd, I love fighting here, and I love having you guys cheer for me. Again, thank you to Melissa. She made it a war, she executed her game plan, she did a phenomenal job tonight, and she frustrated me visibly, but thank you for going toe-to-toe with me, like nobody else would. Thank you very much, you deserve it and a great fight and again thank you Edmonton, you guys make me proud to be and Edmontonian."[10]

Both Hernandez and Mrdjenovich had impressive records of accomplishment coming into their second battle, with the best professional fighters of the era to include such boxers as Belinda Laracuente, Olivia Gerula, Ann Saccurato, Chevelle Hallbeck, Layla McCarter, Erica Annabella Farias, and Lindsay Garbatt.

They were all champions. Willing to travel for bouts, and while Mrdjenovich enjoyed a "home" of sorts at the Shaw Conference Center in Edmonton, in the post-Olympic world of women's boxing, she did begin to contest for titles outside of her comfort zone, including a 2015 defense of her WBC feather title in Panama City against Colombian boxer Francia Elena Bravo, who sported a 19–4–2 record at the time.

While Mrdjenovich's bouts were broadcast in Canada, when Hernandez stepped back over the border to the United States, her fights were not shown on nationally broadcast boxing media. As a case in point, Hernandez fought in a ten-rounder against the veteran journeywoman, Nicole Woods (11–9–2), in July 2012 as a main event, at the Columbus Civic Center in Columbus, Georgia. While not a "barnburner" of a bout, Hernandez won the fight by unanimous decision, and despite being a main event, it was not broadcast.

In their rematch held two years later in Atlanta, there was at least local regional coverage in advance of the fight and highlights that were made available contemporaneously on YouTube. The rematch footage showed the much shorter Hernandez bringing the fight to Woods, and Woods, in turn, looking to use her five-inch height advantage and strength to fight at distance, which gave Hernandez the mixed-decision win.

In speaking about the fight after the bout, Hernandez said, "The game plan always is when you fight somebody tall . . . make them give up their height. And she played well, she was going for it, there was a lot of head butts, but it is what it is, this is boxing, you've got two veterans in there, we're just trying to show that women can do it too."[11]

The third time Hernandez and Mrdjenovich fought, Hernandez entered the ring as the defending champion.

Held again at Shaw Stadium, Edmonton, in May 2013, Mrdjenovich came into the ring bouncing jauntily with a lot more energy than in her last outing. Hernandez repeated her dancing ring walk, happily shimmying along the way.

Similar to their previous match, Hernandez used a southpaw stance, counterpunching Mrdjenovich's straight punches but being caught by body shots in the clinches. With something to prove, Mrdjenovich used her jab more effectively. Hernandez, for her part, fought hard in the clinches to ensure her ability to score points, and was effectively using the left-hand lead, when Mrdjenovich received a gash from an accidental headbutt. Bleeding heavily in the third round, Mrdjenovich brought the fight to Hernandez, only stopping when the referee called a doctor to look at her before the pair fought nonstop till the end of the round.

With further urgency, Mrdjenovich picked up the pace and increased her punch output as she pushed forward on the front foot, and having established dominance, put the round away—with the referee telling her between rounds that he would give her one more round. The red, bloodied face of Mrdjenovich showed her determination as she continued to aggressively push forward and muscle Hernandez as they banged away at each other, leading to a big left hook that sent Hernandez to the canvas from a slip.

Still fighting in the sixth round, the referee allowed the bout to continue as both fighters went toe to toe, with a continuing barrage of punches—showing the determination of the two champions, with Hernandez tagging her opponent as the round ended.

With tears in Mrdjenovich's eyes as the fight was called at the end of the sixth round, Hernandez came to her corner to tell her how sorry she was that she caused the headbutt and that it was not intentional.

After a total war, the audience in attendance cheered both fighters after the bout, with the unanimous decision win, 58–55 57–56, 58–55, called for the new WBC world female featherweight champion, Jelena Mrdjenovich.

In her interview in the ring after the fight, Mrdjenovich started by saying: "I want to thank Melissa so much for giving me this opportunity and putting on a hell of a fight . . . I bet I'm no longer pretty thanks to the Hernandez corner, so thank you very much and I really appreciate you guys in Edmonton . . . through tears, blood and damn near wars."

Continuing, she said, "that cut, I did not want to stop this fight. . . . I trained to go ten rounds of war with Melissa . . . but thank you . . . for putting on a war, and being amazing. . . . "

Responding in kind, Melissa said, "Jelena is probably one of the hardest punchers in the women's game . . . when we came out I saw that . . . anger, that real champ, so I boxed that first and then . . . why not go toe-to-toe, so the cut really made a huge difference . . . because at the end of the day it's my friend. [But after the headbutt] she went for the kill. That's the way Jelena is made, she saw her own blood and it was almost like me smelling blood, she just went for the kill. . . . I wish the cut didn't happen 'cause we were ready."

With the final word, Jelena added, "Melissa's a tough one to hit, first of all; and then second of all, she's legit, she's a world champion, and then we don't go down easy, that's for sure and that's the reason why we're world champions and you know . . . I just wanted to put on a good fight for everyone here, and a good fight with Melissa. We're friends, but we want to put on good fights for women's boxing. . . . "[12]

Though there had been talk between the pair to set up a fourth bout, it never came to pass. But both continued in their remarkable careers in the post-Olympic years with tremendous battles through 2016 when women's boxing pivoted again. For both this meant not only fighting in championship battles but in non-title eight-rounders. Mrdjenovich was able to successfully defend her belt in 2014 and 2015, before a loss to the Argentinian champion, Edith Soledad Matthysse, in Casseros, Argentina, in August 2015. She won back the WBC world feather and added the WBA world feather in a rematch against Matthysse back at home in Edmonton the following March 2016. Mrdjenovich successfully defended both titles through 2019.

Melissa Hernandez's career through 2016 was circuitous, with fewer opportunities for major championship belts and mostly eight-round battles in the United States that were untelevised. She continued to travel, including a unanimous decision loss to Marcela Eliana Acuña, in San Miguel, Tucuman, Argentina in 2013. The main-event bout was a WBO world female eliminator that was broadcast on Argentina's TyC Sports network and went the ten-round distance. The card included a women's four-rounder and was well attended by a sold-out crowd.

In 2014, Layla McCarter and Melissa Hernandez were set to meet for their third lightweight outing at the Orleans Hotel & Casino.

In the run-up to the fight, boxing writer Thomas Gerbasi, an early supporter of women's boxing, wrote a piece for *The Ring* entitled, "The Unseen Trilogy of Layla McCarter and Melissa Hernandez."

The lead of the article laid out in no uncertain terms that "In the world of male boxing, a match between two of the best pound-for-pound fighters in the world would be on pay-per-view or, at the very least, premium cable, aired around the world to fans hungry to see the elite battle it out between the ropes. Add in that the fight is a rubber match, and even more eyeballs would be on it."

He added that because it was a women's boxing bout, nobody would get to see it, except for the tight-knit group of fans in Las Vegas that followed McCarter's prowess in the ring, and viewers of a local series that broadcast fights.

As McCarter, who held world titles in four weight classes, put it, "The state of women's boxing in the USA is sad. Old-school mindsets are keeping us out of the real opportunities. It will take some guys at the top to recognize that women's boxing has depth and talent that needs to be included on major shows to change the status quo."[13]

As the McCarter–Hernandez III main-event non-title eight-rounder got underway, it featured Hernandez's bouncing, shimmying ring walk and subsequent ring antics as she made her way to her corner. McCarter, in her own backyard of Las Vegas, was also loose, and happily greeted the crowd as she entered the ring.

From early in the first round, McCarter began to establish her jab, and in a complement of doubled-up left hooks, she kept Hernandez on the back foot. Toward the end of the second round, in what looked like a knockdown, Hernandez went down, but the referee ruled a slip as the bell tolled. McCarter was able to control the rest of the bout, with occasional flurries from Hernandez, but there was never any doubt that McCarter would end up with a unanimous win. As it was, she won the fight on all three cards, scoring 80–72, 79–73, 80–72.

Speaking after the fight, McCarter noted the key to victory had been in establishing her jab and that since she had fought Hernandez twice before, she was familiar with her style. She added, "My crowd gave me a big boost today, everybody here, family, friends,"

Asked what she was doing to help female boxing in the United States, McCarter said, "[I'm] living the example, you know I'm breaking the ground for the future, trying to establish three-minute rounds for females, and eventually equal pay as well at the top levels."

McCarter and Hernandez were to fight one more time, an eight-rounder at welterweight on the Dontay Wilder versus Chris Arreola card set for July 16, 2016, at the Legacy Arena, in Birmingham, Alabama. Lou DiBella promoted the top of the card, but even with his support for women in boxing, the McCarter–Hernandez battle was not broadcast as part of the main card that went out on Fox in the United States and Sky Sports in the United Kingdom.

In an article in *The Sweet Science*, David A. Avila, another boxing writer who was a strong advocate for women in the ring, made the point that while "It's just one person's opinion but the most skillful fight on the Alabama fight card for the WBC heavyweight title will be the two women clashing for a fourth time."

He further noted, "Fox will televise the Deontay Wilder vs. Chris Arreola fight but not the female clash between two of the best female's pound for pound."

For all of that, Wilder had made the promise to McCarter to put her on his fight card, and he came through.[14]

The fight gave McCarter another unanimous decision win, 78–74, 80–72, 79–73, in what proved to be her fourth and last outing against Hernandez.

As if continuing to prove Gerbasi's point, the opportunities for showcasing women, even with the hugely anticipated boost from the Olympics, was still proving elusive in the United States, just a month before the 2016 Rio Games where women would contest in their second Olympics.

UNDISPUTED AND OTHER EXPRESSIONS OF BRILLIANCE

Cecilia Braekhus's WBC reign at welterweight began in March 2009. By September 2014, Braekhus became the first women's undisputed champion of the four-belt era when she defeated Croatian fighter Ivana Habazin by unanimous decision on a card broadcast across Europe, but with barely a ripple in the United States. Swedish fighter Klara Stevenson was also on the card, winning the interim WBC world super light title.

With Braekhus's win, she not only became the first woman to hold the undisputed crown, but only the third boxer after Bernard Hopkins and Germaine Taylor, both of whom had held that honor at middleweight.

Ahead of the fight, Braekhus said, "This is a massive opportunity for me to cement my legacy as the best female boxer of all time."[15]

Braekhus had already defeated such tough fighters as Anne Sophie Mathis (France), Oxandia Castillo (Dominican Republic), and Myriam Lamare (France) in the run-up to her undisputed crown—one she held until 2020.

As a Norwegian professional boxer who had been adopted from her Cartagena, Colombia, home at the age of two, Braekhus had entered combat sports as a fourteen-year-old kickboxer. She had amassed an impressive amateur career before switching to boxing, where she continued to contest as an amateur until she turned pro with a German promoter in 2007. Throughout much of her early career, professional boxing for men and women was illegal in her native Norway. In 2016, under a groundswell of enthusiasm generated by its native daughter, Cecilia Braekhus, Norway ended its thirty-three-year ban when the law was repealed by the Norwegian parliament. Hearing the news of the repeal, she told a broadcaster, "I believe this might be one of the greatest moments of my life. . . . I am very glad that we've achieved this together.

It's hard to describe all the emotions. In any case, I'm not a criminal in Norway anymore."[16]

Her achievement was momentous and spoke to how sports could achieve and change societal norms. That success was reminiscent of the battles fought and won for the right to box professionally at all, but the universality of Braekhus's achievement in Norway crossed gendered thinking as the pride swelled in her accomplishment as a boxer, period.

That generalized acceptance, however, was proving elusive in such places as the United States and the United Kingdom. Except there were "trickles," such as Shea's appearance on a Shane Mosely's PPV card boxer, Amanda Serrano's six-round super featherweight bout against Kenyan fighter Fatuma Zarika shown on CBS Sports television a few months earlier in May 2015, and the Hardy–Vincent fight in August 2016.

These were proving to be early indications that the seeming ban on broadcasting women's bouts nationally in the United States were beginning to crack, albeit very slowly.

For Serrano, in particular, who was Puerto Rican but fighting out of Brooklyn, New York, and whose talent was beginning to show as one of the hardest-hitting fighters in boxing, male or female, the road to success was in sight, both at home and as a road warrior. She began to capture the imagination of local fans in 2011 with her main-event performance to win the IBF world super feather title as the main event at the Aviator Sports Complex in Brooklyn. The following April she lost an opportunity to gain the WBC world super feather title, resulting in her first loss to Frida Wallberg in Sweden. Serrano went on to fight in the Dominican Republic, where she won two smaller belts in 2013. She contested in six- and eight-rounders before her 2014 win in Argentina by a sixth-round knockout to add the WBO world light championship hardware to her growing collection.

These inconsistencies in opportunity were certainly one of the hallmarks of female boxing, where even with championship belts, fighters were not guaranteed the chance to defend their titles because promoters would not or could not fund the sanctioning fees, venues, or fight cards necessary for such defenses. For Serrano, this meant she needed to chase the opportunities as they arose, wherever they arose, at home or abroad.

She also began to fight on Lou DiBella cards beginning in February 2016, which brought her larger exposure and opportunities to contest for titles and defend them—with a first-round TKO win over Olivia Gerula to capture the WBO world feather title on her DiBella Entertainment outing.

While the Olympics had certainly been a line in the sand with respect to the acceptance of women's boxing on the elite amateur stage, for the women who had been fighting in the pros or just starting out, the payday at the end of the rainbow had not appeared, nor been a consistent plane of opportunity from which to grow their careers. The exceptions continued to be the elite professional boxers in places such as Mexico, Argentina, Japan, and across Europe, where fighters were being given the chance to fight for decent money, on cards that were broadcast across their national markets, and in the case of European fighters, across national boundaries.

Women were also starting to be listened to a bit more, with fighters like Cecilia Braekhus, whose achievements as an undisputed fighter could not be ignored. In that sense, while fighters in the United States and United Kingdom were enormously challenged, there were bouts being held, and applauded by the fans in local markets, even if the larger picture remained elusive.

HONORING THE PAST, BRINGING IN THE FUTURE

The International Women's Boxing Hall of Fame owes its existence to the tenacious insistence that women deserve recognition for their tremendous efforts in the boxing ring—in a "room" of their own, to give a hat tip to the notion first put into the lexicon of sayings by the brilliant Virginia Woolf. The brainchild of pioneer boxer, Sue "Tiger Lily" Fox, the IWBHF was the culmination of the work she'd started recording and documenting the women of the ring on her Women's Boxing Archive Network website (WBAN).

Fox announced "the formative steps towards establishing an International Women's Boxing Hall of Fame" in late 2013. Women had long been recognized in local and regional boxing halls of fame for their roles in and outside the ring. Even though the International Boxing Hall of

Fame housed in Canastota, New York, and considered the "gold standard," had inducted famed promoter and manager Aileen Eaton to the IBHOF in 2002 as a nonparticipant, it wasn't until 2020 that the Hall began inducting female boxers, despite numerous calls to add categories for women's boxing.

From the perspective of Fox, a true trailblazer in all aspects of the sport, the best way to right that wrong was to create a hall of her own.

WBAN had enjoyed a long history of telling the stories of individual boxers, from amateurs through the professional ranks, as well as reporting on fights at a time when they often went unremarked upon in the mainstream boxing press. Aside from reporting on women, WBAN established monthly and yearly awards, as well as a WBAN title belt, first issued to Chevelle Hallback in 2008. Most important of all, WBAN was a community of athletes, promotors, trainers, boxing writers, photographers, and others who supported the right for women to contest in the sport. It was Fox's insistence that women give themselves the accolades they deserve that reverberated through the community and gave a boost to the notion of creating a Hall of Fame dedicated to the triumphs women had accumulated contesting in boxing.

The game-changing inclusion of women in the Olympics was also, undoubtedly, an impetus to recognize and establish where the sport had come from.

In setting up the IWBHF website, Fox noted: "the primary mission of the IWBHF will be [to] call honorary attention to those professional female boxers (now retired) along with men and women whose contributions to the sport and it's athletes, from outside the ring, have been instrumental in growing female boxing."[17]

As Fox went about setting up the IWBHF, she also wanted to approach it differently by allowing members of the public to submit nominations.

"I felt it was fair. I tried to remove myself from the process, and the Board. And didn't want the appearance of favoritism. When it came to the voting," Fox continued, "I started out with the Board, but as time went on, added a range of people, and tried to make it international. People who were knowledgeable and other experts in the field, and even some fans. I had picked up that concept from my police training. They also take people from the community. It gives a different perspective."[18]

Once the nominations were closed, the nine members of the Board[19] of the IWBHF were each given the opportunity to vote on their choices. Those candidates receiving a majority of the votes were inducted—for a total of seven inductees for the inaugural year including Barbara Buttrick, Bonnie Canino, JoAnn Hagen, Christy Halbert, Regina Halmich, Christy Martin, and Lucia Rijker.

The inclusion of Christy Halbert, PhD, an academic in sociology with a strong background in coaching, was particularly meaningful. Halbert had played a pivotal role setting the stage for the addition of women's boxing in the Olympic roster of sports and had served as an Olympic coach for the Team USA Olympic squad at the 2012 London Games.

The first IWBHF ceremony was set for July 10, 2014. Most fitting was the inclusion of the ceremony during the 2014 USA National Women's Golden Gloves tournament, run by inaugural inductee Bonnie Canino, along with her partner and future IWBHF inductee, Yvonne Reis.

Under the auspices of USA Boxing, the tournament included 2012 Olympic bronze medalist Marlen Esparza, winning the finals for the women's flyweight competition, and future 2016 Olympian Mikaela Mayer, winning the women's lightweight competition. Other contestants included Christina Cruz (bantam) and Alex Love (light fly), who had both come close to winning in the 2016 Olympic Trials.

The most notable person to attend—not as a fighter, but to support her USA Boxing teammates—was Claressa Shields. Her appearance on the day of the inaugural award ceremony in a lovely, flowing, orange summer dress and her hair pulled back in a sea of braids, stirred the entire hall of guests and participants. Standing resplendent with a purple ribbon affixed to the gold Olympic medal hung around her neck, she transfixed everyone—here was the future of the sport, in the person of a lovely nineteen-year-old.

As the ceremony opened, Sue Fox noted, "I'm thrilled to have this but when I saw this opportunity to have this in conjunction with the National Women's Golden Gloves, I chose the time to have the induction here . . . because I wanted it surrounded by activities that involve female boxing."

She also expanded upon the importance of the Hall, stating, "The mission is to celebrate our history . . . preserve the legacy of our sport, and to honor our women boxers in the sport. But it is also to honor men and woman who work outside the ring who have significantly contributed to the promotion and development of it."

Noting, "One of our most important goals is to have a physical location for the hall," Fox envisioned a future where boxing fans can come to see "the memories of our boxing heroes, especially the women, who throughout the years have contributed so much to the sport."

The induction ceremony itself came with cheers and tears at the chance to honor women who often went unsung. There was something as well to the sisterhood of brilliant athletes swapping stories that seemed irreplaceable. Inductees, young amateurs, and current professional boxers including Chevelle Hallback, Diane Prazak, Laura Ramsay, Alicia Ashley, Belinda Laracuente, and Sue Reno, among others, all sat together among honored guests, inductees and their families, and assorted others who wanted to participate in the history-first ceremony.

Called to the stage, Barbara Buttrick noted that she was the first to receive her induction. Continuing in a more serious tone and reflecting on the great changes in the sport, she said, "My greatest fight was with the prejudice that was shown to us in those days, and now what I enjoy to see is all these young girls going in the Golden Gloves and the fact that they've been accepted into the Olympics; and now the gyms are full of little girls learning to box."

She ended her brief remarks saying, "This Hall of Fame has taken us all forward and we all look forward to the future."

Each inductee, in turn, took to the stage, with Christy Halbert noting she was appreciative of her role as representing the amateur side of the sport and hoping that it would grow to becoming "a huge stepping-stone" to professional boxing, just as it has been for "male boxers."

Finishing her speech, she brought up Claressa Shields and her accomplishments, but more importantly, how "Claressa had been born at a time when she never knew she couldn't box. That's because of the work, the pioneering spirit, the tenacity" of those who came before and those who tirelessly publicize the accomplishments of women.[20]

Christy Martin started her speech thanking everyone and calling out Bonnie Canino and Yvonne Reis "for stepping up and putting on such a great show for the women, the young women."

Martin, who had survived being "shot, stabbed, and left for dead" by her husband, Jim Martin, a mere two-and-a-half years before, talked about how, getting up off the floor, she had shortly thereafter "gone back to a boxing gym."

She also announced that "in June 2011, when they put me to sleep to fix a broken hand, I had a stroke," adding, "so my boxing career in the ring is done, and I had to say that today just so I make sure it's done."[21]

In her induction speech, Lucia Rijker thanked her fellow participants and marveled at the brilliance of women of the ring. Most poignantly, she thanked Christy Martin, stating, "Thank you so much for being in this world of women's boxing. You were my drive. I needed a focus point, so I wanted to fight you. I wanted to beat you. I chased you. I tried everything. . . . I am sorry of what happened to you, between you and your husband, and God bless your soul and God bless you."

As the ceremony ended, and in recognition of her brilliant achievements in the Olympics, Claressa Shields was called to the stage to speak.

"I feel so honored to be here," she began. "No, I don't get a lot of recognition, but this is a lot of recognition to me. I feel honored. . . . Just know[ing] there were women that paved the way it makes me feel a lot better. That I'm not by myself. They understand the struggle of how hard it is to be a female fighter and be recognized."

She continued: "This is going to give me a lot of motivation for Rio 2016. Boxing is not easy, and not everybody can do it, and for those who know how to fight . . . I want women's boxing's recognition to live on forever and ever."

She finished up, wiping a tear from her eye, and said, "I just feel so honored."

Leaning over, a friend handed her her gold medal. Shields quipped, "This is so heavy I don't wear it all the time."

She stood holding the medal, showing it to the assembled guests and inductees, as the audience clapped and cheered. As she stood beaming with pride in front of the inductees, there was a lovely sensation of not only the continuity of a long, glorious history, but of what the future would bring for the sport.

A success for all involved, Fox was able to manage a second induction event in 2015 that, among others, inducted rivals Laila Ali and Ann Wolfe. Wolfe was unable to attend, but Ali's star power alone made the event a huge success, and embracing the moment, she was generous with her time, standing patiently with each celebrant who waited in line to take a photo with her. The expense and coordination for putting on an event of that magnitude, however, proved very costly, and as Fox contemplated a 2016 celebration, prohibitive.

Other inductees included Jeannine Garside, Dierdre Gogarty, Sparkle Lee, Terri Moss, and Laura Serrano. The magic of the first year was also revived, as the award ceremony expanded to include a Lifetime Achievement Award, posthumously presented to Jose Sulaimán, the longtime president of the WBC, among others.

The costs of putting on an award program were quite prohibitive without adequate sponsorship, and so the ceremony itself was not held again in person until August 30, 2019, in Brisbane, California, and included present and past inductees. With a generous infusion from the WBC, the ceremony was twinned with the Beautiful Brawlers IX all-female amateur boxing show set for the following day, on August 31—an increasingly important showcase for rising amateur stars under the leadership of Bianca Gutiérrez.

The success of the 2019 ceremony proved a boon to the IWBHF. Increased visibility and acceptance also meant the chance to move the ceremony once again, this time to Las Vegas. With the COVID emergency in 2020, the IWBHF, as with other in-person events, was postponed, but the 2021 and 2022 ceremonies, to include a proclamation of a Women's Boxing Day, helped further solidify its place. The sold-out two-day tenth anniversary IWBHF ceremony held on October 6 and 7, 2023, further demonstrated its importance to the sport.

As Sue Fox put it, "The sponsorships just are not there to support women's boxing. You just have to have the love, and not worry about what it's really going to cost you."

Fox has also not been able to realize her dream of a permanent home for the boxing memorabilia she has accumulated and continues to accumulate, but is certain the momentum of women's boxing will realize her dreams.

"The biggest thing that grates my head," she said, "is that the pioneers will never be forgotten. And yes, they all deserve a part in history. Every one of us is a puzzle piece that builds the whole."[22]

CHAPTER THREE

A Truly International Sport

FROM SMALL AMATEUR CLUBS TO FEMALE BOXERS CONTESTING WEAR-
ing the *hijab*, the legalization of women's boxing has had an enormous
impact on the place of women in sport, and the growth and development
of the sport globally. Argentina and Mexico became the home base for
many of the era's boxing champions under the banner of such brilliant
fighters as Zulina Muñoz (Mexico) and Marcela Eliana Acuña (Argentina), among others. With televised fights and decent paydays, Mexican
and Argentinian champions attracted opponents from across the globe
and set new standards for the sport. Norway's Cecilia Braekhus also
continued to hold court in the arenas of Denmark with three of the era's
welterweight belts (WBA, WBC, and WBO), finally becoming the first
female undisputed champion in the four-belt era when she became welterweight champion in 2014, having captured the IBF title over Croatia's
Ivana Habazin by a unanimous decision.

With women having set the stage for "objective" legitimacy of the
sport by the early 2000s, the "major" four-belt sanctioning bodies came
calling. The first of the four majors in boxing to begin sanctioning female
world championship fights was the World Boxing Association (WBA)
on April 8, 2004. The WBA chose to sanction a world championship
main-event minimumweight bout between Canadian fighter Vaia Zaganas and American journeywoman Stephanie Dobbs at the Windham
Inner Harbor Hotel in Glen Burnie, Maryland. A walkover, of sorts,
Zaganas won the ten-rounder by unanimous decision, 99–91, 100–90,
98–92.

By the end of 2012, WBA title holders represented a diverse array of nations to include Argentina, Bermuda, Bulgaria, China, Denmark, France, Germany, Japan, Mexico, Norway, Panama, Peru, the Russian Federation, South Korea, Trinidad and Tobago, and the United States.

The World Boxing Council (WBC) began investing in sanctioning women's championship bouts the following year in 2005. Their inaugural bout pitted Mexico's great Jackie Nava against American Leona Brown in a lopsided contest for the world female super bantam championship, which Nava won by unanimous decision. By the end of the of the first Olympic year of 2012, WBC had added Australia, Hungary, Jamaica, North Korea, and Puerto Rico to the roster of countries with world titlists. The World Boxing Organization (WBO), which had begun to sanction world title bouts in 2009, further added champions from Colombia, Costa Rica, the Dominican Republic, and Thailand. Finally, the International Boxing Federation (IBF), which began bestowing belts in 2011, added Belgium, Italy, and South Africa.

In all, it was an impressive number of nations around the world, but the country sporting the greatest number of champions by 2012 was Argentina, a country that had only legalized the sport in 2001—an extraordinary feat in a mere eleven years.

BOXING IN ARGENTINA

Argentina's national boxing federation (*Federación Argentina de Boxeo,* or FAB) was organized in 1920 ahead of their participation in the 1920 Antwerp Games, having sent featherweight Ángel Rodríguez to compete.

In 1923, their most famous heavyweight, Luis Ángel "The Wild Bull of the Pampas" Firpo, was renowned for fighting a very savage bout against Jack Dempsey. Even with Firpo's loss, which many at the time considered a robbery,[1] boxing was very popular and remained so. Women, however, were not known to participate as practitioners. They were, however, considered to be fervent fans, with "many young women [having] attended matches and . . . [often] rushed to the ring to embrace the winners."[2]

While boxing remained popular over the decades with ebbs and flows, women were essentially absent from the sport, though they did begin to practice and compete in other martial arts and by the 1990s were participating in domestic and international championships across the martial arts disciplines. Formal recognition for women in boxing did not occur until March 25, 2001, when the FAB issued its first boxing license to the future champion Marcela "La Tigresa" Acuña.

An accomplished karate champion, Acuña had left the sport in 1995 to have a child at the age of nineteen. Back in combat sports, she had success as a kickboxer before transitioning to boxing. Her debut bout was in a ten-rounder against Christy Martin in December 1997. The co-main fight of the evening on the WBC world middle bout between Paul Vaden and Keith Holmes, the card, televised on Showtime, was held in Pompano Beach, Florida.

Acuña lost by unanimous decision, having gone down after being hit by a straight right to the chin in the tenth round and popping back up with her arms raised high as if in victory. At the end of the fight, she was lauded for her performance and even with the scores of 100–90, 99–90, 99–90, showed skills and a sense of where her future could go. In only her second fight nine months later, she faced the formidable Lucia Rijker in an IBO super light title bout. She lost by a knockout left hook to the liver in the fifth round but acquitted herself well with excellent lead overhand rights and upper cuts and was praised for her apparent skills by the broadcasters. After back-to-back losses, however, Acuña took a break from boxing, but did express a desire to box again professionally in her native Argentina.

Boxing fans in Argentina had applauded Acuña in her two outings and her boxing acumen against two of the best female fighters in the sport. While boxing for women was not yet legal, in the estimation of Argentinian boxing writer Diego Morilla, "The pressure to regulate women's boxing in Argentina has a name, and that's Marcela Acuña."

Having been denied once, "When she was denied once again, she staged a protest at the local federation and finally achieved her goal of gaining a license and having women's boxing regulated and allowed in Argentina."[3]

Once licensed to box, Acuña was featured in the FAB's first legally sanctioned bout between two women in Argentina. Appearing on April 28, 2001, the four-round undercard bout was held at the 1,100-seat FAB stadium in Buenos Aires. A small venue with two balconies, there were no "bad seats" as the two female boxers contested in the ring. Acuña's opponent was American fighter Jamillia Lawrence, whom Acuña had met during her forays in the United States. Entering the ring, Lawrence sported a 7–3 record and was viewed as a good adversary for the inaugural bout. Acuña managed to win a split decision 37–39, 39½–37½, 39½–37½, and within less than a year faced a succession of boxers from across South America before contesting for the inaugural FAB feather title against fellow Argentinian boxer Patricia Alejandra Quirico, winning that bout in the first round by knockout.

Acuña's early titles included the Women's International Boxing Association (WIBA) world super bantam title in 2004 and WIBA feather in 2004, before capturing the WBA world super bantam in 2006–2010 and the WBC title in 2008–2010, the WBO world super bantam in 2013–2016, and the IBF world super bantam in 2016–2018 and again later in 2018–2020.

The success of female boxing in Argentina became almost exponential as the Olympic Games began in 2012. In discussing this achievement and arguing that the overall number of professional boxers globally had not yet reached real numbers, Argentinian boxing writers and authors Irene Deserti and Yesica Palmetta stated,

> The boxers whose professional debut took place between 2005 and 2010, were having their first World Championship opportunities and winning their first titles. In addition, the first class of amateur boxers were also reaping their first titles as professionals. This caused a "boom" of female boxers in Argentina, in at least 80% of the weight categories, which allowed them to access championships that were vacant with few fights. Several of these championships were defended with other Argentines, which caused the titles to change ownership but not territory.[4]

Given that Argentina perceived it had entered the world of professional boxing later than the United States and European countries such as England and Germany, there was a lot of internal support for women not only to gain access to the sport, but to excel. Traditional barriers to inclusion were pushed open for women to train and become accomplished in the sport both as amateurs competing in the elite levels internationally and with opportunities to gain momentum in the pro ranks. The latter meant that Argentinian boxing cards were thrown open to include female bouts, and over time, with sufficient purses to attract more athletes, and importantly, offer up the sanctioning fees necessary to contest for globally recognized championships.

Morilla also made the point that boxing's appeal as an individual sport in which "'size doesn't matter'[became a] solid alternative for girls," especially from "a certain socioeconomic status," where access to sports such as tennis or field hockey require support that "lower income young girls"just do not have.[5]

With the inclusion of women's boxing in the 2012 London Games, this support accelerated and in the immediate aftermath of the Olympics, fighters such as Yesica Bopp became household names in Argentina as well as internationally recognized as top-ten pound-for-pound boxers. Bopp had begun her career in January 2008, and by November 2009 was the WBA and WBO world light fly champion. She continued to campaign at light fly and retained her WBA championship supremacy with a total of twenty-two title defenses until finally losing a split decision in Panama to the veteran Mexican champion Yesica Nery Plata in March 2022. As with many Argentinian fighters, much of her career was fought in her native Argentina, with fighters from South and Central America, Mexico, the United States, and even the United Kingdom venturing to meet her on her home turf. And while Bopp had suffered three losses across her career, only one had been at home.

Erica Anabella Farias, who was a two-weight champion winning her first WBC world lightweight championship at home against the former American champion Ann Saccurato in 2011, continued to contest at home against Argentinian and overseas fighters until she ventured to Belgium in April 2014 to fight Delfine Persoon. In a particularly physical bout, with both fighters losing points for headbutts, Farias suffered her first defeat. A highly anticipated matchup, the shock of the loss pushed Farias to expand her skill set. She jumped up to super light, and after a quick TKO win in a six-rounder at her new weight, faced fellow countrywoman Alejandra Oliveras, a three-weight champion at feather, light, and super light, to contest for Oliveras' WBC world super light title. The fight itself was a main event contested in Cancun, Mexico, a first for two Argentinian fighters, and was shown on the Fox Español network.

Through 2015 and 2016, Argentinian women continued to excel in the sport, with momentous victories by fighters such as Daniela Bermúdez, whose knockout win over Tomomi Takano in Japan even brought the Japanese fans to their feet. Soledad Matthysse also had a historic battle in Argentina against Jelena Mrdjenovich. The unification bout netted Matthysse the WBA and WBC world feather titles, although she lost in a rematch the following year in Edmonton, Canada—Mrdjenovich's home turf, as previously noted.

Other huge wins included Marcela Acuña's spectacular knockout of the year in the tenth round of the vacant IBF world super bantam championship fight against fellow countrywoman Yesica Marcos. Having peppered Marcos with a series of left jabs and feints, Acuña let loose with a lead straight right that hit Marcos' chin followed by a cuffing left hook as Marcos dropped to the canvas, banging her head a couple of times. She made a game effort to get up from her supine position but was counted out by the referee. Acuña was ecstatic with the win, holding on to her trainer as he carried her in the ring, and thereby added another title to her growing collection.

Daniela Bermúdez also drew further accolades for defeating Mexico's iconic Mariana "Barbie" Juárez at Mexico City's Arena Coliseo in a ten-round main-event showdown. Bermúdez won on the cards, 96–94, 97–93, 97–93, in what many in the crowd thought was a spectacular upset performance. In a very physical bout, Bermúdez was able to stun with hard overhand right shots and unrelenting combinations in the later rounds. Even the announcers had the fight even through eight rounds but giving Bermúdez the edge coming into the tenth round. With the win, Bermúdez established herself as among the best in boxing.

Wins of this sort in Argentina and across the globe helped to further establish the dominance and respect of Argentina as a female boxing empire. Women at the higher levels of the sport could also reasonably expect to earn a decent living from the purses they received from the sport along with some endorsements. The stresses on the economy in Argentina, which resulted in higher interest rates and a lot of fluctuations in the exchange rate between the Argentinian peso and other world currencies, however, had deleterious effects. This was especially so for foreign fighters who were looking for higher paydays or at the very least to be paid in US dollars or other such currencies. As it was, women's earnings were much lower than their male counterparts domestically, and according to Deserti and Palmetta, could be as much as 70 percent lower—with some exceptions for the elite female fighters who were able to negotiate more favorable terms with their promoters. The pay gap even at that level was substantial, as was the case across the board for women contesting in the sport. The popularity of the sport, even though there was considerable national support and featured placements on fight cards, still suffered in comparison to male boxers despite the excellence of the fighters.

BOXING IN MEXICO

Boxing for women in Mexico had been practiced in the early decades of the twentieth century to great popularity, with the renowned boxers Margarita "La Maya" Montes and Josefina Coronado among two of its practitioners in the early 1930s. La Maya famously battled men as well, and achieved stature as the Pacific Coast champion.[6] The American Vaudeville boxers Emma Maitland and Aurelia Wheeldin also came to Mexico to box on stage at the Teatro Politeamo in Mexico City in late October 1928. Whether they participated in local "smokers" is unknown; however, it was not uncommon at the time for the pair to appear in such events, and women in Mexico were beginning to make their own first forays into the ring by the late 1920s. The sport of women's boxing was eventually banned by presidential decree by the new president, Miguel Alemán Valdés, on December 5, 1946—as an imperative to protect female bodies from alleged (though unproven) damage to their sexual organs—along with his more conservative views of the roles of men and women in society.[7]

By the 1990s, with the rise of boxing in the United States, women began to find their way into the ring across the Mexican Republic. The exploits of Mexico's famous boxing daughter, Laura Serrano, in the mid- to late-1990s across the border in the United States, began to capture headlines and interest. Serrano's first bout in May 1994 had been against Christy Martin. The six-rounder was televised on a Don King Promotions PPV card that included the great Mexican national boxing icon Julio Cesar Chávez. That alone had a lot of eyes on it, and with Serrano's excellent boxing skills, she began to draw a following, especially after having fought the better-known Martin to a draw.

Serrano's next fight a year later was a ten-rounder for the WIBF world light championship, which she won by TKO in the seventh round against Irish boxer Diedre Gogarty. The bout was the co–main event on WIBF's all-female card, held on April 20, 1995. The buildup to the card had been tremendous; however, it happened to occur the evening after the notorious Oklahoma City bombing at the Alfred P. Murrah Federal Building, considered the deadliest act of domestic terrorism in the United States, in which 168 people lost their lives, which meant the news coverage was scant at best.

The confluence of history aside, Serrano became the first Mexican woman to win a championship boxing title—and even fought on a card in Tijuana in 1996 purportedly to honor the Mexican "grandmother" of the sport, Margarita "La Abuelita Bejines" Barajas, who'd begun boxing in the 1940s, and in Ciudad Juárez in 1998, with the ban still in effect— although it was generally only illegal in Mexico City at that time. Her visibility also influenced other Mexican women to take up the gloves and appear on a series of cards in Guadalajara.

With her title, Serrano became a renowned—if inconvenient—figure in boxing, whose next big battle was against the maintenance of the ban against women in the boxing ring. Dr. Horacio Ramírez Mercado, the influential Mexico City Boxing Commission's medical services chief, had espoused the idea that "'from the anatomical point of view,' boxing was 'not an appropriate activity for the female sex' because 'even if women used a certain type of protection, blows would somehow affect them in the short, medium or long term.'"

With Serrano's win, however, Mercado had changed his rhetoric to some degree, stating, "now that Laurita [a diminutive for Laura] won the world title, we have received requests for it to be accepted. We need to do a multidisciplinary study. . . . "[8]

Serrano was eventually added to the newly formed "special commission," which included psychologists, medical practitioners, and gynecologists—in itself, of interest. For her troubles, Serrano's inclusion not only netted her a death threat, but a patronizing suggestion that she quit boxing altogether. Having gained her law license by studying to become an attorney at the Universidad Nacional Autónoma de Mexico, Serrano was not backing down. She became very invested in overturning the ban, pointing out the fallacy of statements to the effect that women were endangering their health by boxing.

"It is contradictory to oppose the regulation of women's boxing by arguing that it is in the interest of their protection," she said, "when in reality they are left in an utter state of defenselessness, leaving them in the situation where they have to accept clandestine bouts that offer absolutely no guarantees."

She punctuated this argument, noting, "Women have been studying, working and preparing themselves for their fulfillment as a human being in all spheres: the political, academic, scientific, artistic, and in sports."[9]

Serrano's perseverance was spurred on by the cancellation of a popular fight card that was to have included the great Julio César Chávez, and a rematch between Serrano and Martin, put on by their shared promoter, Don King. The cancellation, which had even gained the support of the WBC's then president, Jose Sulaimán, plus the momentum of increasing interest and support for women in the sport, led to the ban being overturned on April 15, 1998. A statement issued by the government noted it had been dropped based upon a "judicial interpretation," citing it violated the "1992 constitutional reform proclaiming equality between the sexes."[10]

Mexico's explosive growth began in earnest almost immediately after the first fights were contested in early 1999, in Mexico City, and in those places across the Republic that had begun to push against the ban by either ignoring it or in those states where it had been illegal, overturning those bans in advance of the nation's most influential boxing commission.

Similar to the momentous rise of women's boxing in Argentina, by the time of the 2012 London Games, Mexico was also very well represented in the annuls of champions from the major sanctioning organizations.

With such brilliant boxers as Mariana "Barbie" Juárez, Jackie "Princesa Azteca" Nava, Anabel "Avispa" Ortiz, and Ana Maria "La Guerrera" Torres leading the way, the opportunities seemed limitless. All four boxers created brilliant careers contesting most of their fights in Mexico, and most especially their world title fights, with an impressive array of talent coming to Mexico to fight, along with the creation of a "rivalry" of sorts between Mexico and Argentina.

By 2012, the popularity of the sport in Mexico had even grown to the point where American boxer Alicia "Slick" Ashley, in a defense of her WBC world super bantam title against Mexican boxer Maria Elena "The Rush" Villalobos, was the "A" side main event on a card in Mexico City.

Ana Maria Torres, an early champion of the new era, had her last successful defense of her WBC world super fly title in March 2012, the same month of the Ashley fight, just before the start of the London Games. Torres had a "monster" reputation and skills to match, an important marker for younger fighters.

Juárez and Nava, who respectively began boxing as professionals in 1998 and 2000, were early pioneers of the sport in Mexico, benefiting from the lifting of the ban at the start of their careers in the sport. Their sensational boxing prowess, however, gave rise to an industry and paved the way for its subsequent growth, not only through their evident talent, but having straddled the period well into the early 2020s, they provided continuity and ultimately legitimacy to the growing prominence of women in the ring.

Ortiz started much later, in 2007. She'd had some success in the nascent Mexican amateur boxing program. The support of women in the amateurs, however, was suspect.

In an interview in late 2005, Ricardo Contreras, then president of the Mexican Federation of Amateur Boxing, stated, "Men are structurally better prepared for punishment. . . . [I]n our sport it is not only physical integrity that is exposed when going to compete, but life itself. There have been deaths in professional boxing recently and I think that it is a matter to be reckoned with by the ladies who are going to practice this sport, right?"[11]

Teasing out the seeming contradiction of creating opportunities while undermining the support, writer Hortencia Moreno noted "the possibility to practice a sport does not automatically lead to the creation of narratives . . . since the sports hero" requires acceptance through "four dimensions of social life." For Moreno, those include public acceptance equating to a strong fanbase; the continuing support of national sporting institutions; private enterprise—to support professional practice of sports—which in boxing terms is the apparatus of managers, promoters, trainers, and the like; and the fourth, the media.

Taking it one step further, she theorized that the male–female dynamic in Mexico was very much in play, such that a female boxer might still need a male "family member" to gain entry to a boxing space and, in her view, continue to exert a systemized form of social control.

While some fighters, such as Serrano, had gone their own way, the challenges of developing opportunities, gaining places on boxing cards, and garnering popularity were dependent on an apparatus of promoters, managers, trainers, boxing media, and television executives, among others, that was male dominated. A factor that was true worldwide.

In looking at Nava's career, her first taste of combat sports was as a practitioner of limalama, an American–Polynesian contact sport, starting at the age of twelve. She achieved her black belt at seventeen and had already begun kickboxing in Tijuana at age sixteen. She went on to become a Muay Thai featherweight champion and turned professional in boxing in May 2001. Her entry into boxing seemed to belie Moreno's thesis of male dominance, but certainly her ongoing career was dependent upon the growing apparatus of promotion and media support that was decidedly a male enclave across her career.

Aside from her interests in martial sports, Nava studied architecture at the Tijuana Institute of Technology, gaining her undergraduate degree in 2003, and became a member of the legislature representing Baja, California's, eighth congressional district from 2015 to 2018.

Nava retired after her last fight in a ten-round bout against an Argentinian journeywoman fighter, Gloria Yancaqueo, in October 2022—her first fight outside of her native Argentina. Barbie Juárez, as she is known across Mexico, lost in a battle with Nava by unanimous decision for the vacant WBC diamond super bantam belt—honorific for both fighters who across their careers had brought so much to the game but had never met in the ring.

BOXING IN ASIA

A quick look at the early titlists by the four major sanctioning bodies not only reveals the dominance of champions from Argentina and Mexico but a preponderance of champions from across Asia. Countries represented included India, Japan, North Korea, South Korea, and Thailand, most particularly in the lower weight classes.

The first women's amateur boxing championships were held in August 2001. The medal table included eight countries representing a cross-section of Asian nations, adding China, the Philippines, Chinese Taipei, and Sri Lanka to the boxing powerhouses noted above. The following November, at the 2001 World Women's Boxing championships, China, India, and Turkey were represented on the medal stand, with China and Turkey taking gold and bronze, and India grabbing a silver.

This early representation grew in significance in India, where boxer Mary Kom's prowess spurred an industry of sorts for women to participate at the amateur level in the sport. Often from poor families, their inclusion on national teams was hard won, but the fight for recognition and respect from the team and their families was a continuing struggle. The early wins of team members at international competitions did mean that the opportunities for further growth and development within the sport began to materialize to an ever greater degree. The culmination of the investment in women on the Indian national team was Kom's bronze medal win at the 2012 London Games. By this time married and the mother of two boys, Kom had also became the subject of a big-budget Bollywood "biopic" that celebrated her struggles and triumphs in the ring. Believing her story was universal, the film had its premiere at the Toronto International Film Festival to excellent notices. In India, the film enjoyed the highest opening weekend of any film featuring a female protagonist. The film also enjoyed good reviews, with a plot line that roughly followed the contours of Kom's career from her humble beginnings in Rural Manipur, India, through winning gold in the pin weight division at the 2008 International Boxing Association (AIBA) Women's World Boxing championships held in Ningbo City, China, following the 2008 Beijing Games. It should be noted, in addition to Kom's gold medal, Indian women won one silver (featherweight) and two bronze medals (flyweight and light bantamweight) at the 2008 tournament, a testament to the excellence of the team.

As for Olympic success, Kom was unable to repeat it in 2016. At the delayed 2020 Tokyo Games, however, Lovlina Borgohain brought home India's second women's Olympic bronze medal when she won a split 4–1 decision against the heavily favored Taiwanese fighter Chen Nien-chin. The bronze at welterweight had the added significance of being the first medal awarded as the weight class had been added as part of the expansion to five weight classes for the 2020 Games.

The Indian women's boxing team itself was featured in the 2016 documentary *With This Ring*, by filmmakers Ameesha Joshi and Anna Sarkissian, covering the years 2006–2012, which laid out in stark realism the challenges women faced to pursue boxing.

Despite success as elite amateurs, Indian women have not been able to translate it to winning championships at the professional level. This might change as more and more women begin to consider whether the expanding opportunities in the sport make it worthwhile to pursue.

Japan's entry into professional boxing began with the development of the Japan Women's Boxing Commission (JWBC). The commission was started in 1999. Mary (Marie) Speed from New Zealand became the chairperson backed by its manager and chief proponent, ex-kickboxer Toshihiro Yamaki, who achieved fame and a strong following. The organization itself was private and not affiliated with the official Japanese Boxing Commission (JBC).

The first women to begin to compete were primarily coming from kickboxing, and while the JWBC bouts were not officially sanctioned, the shows, which could be labeled as "underground," were popular.

At approximately the same time, there was a push for participation in the amateurs. Boxing journalist Yuriko Miyata noted the earliest amateur event documented was the "'sparring competition' started unofficially by a pianist and a boxing trainee Chie Hara in Osaka in 1996 renamed [the] 'All Japan Women's Amateur Competition' in 1999."

One of the competitors in that event, Etsuko Tada, went on to win a bronze medal in the first Asian championship, in 2001. With that success, Japan's Amateur Boxing Federation (JBAF) officially recognized female amateur boxing, naming Chie Hara as the female department chairperson. They also established a national female championship two years later, in 2003.

Spurred on by achievements in the amateur program and by the WBC's decision to award female championships beginning in 2005, the JBC agreed to license professional female boxers in late 2007. It must be noted that Japan's strawweight fighter Nanako Kikuchi won the WBC strawweight title on November 7, 2005, in Bangkok against Thai boxer Siriporn Taweesuk, until she lost the fight against Carina Morena in California in 2007. Prior to winning the WBC title, in September 2004, Kikuchi had also won the Japanese women's minimumweight title against Marika Watanabe, in Kyoto, Japan. While the card was unsanctioned, the WIBA had put on two world title bouts, with Japan's Fujin Raika winning the WIBA world feather title by defeating American Melissa Fiorentino by unanimous decision, and Yuko Sodeoka fighting American fighter Yvonne Caples to a draw for the WIBA world minimumweight.

The first officially sanctioned fights under the auspices of the JBC occurred in Tokyo on May 9, 2008, at Korakuen Hall. An all-female fight card, it featured 10 four-round and six-round bouts. Many of the fighters on the card already sported win–loss records. The main-event bout featured Fujin Raika, a veteran who came into the contest with a 17–3–1 record having lost a WBC world super feather title shot to

Jelena Mrdjenovich the year before and holding the WIBA world light weight title. Her opponent in the bout was American fighter Natalie Brown, who entered the ring with a 5–0 record having previously fought four-rounders. Raika prevailed in their bout, winning by mixed decision. Other future champions on the card included Naomi Togashi, who went on to win the WBC world light fly title the following year in May 2009, and most impressively, Momo Koseki, who won the WBC world atom-weight title by TKO in August 2008 and sported seventeen successful defenses before she retired from the sport in 2018.

Etsuko Tada, who debuted on the 2008 card, was another future champion who went on to claim the WBA world minimum title from 2009–2013, the IBF world mini fly from 2015–2017, and the WBO world mini fly from 2018–2019, and again from 2020–2021.

Despite the talent Japanese women showed on the world stage, Miyata noted, placement on cards was challenging, as most promoters did not support women in the ring. She added that, despite this, "The Japan Pro Boxing Association (JPBA), the union of boxing organiza-tions . . . help[ed] to put on female events," including paying the nec-essary sanctioning fees for world title events. Female boxers needed this assistance because it was not possible to earn a living from boxing. Fights were also not televised for the most part except for Sky A Sports, which televised female bouts in the period from 2008 to 2014.

With the 2012 Olympics, "schools began having female boxing teams" at the high school and college level, and on the professional side, women did get attention in the press and gain some popularity at boxing events, most especially the title fights.[12] While no Japanese woman com-peted in the 2012 or 2016 Games, the delayed 2020 Tokyo Games were a different story. Boxer Sena Irie won gold at featherweight, while boxer Tsukimi Namiki competed and eventually prevailed with a bronze medal. Even with success in the Games, however, neither fighter has opted to turn professional, with Irie deciding to leave boxing altogether to pursue a graduate education studying frogs. She noted: "I'm a fan of the Japanese common toad and want to research its ecology. I want to study hard and spread the word about it."[13]

The Olympics garnered headlines and a reimaging of women's boxing as a viable if niche sport. It also became more of a mainstay in popular culture, with two back-to-back, if decidedly different, films with female protagonists.

The first entry was the film *Small, Slow but Steady*, based on the memoir *Do Not Lose* by deaf female boxer Keiko Ogasawara, who fought between 2010–2013 with a 3–1 record. The film entered the annuls of the boxing genre as a tone-poem to the sport and its practitioners, artfully told by Japanese director Shô Miyake to excellent notices worldwide in 2022 and including a showing at the Tokyo International Film Festival. According to the review in the *Japan Times*, it was noted as "as a featherweight, but it packs an undeniable punch,"[14] with exceptional storytelling focused on the challenges of prevailing in a sport in silence. The film explored the relationship between the fighter and her trainer as well as her own sense of displacement as COVID raged and the gym she knew as her safe place was threatened with closure.

Miyake's film was followed by the more conventional drama *Red Shoes*, by director Toshiro Saiga. Targeted for a mass audience, *Red Shoes* tells the story of Manami Ota, who wants to follow in the footsteps of her boxer father but his untimely death when she was a young girl still haunts her. Having lost her husband to cancer, Ota must raise her young daughter on her own while pursuing her desire to enter the boxing ring. With melodramatic flair and through a sequence of misfortunes, she loses custody, but prevails in the end as she fights for a boxing championship. While not particularly artful in its execution, the film garnered popularity at the box office and pushed the acceptance of female boxing to coincide with the prestige of the Olympic wins.

New young Japanese fighters continue to stand out as boxing champions in the footsteps of the pioneers of Japanese women's boxing. Fighter Mika Iwakawa has prevailed as the IBF world atom champion, and most recently Mizuki Hiruta, who won the WBO world super fly belt in December 2022 along with a successful title defense. While these fighters continue to grapple with the uncertainties of fight opportunities and other incumbent issues, they are proving that women do have a place in Japanese boxing.

Part II

2017–2019

The years 2017–2019 saw a dramatic shift in women's boxing. For one, such amateur boxing stars as the United States' Claressa Shields and Ireland's great boxing talent, Katie Taylor, turned professional, thus upending the sport's professional "applecart." While it was no secret that most female boxers fought for small purses with little opportunity, Shields and Taylor both were able to make more demands in terms of their promotional deals. This also opened the doors for more televised visibility, with Taylor signing with Eddie Hearn's Matchroom Boxing and their new streaming service DAZN Boxing and Shields signing with Dmitry Salita's Salita Promotions and appearing on Showtime. Shields and Taylor both demonstrated enormous talent, and by 2019 each had joined the ranks of elite boxing by becoming undisputed champions: Shields as middleweight on April 13 in Atlantic City, and Taylor as lightweight on June 1 at Madison Square Garden. The visibility of these two giants in the sport gave new impetus to other champions to fight and demand more visibility and higher paydays with varying levels of success. It also brought new promotional players into the mix, with more opportunities for new fighters to join the professional ranks. Young girls and adolescents also felt a stronger drive to take up the sport, as a new generation joined seasoned amateurs in the run-up to the 2020 Tokyo Games.

CHAPTER FOUR

Being Seen

THE SUCCESS OF THE 2016 OLYMPIC CYCLE BROUGHT NEW GLOBAL
players to boxing promotion that began to impact how women's fights
were seen. In particular, the United Kingdom's Matchroom Boxing
picked up the gauntlet to support female boxing in the period between
2017–2019. That commitment had a tremendous impact on the sport
as 2012 and 2016 Olympic stars transitioned to the professional ranks,
whether signing with Hearn or not. Irish fighter Katie Taylor became the
first female Olympic star to sign with Matchroom in late 2016, followed
by British Olympian Natasha Jonas in 2017. Two other British Olympians turned professional in 2017: Nicola Adams and Savannah Marshall,
each of whom chose their own unique promotional relationship.

In the United States, Olympian Claressa Shields turned pro in the
fall of 2016 and was joined by teammates Marlen Esparza and Mikaela
Mayer in 2017. Esparza and Mayer chose to sign with two established
promoters, Golden Boy Promotions and Top Rank Boxing, respectively.
Their early outings in the period of 2017–2019 soon began to have an
impact on women's boxing, with Esparza fighting in a three-minute-
per-round title fight, and both appearing regularly on television and/or
streaming services. Pros such as Amanda Serrano and Heather Hardy,
though, were met with mixed success on their campaigns for recognition
and opportunity, as were such boxers as the veteran champions Layla
McCarter and Kali Reis, who continued to push for spots on cards. Many
promotional companies continued to feature men-only boxing cards.
The primary reason cited has been the economic viability of investing in

female fights, and the belief, however mistaken, that there is not enough talent to anchor such cards.

Class Is In

The Olympians—Claressa Shields (United States), Katie Taylor (Ireland), Marlen Esparza (United States), Nicola Adams (United Kingdom), Natasha Jonas (United Kingdom), Mikaela Mayer (United States), and Savannah Marshall (United Kingdom)—all turned pro in 2016–2017, demanding higher pay and visibility on fight cards, some with success, and some less so, after the 2016 Rio Games.

Claressa Shields' debut professional bout came first on November 19, 2016, on the undercard of the Andre Ward/Sergey Kovalev HBO World Boxing PPV show at the T-Mobile Arena in Las Vegas. Though not shown on the main card, her bout was livestreamed on HBO Boxing's YouTube channel and broadcast on the PPV events channel prior to the official telecast of the main card, an otherwise rare occurrence for female bouts. Her opponent in the four-rounder—Franchon Crews-Dezurn, the eight-time USA Boxing national champion—was also making her debut in the ranks of the pros after an eleven-year, 56–19 amateur career.

In the run-up to the fight, Shields expressed confidence, saying, "I can't wait to perform for my fans on Nov. 19th. Franchon Crews has an outstanding amateur background, but I'm a once-in-a-century fighter and I fear no one. It will be a great night for women's boxing, a night that I hope will be remembered as one that changed the course of history."[1]

The fight came early on the card, with the commentators immediately querying whether Shields could make the transition to the professional game.

A stinging overhand right that scored as Shields came forward at the opening bell followed by a sharp jab gave the fans in the stands no doubt that she was in the ring to make a statement. With both fighters throwing leather, one of the announcers was quick to point out "this isn't amateur style boxing," while making further note of the "blazing hand speed" shown by both boxers. Shields was also favorably compared to Laila Ali, as showing a "similar" fight style.[2]

Given where women's boxing was in the United States in late 2016, with a virtual blackout of their matches on mainstream sports media, such comparisons made sense. Both were fighting in similar weight classes, and since Ali's retirement from boxing in 2007, no one in the world of women's boxing had crossed over into popular culture in quite the same way. Moreover, Ali's retirement also coincided with the loss of visibility in the sport on mainstream boxing media, which further lessened the chance for women to break through. With Shields touted as the "most decorated female amateur in American history" by one of ESPN's premier boxing pundits, Dan Rafael, the stage had been set for excitement and a "look see" for boxing fans who might not have seen her momentous triumph in the Olympics.

Across the four rounds, both fighters were intent on giving their all. The second round made it clear Shields would come out of the bout triumphant, and more so after connecting with a stinging overhand right at the end of the third round. The fourth round proved to be Crews-Dezurn's best as she pressed Shields and unleashed her inner "dog." Still, Shields connected with some hard shots, and prevailed with a unanimous 40–36 score on all three judges' cards. More to the point, Shields established herself as a presence in the sport, and by choosing Crews-Dezurn as her opponent—who, in later years, she noted hit her with the hardest punches she ever felt in her career—Shields made the statement that she was willing to take on the toughest opponents in her weight class.

"It feels so good to have just made my pro debut," Shields said. "This is what I've been training for. I'm faster and I hit harder. And I'm the better fighter. But Crews brought 100 percent, and I respect her for that."[3]

Claudia Trejos, one of very few female boxing broadcasters, noted on ESPN that Shields had made "an extraordinary debut," having "dealt with Franchon Crews[-Dezurn] in the best way possible."[4]

Coverage of the pro-debut bout even included a piece in the UK's *Guardian* newspaper, making note that Shields had "landed 76 of 214 punches (35.5%), compared to 27 of 183 (14.8%) for her opponent." The article made the point that "Shields wants to elevate women's boxing the way Ronda Rousey propelled women's MMA from a sideshow to headline attraction," adding that "Rousey . . . benefitted from the full backing of the UFC, which put the same marketing and promotional heft behind its female fighters as their male counterparts."[5]

Without similar backing, however, and given the debut battle was a one-off promotional deal with Roc Nation Sports, the work necessary to make such goals a reality would take time and effort while pushing against the stream of the current boxing promotional landscape.

Shields had signed a management agreement with former HBO Boxing executive Mark Taffet. She further solidified her place in the sport when she signed with Salita Promotions, run by retired professional boxer Dmitry Salita, whose successful career as a welterweight gave him unique insights into the needs of the fighters he represented.

It took until June 2017 to finally ink the deal, having already worked together on a one-time basis for her second bout on March 10 at the MGM Grand in Detroit and broadcast on *Showtime Boxing*—only the second female bout after Amanda Serrano's debut on the network in January. Shields captured the NABF middle title in the four-round bout, obtaining her first TKO win in the third round over Hungarian journeywoman Szilvia Szabados (15–8–0).

Katie Taylor's debut bout came about a week after Shields, appearing on a fight card at London's Wembley Arena on November 26, 2016.

Having signed a promotional deal with Matchroom Boxing's Eddie Hearn and manager Brian Peters, Taylor was poised to take the boxing world by storm. Moreover, in choosing to work with Hearn, she had set her eyes on something more than just her personal growth in the sport, but with the intention of leading a vanguard of women's boxing talent on Matchroom's future roster of female boxing stars and prospects.

Taylor noted, "When I first dreamt of Olympic gold, female boxing was practically unknown. Now because of my journey and the incredible supporters who came along with me, female boxing is as much part of the fabric of the Olympics as its male counterpart. Now I want to do the same for the professional sport and I hope those who have supported me along the way will come with me."[6]

During fight week, promoter Eddie Hearn stated it this way:

It's not about women's boxing breaking through. It's about the product breaking through. What that means is if you are entertaining, you are entertaining. It doesn't matter if you are a man or a woman. It's completely irrelevant.

On Saturday I was in Las Vegas with Claressa Shields. The only thing that was missing is they put her on at 5:30 in front of 10 per cent of the crowd. She was entertaining and that's what I believe Katie Taylor will bring to the world of boxing.[7]

Along with the announcement of Taylor's debut on November 26, she was also inked in to have a second bout on the December 10 at the Manchester Arena on the same card as Anthony Joshua's IBF heavyweight defense against Eric Molina. Set for an aggressive start with back-to-back fights with a mere two weeks in between, Taylor and her team were of a mind to aggressively pursue a winning record that would allow her to contest for a major belt within her first year as a professional.

Taylor's foray was also fraught with the tensions she brought that punctuated her exit from the amateurs. Her loss in the preliminary rounds of the 2016 Rio Games was controversial but nonetheless, devastating (see chapter 1, endnote 41). It had come after the very public split with her father and coach, Peter Taylor, in the form of a personal family drama writ large. His departure meant that she not only lost the relationship with her father, but her lifelong boxing coach and mentor. Taylor had been candid in revealing the extent of the devastation the split had caused her and how much it had affected her game and even her love and devotion to boxing.

"My dad was obviously my coach ever since I started boxing as a ten-year-old. We spent every single day together getting ready for big fights and big competitions. We made a great team, that's for sure. Unfortunately, he stepped away from the family and . . . it was a huge breakdown of the relationship. . . . That just brought so much heartache."

Reflecting more on the impact it had had on all her life, she said, "Life is about mountain tops and valleys and it's great being on top of the mountain, but the valleys are the place that maturity, and . . . character is built as well, and I knew after the Rio Olympics I needed to change something."[8]

The road back was to be her professional career.

A new beginning that included her new management team and trainer, all of which helped bring the spark of excitement into the sport for her.

Taylor's first bout was against Karina Kopinska [Smalenberg], a skilled Polish journeywoman fighter. Sporting a 7–14–3 record, the win for Taylor was very likely. Nonetheless, the moment was not lost on Taylor, as she made her way toward the ring with a stoic face alongside her American trainer, Ross Enamait, whom she'd joined in Connecticut shortly after her loss in the 2016 Rio Games. Eddie Hearn also made the ring walk with her, his facial expression showing a similar enigmatic stoicism.

In the hubbub of the excited crowd, the Sky Sports announcers made note that it was a big night, capping off a momentous week in professional boxing as two of the best Olympians were making the back-to-back pro debuts. The announcing team was also joined by Team GB 2012 boxing Olympian Natasha Jonas, who was herself considering whether the time was right to step back into boxing and turn pro after leaving the sport the year before.

With no apparent jitters, Taylor immediately got to work in her debut six-round super featherweight bout, quickly establishing her jab, her hand speed, her footwork, and her stinging shots to the head and body of her opponent. The second round showcased more of Taylor's elite abilities in the ring. In awe of her shot selections and ring generalship, one of the announcers made the point that her skill level was such that it didn't matter if a fighter was a man or a woman and that one day the sport would just be collectively referred to as "boxing."

Jonas further opined that it was the quality of sparring with men and elite women that was adding to the high level of skill being exhibited by women coming into boxing, and as if to second her co-announcer, noted in the UK, "We are now treated as boxers and not just as females."[9]

With the third-round stoppage following a veritable beat-down, Taylor had established herself as a skilled force to be reckoned with in the sport and as having easily transitioned from her 176–12–1 amateur standing to a 1–0 professional with no questions as to her ability to fight in the pro game.

Marlen Esparza, the Team USA 2012 bronze medalist, though planning one last hurrah as an amateur at the 2016 USA national championships in December 2016, sent out a brief tweet on the Twitter social media platform at the end of October stating, "I am going pro. We will be announcing soon."[10]

Having won the silver medal at the nationals, Esparza retired from the amateurs and promptly announced she was signing a multi-year promotional deal with Golden Boy Promotions, the first female boxer to join their stable of fighters.

"I recently told my fans that I was going pro, and I am happy to announce that it will be the world's best promotional company—Golden Boy Promotions," Esparza said. "I am excited to get back into the ring as soon as possible and start climbing the ladder towards winning a professional world title."[11]

In seconding the excitement, Golden Boy president Eric Gomez noted the promotional company was committed to promoting women in the sport, with the belief that Esparza "is someone who can revolutionize women's boxing in the U.S. and bring awareness and excitement."

Gomez also admitted, "Women's boxing has been very successful around the world but we're a little behind in the U.S. She is a smart young woman, and she can fight."

Reiterating Golden Boy's commitment, CEO Oscar De La Hoya said, "At Golden Boy Promotions, we pride ourselves on developing fighters and transforming them into the best of the best. We look forward to doing the same with Marlen."

The public relations aside, Esparza told an interviewer, "I chose Golden Boy because they seemed [to] actually care more about my career" than other promotional firms to whom she had spoken. During negotiations, Esparza also felt Golden Boy was willing to listen and would work to market her evident boxing skills to further her boxing brand.[12]

Having signed with Golden Boy, Esparza's first pro fight was set for March 23, 2017, at the Fantasy Springs Casino in Indio, California, against a 0–2 southpaw fighter from New Jersey named Rachel Sazoff.

Esparza prepared for the fight alongside British two-time Olympian Nicola Adams, who was also preparing for her pro debut set for the Manchester Arena in England on April 8, 2017, against Virginia Noemi Carcamo (4–2–1) a skilled boxer from Argentina.

Esparza and Adams both trained at Vigil Hunter's training camp and at the SNAC facility for strength and conditioning training. Esparza noted, "We do work together and it's all technical. But when we spar, we spar with guys because we both prefer it. It's a lot harder with the guys, it's just a lot more difficult."[13]

Of her upcoming pro debut, Adams told a reporter, "I love creating history and every time I step in the ring, I pretty much get to do that. So, it is a good motivation. I never get tired of challenges—I guess it's just the thought of being able to make history that makes it exciting for me."

A unique figure in British sports who with her second gold medal at the 2016 Rio Olympics had crossed over into the public's imagination, Adams was a hot prospect for any promoter. She eventually signed with the famed British promoter Frank Warren, who had only a few years before vowed never to promote women. It was Adams's second gold medal, however, that made him an instant believer in women's boxing, and he signed her with the sincere belief that she would be a professional world champion in short order.[14]

A few days ahead of her pro debut, Esparza spoke with boxing writer Gabriel Montoya. For Esparza, the most surprising part of the experience preparing for her fight was the transition from the amateurs to the pros.

"The transition is the hardest part," she said. "I'm more worried about the actual transition from the amateurs to the pros than I am about the actual fighting right now and I know I need to settle my style down a little bit more.

"What gets me so nervous is the actual thought of just the change. The structure is different, how you proceed is different . . . You kind of get thrown into the fire and I didn't expect that at all, so now I'm . . . excited to find my way and to find the structure within the pro game, and what are my regimens, who is my team going to be, what am I about."

Esparza also opined that the structured rules of the amateurs and the approach to how to move up the ladder in the sport took away some of the excitement of boxing.

For Esparza, the pro game was more about winning—and not only winning, but ensuring that she demonstrated her best, round by round.

"It's not you're only as good as your last fight, but you're only as good as your last round."

Expanding on it a bit, she said she liked the idea of "pay[ing] attention to the small stuff" that would make her performance that much better.

Asked about why she'd decided to turn pro, Esparza said, "I do think it is a good time . . . in the sport, with Ronda Rousey, people did want to watch her, people did respect her, because of that a lot of the girls [in boxing] are getting more attention. And people that have been fighting like Heather Hardy they're acting like they're brand new, but they've been around, it's like, where have you guys been."[15]

Esparza's debut fight proved to be very one-sided. She was able to make liberal use of her full repertoire of punches with flurries of hard jabs, right hooks, and straight rights that rocked her opponent repeatedly. She came away from the four-round battle with a unanimous 40–36 decision on all three judges' score cards, and the sense that she was certainly as good as her last round.

Two weeks later in the run-up to Nicola Adams's debut bout, promoter Frank Warren penned an opinion piece. "The Leeds flyweight changed my mind about women's boxing and now she is going to bring new fans to the sport," he said. "I am delighted to be playing a part in what is sure to be an exciting journey."[16]

Adams's debut was also very one-sided, providing fans with a showcase of her slick boxing, shot selection, and excellent foot work—and winning all four rounds handily. Still, Adams had to work for it against an experienced fighter and in a postfight interview noted, "I was a bit too eager to get the stoppage because I wanted to entertain the crowd, but she was tough and she was hanging in there, literally at the end."

Boxing writer Nick Parkinson also opined, "Adams' boxing skills were a joy to watch in the third and fourth rounds and she was just too quick for Carcamo, who proved too tough to crack over four rounds."[17]

Team GB 2012 Olympian Natasha Jonas was the next to announce she was turning pro, wanting to "strike while the iron is hot." Having signed with Eddie Hearn's Matchroom Boxing, she also came to be under the tutelage of renowned British trainer and 2015 *Ring Magazine* Trainer of the Year, Joe Gallagher.

Jonas had lost to Taylor in the quarter finals of the 2012 Olympic Games and continued to compete on Team GM through the middle of 2014—leaving the team to have a baby before finally retiring in 2015 after an injury.

In deciding to turn pro, Jonas said, "An opportunity came about. I thought about it, and it was too good an opportunity to turn down!"

She'd also been clear on the debt she owed.

"Katie [Taylor] was the reason I could turn pro. When I said goodbye to the amateurs, I was saying goodbye forever because there was no pro scene, there was none of that. And then because of Katie, there was then an opportunity and a space in the market. I then thought I can go back but before that, there wasn't an option there."[18]

Asked about a potential fight with Katie Taylor down the line, Jonas was clear in her thinking about her. "Katie Taylor's always set the bar in women's boxing, and everyone's always aspired to be like her. Whenever she goes, whatever she's done, she's always a good example. I've said I'm not here to be in anyone's shadow, but I take my hat off to everything she's achieved in boxing."

She also spoke to the challenge of fitting in motherhood with training. "I have a massively supportive family, they all chip in and help, and like most working mothers, you drop the baby off at nine and you come back at five . . . it's just that my work is a little bit different."[19]

For her first bout, Jonas was set to Monika Antonik, 1–3–0, a fairly novice boxer from Poland. Broadcast on Sky Sports, the southpaw Jonas showed off her skills very early in the four-round lightweight bout, keeping Antonik on the back foot throughout her onslaught. The referee, having seen enough punishment, waved off the fight at 1:32 of the first round to give Jonas the stoppage win.

Demonstrating great technical skills, Jonas had previously said, "Training with Joe [Gallagher] has been fantastic. Training alongside some of the best fighters in the country, world champions and unbeaten boxers, I am watching them and picking up their good habits. I've been out for a long time, but I feel ready to go now."[20]

Her performance made it clear that she had inculcated a range of new skills on top of those she'd already garnered through hard work and diligence throughout her amateur career.

For Mikaela Mayer, the 2016 Team USA Olympian, the decision to turn pro was one of balancing a shot at the 2020 Games, with turning pro.

"I loved competing as an amateur, but I've always been the type where my ambition comes from having huge dreams, dreams that scare me," Mayer told the Associated Press in a phone interview. "I just felt I wanted a bigger stage, more of a challenge. But it was a really hard decision for me. I went back and forth with it for months."

Mayer went on to note that "After the Olympics, I felt an emptiness. I didn't feel I got everything I was going to get out of the Olympics, and not just because I didn't medal. I just thought there was going to be more. The Olympics were over, and I was kind of in the same position I was before."

Having signed with manager George Ruiz, she was offered an opportunity to speak with Top Rank and jumped at it.

"We sat down with Top Rank, and they were the first promoter to make me think they saw the vision," Mayer said. "Other promoters, you don't believe, you don't see. Top Rank did, and within a matter of weeks, we got it done."[21]

Mayer's first fight was against the novice Wisconsin 0–1 fighter, Widnelly Figueroa. The four-rounder was on the undercard of the Lomachenko–Marriaga WBO world super feather title fight at the Microsoft Theater in Los Angeles.

From the opening bell, Mayer, with long-term coach Al Michael in her corner, immediately showed her pedigree as a fighter, using her considerable height to her advantage over her opponent. Executing picture-perfect jabs to set up her array of punches, Figueroa was on the backfoot throughout the bout. Clearly outclassed, Figueroa took a huge left to the body and sunk to her knees as Mayer continue to rain punches until the referee waved off the fight at 1:15 of the first round, giving Mayer the KO win.

Speaking after her triumphant debut fight, Mayer said, "I thought I was going to feel a little more nervous, but I actually felt calm."[22]

The last of the British Olympians to sign and debut was Team GB's Savannah Marshall. Leaving Great Britain for the United States, Marshall signed with Mayweather Promotions, joining LaTondria Jones and Layla McCarter as only the third woman to sign with the marquee boxing promotional company.

The announcement came at a press conference for the upcoming Gervonta Davis fight, clearly taking Marshall by surprise. In the aftermath of the announcement, Marshall told an interviewer she'd been approached with the idea of joining Mayweather, and as she put, "he'd come up with the goods and he's really helped me a lot," noting she'd be based in Las Vegas and would be moving there at the end of June 2017.

Regarding the timing, Marshall said, "I think women's pro boxing just needed a couple of big names to [turn pro] and I think Nicki [Nicola Adams] and Katie [Taylor] have done that." She also noted she hadn't boxed since the Olympics in August 2016, and said, "I'm bored now."

Marshall had already been much ballyhooed for having defeated Claressa Shields in the amateurs in 2012; speaking to that, Marshall hoped they would cross paths in the pros: "I'm the only loss she's ever had, so it's gonna eat away at her till she gets that win."[23]

Her actual pro debut came on August 26, 2017, at the T-Mobile Arena in Las Vegas, as the opener on the Nathan Cleverly–Badou Jack WBA world light heavy card. The card also quite famously featured Floyd Mayweather's bout against the Irish MMA star, Conor McGregor.

Set to box the battle-tested southpaw fighter Sydney LeBlanc (4–3–1) from Louisiana, the journeywoman professional fighter had already shared the ring most recently with Claressa Shields in a very tough WBC silver middleweight eight-rounder in June, and contested Franchon Crews-Dezurn in a four-rounder just two weeks before.

For Marshall's part, with her boxing skills honed in the gym by trainer Peter Fury (as she had not yet moved to Las Vegas as originally intended), Marshall was able to control the ring and easily outpointed LeBlanc using her jab to great effect over the four rounds of the contest. What distinguished the fight was it was contested using three-minute rounds—a rarity among women's boxing battles but allowable in Las Vegas even for championship fights except for WBC bouts, which will not sanction three-minute rounds.

Having clearly dominated the fight, Marshall was awarded a unanimous decision, with all three judges scoring the contest 40–36.

"I feel brilliant," said Marshall after the fight, adding, "I'm really glad it was three-minute rounds because I prefer that over two-minute rounds. She was really tough like I knew she would be. I'm glad that I got out of there with a win against a top-class opponent."

Still thrilled about her win, she exclaimed, "I've been looking forward to this all week, so I'm really excited about my performance. The build-up this week has been great."[24]

Of her time preparing for her debut platform, some years later Marshall said, "In my first camp I was telling [Peter Fury] I'm going to Mayweather Promotions and going to live in America," she recalled. "Every now and again he would say, 'you just look after yourself out there because this pro game is not what it seems.'

"For weeks he kept mentioning it and drilling it into me. At the time I was thinking, 'ah well, just wait until I get to America, you'll see'—but I learnt that professional boxing is a dirty business and sometimes it's not just about the actual sport."[25]

A PRO, IS A PRO, IS A PRO

Marlen Esparza's comment about the women who had been holding the baton for the sport had proven time and again to be spot on: "they're acting like they're brand new, but they've been around, it's like, where have you guys been?"[26]

American fighters such as Amanda Serrano, Heather Hardy, Layla McCarter, Kali Reis, and dozens of other skilled boxers who'd not gone the amateur route were continuing to be left to fend for themselves and fight mightily for opportunities wherever they could find them.

For Amanda Serrano, fortune seemed to have finally begun when on January 14, 2017, she stepped into the ring to defend her WBO world super bantam title and contest for the WBC diamond belt against the tough Mexican fighter Yazmin Rivas (35–9–1, 10-KOs).

Rivas, the former IBF and WBC world bantam champion, had sustained some losses, but came through the ropes of the ring at Brooklyn's Barclay's Center, ready to fight under the bright television lights of *Showtime Extreme*, a branded boxing show and first for women on the network since 2000 (for non-pay-per-view shows).

At the weigh-in the day before, Serrano had been asked about the significance of the fight.

"I'm doing this for women's boxing," she said. "We've been here long enough, we deserve to be on this stage, and for all the hard-working women out there, all types of women in a male dominated sport, we are going to show that we deserve to be here, and this is our time."[27]

Despite that opportunity to speak at the press conference two days before the fight, Floyd Mayweather, the show's main promoter, had refused to allow Serrano or Rivas to take questions or say anything after their brief photo opportunity in front of the waiting boxing media.

"Let the guys do that," said Mayweather before ushering them off the stage as two of the co-promoters, Lou DiBella and Eddie Hearn, looked on in stunned silence.

The excitement of fight night, however, belied any of the potential for lingering tensions. From the opening bell, both women came out banging, throwing hard body shots and combinations in an unrelenting slug fest through all ten rounds. The traditional Puerto Rico versus Mexico rivalry was alive and well in their bout, with superb ring skills on display even as Serrano started to pull ahead with the cleaner, more effective shots. As a sign of the mental and physical toughness of both fighters, neither went down despite the withering head and body work on display.

Winning the contest by unanimous decision, the fight scores, 97–93, 98–92, 99–91, with perhaps a bit of a nod toward Serrano in the scoring, nonetheless showed just how dominant Serrano's performance had been.

The fight stats also demonstrated Serrano's control over the fight, documenting that she had thrown a total of 628 punches to Rivas's 539. In terms of her percentage of punches landed, Serrano clearly had the edge, with 33 percent of her punches hitting their target to Rivas's 20 percent, but it was in her power punches where Serrano's real dominance showed through with a connect rate of 42 percent.

Having put on a brilliant performance in her war against Rivas, in a postfight interview, Serrano said she had wanted to win by knockout, but conceding that it had gone the distance, said, "She hit hard, but I hit harder. I could hear her breathing in between rounds, and I knew I had her."

Exuberant from her win, Serrano also proclaimed, "It was a great night for women's boxing, and I hope it keeps getting bigger and bigger."

That great night, however, did not necessarily translate into their pay rates, with Rivas heading home to Mexico with $15,000 and Serrano receiving $17,500.

The inequities in the boxing fees compared to their male counterparts aside, the fight was an important marker in the long climb back to showcasing women's contests on nationally broadcast televised boxing shows. As pointed out by Katie Richcreek in her article for ESPN, "The last women's world title fight on English-language television in the U.S. was Mary Jo Sanders' defeat of Valerie Mahfood by unanimous decision to retain her International Boxing Association female middleweight title on March 30, 2007, on ESPN2."

Richcreek also noted the week before ESPN2's last broadcast, "Fox Sports Network televised Holly Holm defeating Ann Saccurato to win the IBA female world welterweight title, the WBC female world welterweight title, the WBA world female welterweight title and the International Female Boxers Association world welterweight title."[28]

Serrano's next outing, on April 22, 2017, was her historic attempt at capturing a major title in a fifth weight class. Slated for broadcast on Showtime, Serrano fought for the vacant WBO bantamweight title against Dahianna Santana of the Dominican Republic, who came into the fight with a 35–8 record.

On the undercard of the Shawn Porter–Andre Berto card at Barclay's Center, trouble brewed when Santana came in significantly overweight. Serrano and her team, however, were undeterred, and along with the sanctioning body agreed to go forward with Serrano being given the assurance she would become the new title holder if she defeated Santana.

Stepping into the ring, Serrano dominated Santana throughout with vicious body shots and combinations. The unrelenting assault led Serrano to gain a TKO win at 1:14 seconds of the eighth round, with two near stoppages in the earlier rounds and a point taken away from Santana for holding in the fourth round.

Despite her history-making win, the paydays for both women were significantly less than the previous Showtime bout, with Santana slated to earn $6,000 and Serrano, $12,000. Serrano, however, took it all in stride in her public statements, declaring, "I'm so proud to be a Puerto Rican. I'm so proud to be a Showtime fighter. I'm just so happy for this moment . . . just to be a five-division world champion, I could retire today and be the happiest woman alive."[29]

Heather Hardy (18–0) also fought at Barclays Center on March 4, 2017, in a defense of her WBC international featherweight belt, against the Hungarian boxer Edina Kiss (13–2). It was the first chance she'd had to box since defeating Shelly Vincent the previous August, due to the lack of opportunity to get placed on a boxing card.

The fight as contested was the opening bout on the Danny Garcia–Keith Thurman welterweight extravaganza. While initially promised a spot closer to the main card, this was changed at the last minute. As a result, Hardy began to frantically text friends, family, and fans that the fight was now the first of the night. Particularly galling was the fact that the fight ended up starting before the fans were even allowed to be seated—and despite the main card being shown on CBS television, Hardy's undercard battle was not broadcast.

The last-minute drama aside, Hardy was able to settle herself into fight mode. She was determined to win against Kiss, who had been bandied about as a hot prospect, with some pundits even opining that Hardy was the underdog against her.

As the fight got underway, Kiss was quickly outmaneuvered by a dominant Hardy, keeping Kiss on a defensive footing across the eight rounds of their battle. Hardy was applauded mightily by the growing group of her fans who'd been able to see at least a part of her fight and were particularly gratified to see Hardy's hand raised in the air following her unanimous decision with the scores 88–72, 88–72, 79–73.

Hardy had already begun to consider other options, including a fall back to her kickboxing days and the potential for a higher payday as an MMA fighter. Like the rest of the female boxing world, the quick ascendency of women's MMA as a viable and lucrative sport was not lost on her. With the success that Holly Holm was enjoying as a crossover athlete from boxing to MMA, and her unexpected dramatic win over Ronda Rousey on the UFC 193 card in November 2015 that also brought her the world bantamweight title, it seemed a viable if daunting option.

Determined to explore the feasibility, Hardy started to train in earnest, having been approached with an opportunity to debut in the sport on the Invicta FC21 card in Kansas City, Missouri, set for January 21, 2017. With a mere eight-week camp and muscle aches and bruises where she never knew they could exist, she felt ready to try her luck and was set to travel out of Brooklyn, a first for her. Four days before the fight, however, her opponent, Brieta Carpenter, also set to make her MMA debut, withdrew due to an injury—and the fight was indefinitely put on hold.

Even with the fight placement debacle at Barclay's, Hardy knew a win was a win, and she moved forward to rematch against Edina Kiss on DiBella Entertainment's Broadway Boxing show at Brooklyn's historic Paramount Theater a mere two months later on May 18, 2017. A showcase for Hardy, she was the main event on the four-fight card, which gave her fans, many of whom had waited in vain on long lines snaking around Barclay's to see her last fight without ever actually seeing her in the ring. With typical fortitude, Hardy outworked Kiss again, capturing the eight-round unanimous decision with the same scores as their first bout, 80–72, 80–72, 79–73.

Immediately afterwards, however, Hardy announced she would have her debut MMA fight at Madison Square Garden on the Bellator 180, June 24, 2017, card. She noted she would also continue to box but wanted to give MMA a chance—especially given there were much greater prospects to earn money as a fighter, the potential for more promotional opportunities, and importantly, the chance to be seen by a wide audience and thereby gain new fans.

Speaking to the press, Hardy's promoter, Lou DiBella, began his remarks saying, "Heather's going to make her MMA debut."

He emphatically stated, "And a credit to the people involved, it wasn't something that was done behind my back, it was something done together. She deserves an opportunity to make the best living she can for her family, she's a great athlete and she's been training with some of the best people in MMA, and I'm convinced that she can really do it. Tonight, was partially to make the point that she's not leaving the ring, we're going to get a world championship in boxing in the next six or eight months, but she's going to pursue her desire to get involved in mixed martial arts."[30]

In the run-up to her MMA debut, Hardy expressed that she was thrilled with the idea of fighting at Madison Square Garden, an opportunity that had so far eluded her in boxing.

Asked whether she would sign with Bellator, Hardy stated, "Because I am promoted by Lou DiBella with my boxing, [I] will be the first two-sport co-promoted athlete . . . and he is working things out legally now so this can happen."

She also emphasized that there was more equity in the pay MMA fighters received at the lower levels of the sport, stating that when it comes to boxing, "there really [aren't] a lot of opportunities for women. I'm a two-division [boxing] champion, 20–0, selling $40,000 in tickets myself for my fights, and I'm finding trouble getting television time because networks don't want to televise female fights.

"MMA is so much more evolved than boxing." she continued. "Ronda Rousey is the most known of all [though there are many more] and Dana White took a chance to put her on a tremendous card and said let's see what happens. [And it worked.] People love her."

By contrast, she said, "I just boxed on the Thurman–Garcia card. Why not put Heather Hardy on TV? Do you think that people will turn their televisions off? Somebody needs to take initiative to make a change. That's what they did in MMA and women are seen as athletes." She continued, saying that as a champion athlete in boxing, "I'm barely making $10,000 for my title fights . . . and my debut with Bellator will be more than I've ever made in boxing."[31]

Layla McCarter, a perennially highly ranked welterweight fighter with a strong pedigree of opponents as she marked nineteen years as a pro in the sport, spoke to an interviewer in January 2017 about the hope for a fight as early as February on a Mayweather Promotions card.

Making note that she was ranked third overall as a welterweight, she pointedly asked to be considered for a bout against the number one ranked undisputed champion, Cecilia Braekhus, following the upcoming battled with number two ranked Swedish fighter Klara Svensson.

McCarter said, "This year, I just want to stay busy, I want to get more active [at least four times this year], and I want to have some high profile [fights] as far as TV. Showtime said they are televising women's boxing this year, and some of the other networks as well, I'm thinking this might be a big year for women's boxing."[32]

McCarter was finally given the chance to box the Hungarian fighter Szilvia Szabados (16–9) in an eight-rounder at Sam's Town Hotel & Gambling Hall in Las Vegas on April 29, 2017. The fight was the opener of a PBC card on Fox Sports, giving both women the opportunity to show off their skills and make a statement.

A favorite in Las Vegas, McCarter started off strong, swarming Szabados with a flurry of punches that pushed her toward the ropes and hitting her opponent with lead hooks as the opportunities opened in front of her. Szabados, though, was not content only to eat leather, and let loose with straight rights and left jabs of her own to catch McCarter.

The four-division world champion, McCarter began to catch her rhythm to dominate the fight starting at the end of the second round, exciting the fans in the stands. Fought at two minutes per round, the announcers pointed out that McCarter had been the first woman in Las Vegas to fight in contracted three-minute, twelve-round championship fights—and continued to advocate for three-minute round bouts. McCarter was not in the position to dictate the number of minutes per round in her fights, a position she had been in years before when she wielded more agency in the sport and, as it was, took the opportunities that became available.

As the fight edged into the later rounds, Szabados had given to tactics including hitting McCarter repeatedly in the back of the head. She was warned by referee Tony Weeks, who finally deducted a point from her early in the seventh round. Back in action, McCarter let loose with an unrelenting series of left hooks to the body of Szabados. Doubling over in evident pain, Weeks pushed in to waive off the fight, giving McCarter the TKO win at 0:56 of round seven.

The victory, however, did not set her up for a title opportunity against the undisputed champion, Cecilia Braekhus, nor eliminator bouts for any of the four sanctioned titles. In fact, McCarter's next bout wasn't until December 22 in Mexico City, where she had traveled for an eight-rounder against a novice Mexican fighter—and a continuation of McCarter's unsuccessful campaign for boxing opportunities.

Kali Reis, who proudly lauded her Native American (from Cherokee, Nipmuc, and Seacoke Wampanoag tribes) and Cape Verdean descent, started her boxing career in small club fights in the New England area, encouraged by teammate and self-described fellow misfit Shelly Vincent. Reis became a boxing road warrior starting in 2014, taking the opponent role in title fights across Europe including a WBO middleweight bout against Christina Hammer which, though Reis lost, saw her land a memorable overhand right in the tenth round that sent Hammer to the canvas.

By 2016, Reis had become the WBC world middleweight champion, having defeated Maricela Carnejo by split decision on a female-dominated card contested in Auckland, New Zealand, on April 14. The veritable who's who of East Coast fighters on the card included Ronica Jeffries and Melissa St. Vil, both of whom fought out of Brooklyn's Gleason's Gym and came home with WBC silver feather and WBC silver super feather titles, respectively. To round out the group were the two journeywoman fighters Nydia Feliciano and Noemi Bosques, both of whom lost close decisions against their respective local opponents.

Reis went on to be defeated in a closely fought unification—a battle for the WBC and WBO middleweight titles in a rematch with Christina Hammer at Munich's Ballhaus Forum on November 5, 2016. The co-main event battle generated a lot of interest in Germany and was broadcast live on Sky Germany PPV—but not shown in the United States. Of interest is the fact that Reis had fought and won an untelevised non-title eight-rounder against Althea Saunders on July 16 back at the Twin River Event Center in Rhodes Island, having not been able to gain traction for a sanctioned title defense despite holding the prestigious green belt.

After the loss of her title, Reis did manage to keep active with three separate six-round bouts in May, October, and November 2017, two of which were at the Mohegan Sun Casino in Connecticut, promoted by Joe DeGuardia and shown on local outlets, and one at the Mayflower Hotel in Washington, DC. What Reis was not receiving were opportunities to fight on nationally broadcast fight cards despite the inroads of fights being televised on Showtime and Fox Sports.

In the United States, the only fighter who was truly managing to find those kinds of opportunities was Claressa Shields, who upon capturing the WBC silver middle title in June 2016 was set up to contest for the vacant WBC and IBF unified super middle world titles against the current IBF champion, German boxer Nikki Adler.

The card was fought on August 4, 2017, just under a year since Shields had captured her second Olympic gold medal. Broadcast as the main event from the MGM Grand in Detroit, Michigan, the fight was aired by *Showtime After Dark* as the Main Event, a first for the network and one of the few fight cards historically with a female boxing match broadcast as the main event.

And Shields did not disappoint. She gained a huge stoppage win at 1:34 of the fifth round.

"I worked real hard in the gym, I trained, I ate right, I went to sleep on time, I was real focused," Shields said. "I blocked all negativity. Getting the knockout gave me joy."[33]

Claressa Shields, Alicia Ashley, and Heather Hardy attend a live WNYC panel discussion on women's boxing after Shields was chosen as one of the three Team USA Boxing Olympians ahead of the 2012 London Games. The Green Space, New York, February 10, 2012.
MALISSA SMITH, FROM THE COLLECTION OF THE AUTHOR

Lucia Rijker and Christy Martin were two of the inaugural inductees to the International Women's Boxing Hall of Fame, Fort Lauderdale, Florida, July 10, 2014.
MALISSA SMITH, FROM THE COLLECTION OF THE AUTHOR

In the fight billed as McCarter–Hernandez III, the best fight between pound-for-pound boxers no one would ever see, Layla McCarter (35–13–5, 8-KOs) throws a power jab at Melissa Hernandez (19–5–3, 6-KOs) in the rubber match to take the UD win and bragging rights in their trilogy. Orleans Hotel & Casino, Las Vegas, November 21, 2014.
MARY ANN OWEN

WBC's Jill Diamond and super-bantamweight champion Alicia Ashley attended the 2015 IWBHF second induction event, Fort Lauderdale, Florida, July 11, 2015.
MALISSA SMITH, FROM THE COLLECTION OF THE AUTHOR

Claressa Shields sporting her two gold Olympic medals ahead of her professional debut, Las Vegas, November 14, 2016.
MARY ANN OWEN

Franchon Crews-Dezurn delivered a straight right to opponent Tiffany Wooward, winning their six-round bout by unanimous decision on the undercard of the Claressa Shields–Tori Nelson main event. Turning Stone Resort & Casino, New York, January 12, 2018.
TERRELL GROGGINS/MY ART MY RULES

Shelito Vincent, ahead of her WBO world featherweight title match with Heather Hardy. Manfredo Boxing Sports Fitness, Smithfield, Rhode Island, October 13, 2018.

Heather Hardy sporting a cut above her left eye as she wears her WBO world featherweight belt. Gleason's Gym, New York, October 29, 2018.

MALISSA SMITH, FROM THE COLLECTION OF THE AUTHOR

In the final bout of HBO's storied history in boxing, Cecilia Braekhus (35–0, 9-KOs) retained her undisputed welterweight championship by easily outboxing Alexandra Magdziak-Lopes (18–5–3, 1-KO) over ten rounds. Stub Hub Center, California, December 8, 2018.

TERRELL GROGGINS/MY ART MY RULES

Helen Joseph after twelve rounds of sparring. Mendez Gym, New York, October 9, 2019.
MALISSA SMITH, FROM THE COLLECTION OF THE AUTHOR

Women's boxing champions Melissa St. Vil, Heather Hardy, and Ronica Jeffries pose at Gleason's Gym, New York, October 9, 2019.
MALISSA SMITH, FROM THE COLLECTION OF THE AUTHOR

Melissa Hernandez (23–7–3, 7-KOs) readying for her bout against Chantelle Cameron (13–0, 7-KOs), Gleason's Gym, New York, April 19, 2021.

MALISSA SMITH, FROM THE COLLECTION OF THE AUTHOR

Sue "Tiger Lily" Fox, president of the International Women's Boxing Hall of Fame, displaying the Women's Boxing Day proclamation issued by Las Vegas mayor Carolyn Goodman. Orleans Hotel & Casino, Las Vegas, August 14, 2021.

MALISSA SMITH, FROM THE COLLECTION OF THE AUTHOR

IWHBF 2019 inductee Lisa Holewyne, boxing referee Kenny Bayless, and IWBHF 2014 and IBHOF 2020 inductee Christy Martin having fun ahead of the IWBHF 2021 induction ceremony. Orleans Hotel & Casino, Las Vegas, August 14, 2021.

Scottish fighter Hannah Rankin (11–5, 2-KOs) celebrates becoming a two-time world champion after beating Swede Maria Lindberg (19–8–2, 10-KOs) by unanimous decision to take the vacant WBA and IBO female world super-welterweight titles. Tottenham Hotspur FC Banqueting Hall, England, November 5, 2021.
JIM DIAMOND PHOTOGRAPHER

Katie Taylor (20–0, 6-KOs) and Amanda Serrano (42–1–1, 30–KOs) at the press conference announcing their historic Madison Square Garden Arena main-event undisputed lightweight battle alongside promoters Eddie Hearn, Matchroom Boxing, and Jake Paul, Most Valuable Promotions, New York, February 2, 2022.
MALISSA SMITH, FROM THE COLLECTION OF THE AUTHOR

Katie Taylor (20–0, 6-KOs) and Amanda Serrano (42–1–1, 30-KOs) displaying all the belts, alongside promoters Eddie Hearn, Matchroom Boxing, and Jake Paul, Most Valuable Promotions, Madison Square Garden, New York, February 2, 2022.

Franchon Crews-Dezurn in her undisputed super middleweight bout against champion Elin Cederoos on the undercard of the historic sold-out Katie Taylor–Amanda Serrano undisputed lightweight main event. Madison Square Garden Arena, New York, April 30, 2022.

Claressa Shields (13–0, 2-KOs) makes a triumphant entry in a costume inspired by Apollo Creed, before her undisputed middleweight win against British boxer Savannah Marshall (12–0, 10-KOs) at the head of the historic sold-out all-female card at London's O2 Arena, England, October 15, 2022.
RAKEEM NOBLE

IWBHF pioneer inductee Dar Buckskin and IWBHF 2019 inductee Martha Salazar at the ninth induction ceremony, Orleans Hotel & Casino, Las Vegas, October 22, 2022.
MALISSA SMITH, FROM THE COLLECTION OF THE AUTHOR

Some members of the IWBHF class of 2022 inductees at the ninth induction ceremony, Orleans Hotel & Casino, Las Vegas, October 22, 2022.
MALISSA SMITH, FROM THE COLLECTION OF THE AUTHOR

Amanda Serrano (43–2–1, 30-KOs) being interviewed at the weigh-in ahead of her undisputed battle with Erika Cruz (15–1, 3-KOs), Madison Square Garden Theater, New York, February 3, 2023.
MALISSA SMITH, FROM THE COLLECTION OF THE AUTHOR

Alycia Baumgardner (13–1, 7-KOs) and Elhem Mekhaled (15–1, 3-KOs) weigh-in ahead of their super featherweight undisputed showdown, Madison Square Garden Theater, New York, February 3, 2023.

Alycia Baumgardner (13–1, 7-KOs) facing off against Elhem Mekhaled (15–1, 3-KOs) in the first round of their super featherweight undisputed showdown. Baumgardner won by unanimous decision, Madison Square Garden Theater, New York, February 4, 2023.

British boxer Raven Chapman (6–0, 2-KOs) continues her rise to a world title shot as she beats former Peruvian world champion Linda Laura Lecca by unanimous decision to retain the WBC (international) featherweight title in her first ten-rounder, York Hall, Bethnal Green, England, March 25, 2023.

Mikaela Mayer media workout, Brong Boxing Gym, Camberwell, England, April 13, 2023.

CHAPTER FIVE

Breaking the Ceilings

WHILE THE INCREASE IN OPPORTUNITIES FOR WOMEN TO BOX PROFES-sionally became evident, a continued lack of placement on major fight cards, the pay gap between male and female fighters, and issues related to promotion, matchmaking, and sanctioning organizations still plagued the years 2017–2019. Fighters such as Seniesa Estrada were caught in between, having competed in the amateurs before the Olympics but turning pro in an era that still undervalued women in the ring.

Those struggles aside, there were also old guard fighters such as Cecilia Braekhus who were able to break through glass ceilings that had seemed insurmountable even with the strides being made by the Olympians. This included the first-ever broadcast of a female fight on HBO Boxing for the undisputed welterweight title battle between Braekhus and Kali Reis in 2018. With that glass ceiling broken, Heather Hardy's gutsy outreach directly to HBO Boxing saw to it that her WBO world feather title bout at the Madison Square Garden theater against Shelly Vincent would be only the second female bout televised by HBO. Moreover, for HBO's final card, Braekhus was given the place of honor at the head of the card.

Boxing media also began to demonstrate a growing crescendo of positive representations of the sport, as well as a hearty respect for the women who donned the gloves to enter the ring. This included the announcement of the BWAA Christy Martin Award in 2017 in recognition of the female fighter of the year—with the first ever awarded in 2018 to Cecilia Braekhus.

UNDETERRED

Back in 2005, writer Kurt Streeter wrote a five-piece, front-page feature series for the *Los Angeles Times* about boxer Seniesa "Super Bad" Estrada. The series was published just after her thirteenth birthday and chronicled her journey in the sport from the tender age of six.

"Do girls box? she asked, turning to her father one evening.

Is it OK for girls to box?

Well, yeah, mija, they do, he answered. *Sure, it's OK for girls to box."*[1]

The query to her father has been repeated across the arc of Estrada's journey in boxing—a moment that she says has defined the person she was to become.

Her first forays in boxing came in the small gyms in and around East Los Angeles (East LA) eventuating in her 7–1 amateur record. Estrada had won both the 2007 and 2008 Junior Olympic national championships at light fly and fly, respectively, before going on to capture the 2009 USA Boxing women's national fly championship in June 2009.

The winner's podium in 2009 included future 2012 Olympians Marlen Estrada, who captured the light fly honors, and Queen Underwood at super light. Given Estrada had competed in both fly and light fly categories, it should be noted she had never faced Esparza in the ring as an amateur—this would only come later in the pros. Estrada went on to compete in a tournament in Ecuador a few months after winning the national title. With her loss also came the decision not to pursue further amateur opportunities, opting instead to turn professional in 2011—and due to an injury choosing not to dip back in to compete for a place on the Olympic team. With that decision, she left the sport entirely until 2014, taking "community college classes and work[ing] a string of low-paying jobs, including as a server at an ice cream shop."[2]

By September 2017, Estrada had put together a 10–0 professional record, including a knockout win at 0:38 seconds of the first round of her ninth pro fight—and a solid fan base from her beloved East LA.

Estrada's decisive win on the cards in her eleventh fight over Mexican fighter Anahi Torres in the late afternoon sun at the StubHub Center was another in her string of achievements. On the undercard of an HBO Boxing card, it brought her more fully to the attention of Golden Boy Promotions, leading to a multiyear contract signed in January 2018— only the second female boxer to have joined their roster of fighters after Marlen Esparza. As Estrada put it, this was "18 years of hard work, dedication & sacrifice. Ready to show the world who I am"—all with the idea that Golden Boy could well look to set up a rivalry between their two marquee fighters.[3]

This was not, however, her first encounter with Golden Boy. Back in November 2010 (following Kaliesha West's successful WBO title fight on a Golden Boy PPV card in September), Estrada had won a tough, three-round amateur bout on a Professional-Amateur (Pro-Am) Golden Boy card at Club Nokia in Los Angeles. The only female bout of the evening, she fought the much heavier, Fresno-based fighter Shanne Ruelas in a crowd-pleasing slug fest ahead of the pro side of the card, which left the fans clamoring for more. In a postfight interview, Estrada still had the dream of going to the Olympics.

"I am staying amateur to try and make the 2012 Olympic Team. I am excited for the long journey I have ahead of me in order to get there," she said.[4]

Seven years on, and having turned professional ahead of the Games, Estrada's first professional bout under the Golden Boy banner saw her head up a show in the popular LA Fight Club series at the Belasco Theater. Billed as the main event, Estrada had a lot to prove. As a non-title fight, the bout was set for eight-round, two-minute rounds in front of an excited, friendly crowd.

In only her second appearance at the LA Fight Club, where she'd won a unanimous decision in a six-rounder two years before—though suffering her only knockdown—Estrada was pitted against Mexican fighter Sonia Osorio (11–4–1, alternatively 8–5–1 and 10–5–1). To further promote their hot prospect, the fight was shown live on Golden Boy's Facebook channel, Estrella TV, and Ring TV.

"I am very excited and ready to make my Golden Boy Promotions debut in my hometown," said Estrada. "I've been working harder than ever to put on a great performance for my fans and for those who have not seen me fight. I hope to entertain and gain many more fans throughout my career with Golden Boy Promotions, and I can't wait to kick off 2018 with a great victory."[5]

The viewers at home were treated to the raucous excitement of the packed venue, cheering as both fighters were introduced but saving their most adoring demonstrations of support for Estrada, the pride of East LA. In an effort not to disappoint, Estrada was poised to fight as the bell opened, and proceeded to put on a boxing show. She outshined the skilled and accomplished Osorio with a range of punches, exquisite footwork, and in the tradition of her trainer, Dean Campos, an unorthodox style of boxing that relied more on feints, switching stances, counterpunching, and right- or left-hand leads rather than the traditional use of the jab, opposite hand, straight punch combination.

Estrada had been training with Campos since her early amateur days—and on through lean years when it came to money and opportunity in the pros. From Campos's perspective, even though the 2012 London Olympics had started to turn the tide in the sport, he firmly believed that Ronda Rousey's achievements with the UFC made the difference even as Olympians started to turn pro.

"I told [Seniesa], 'You know what, believe it or not, this is going to open the door for women in boxing,'" Campos said. "She goes, 'You think so? It's MMA.' I told her it doesn't matter. They're going to start seeing that a girl can headline, and they're going to at least start putting girls on the undercards."[6]

As early as 2016, Estrada made appearances on the undercard of major fights at venues such as the Forum in Englewood, California, bringing fans to the arena long before the main card in much the same way as fighters such as Heather Hardy, Amanda Serrano, and Shelly Vincent on the East Coast. Ahead of her appearance on the undercard of the April 2016 Golovkin–Gonzalez HBO event, Estrada said, "Most people who don't know me or have never seen me fight, wonder why I'm here and wonder who I am, but nobody knows my 16-year journey that I've been on, and that I've had over 100 amateur fights. What I just want to continue to do is just prove why women deserve these opportunities and to prove why we belong here and just put on a great show."[7]

Challenges aside, she'd managed to have three fights in 2016 and again in 2017 before Golden Boy Promotions signed her.

Still, Estrada's debut win as a Golden Boy fighter was sweet. "I knew she was a tough opponent but I tried to mix it up as best as I could," said Estrada. "Tonight was special and I'm ready to represent women's boxing."

She added: "I'm so blessed to have so many people come out and support me. I was happy to fight in my hometown and have my supporters here."[8]

Marlen Esparza's early success fighting on Golden Boy cards also helped to pique interest in Estrada, both as a foil but also to capitalize on the perceived potential for pushing women on fight cards. While Esparza's first bout had been a two-minute-per-round fight against Rachel Sazoff, Esparza's second and third fights were contested at the T-Mobile Arena in Las Vegas, which gave her the opportunity to fight three-minute rounds—long legal in Las Vegas, thanks to the pioneering efforts of Layla McCarter before her.

For Esparza and her Golden Boy promoters, it was also an opportunity to push the viability of female boxing given the perceived notion that fighting two-minute rounds somehow lessened the legitimacy of women's boxing as a whole.

"Finally!!! Everyone, I will be fighting 3min rounds no more 2min!! To top it off I will be fighting May 6th on the Canelo/Chavez undercard!" Esparza announced on Twitter.[9]

In a follow-up tweet, she wrote, "ITS TIME! Im excited and ready to announce Ill be fightin 3min rounds like the men! May 6th ON The Canelo/Chavez undercard."[10]

As she had noted, Esparza's first three-minute outing was on the undercard of the Canelo–Chavez Jr. HBO PPV card. Contesting against fellow Texan Samantha Salazar (2–3–1) for 4 three-minute rounds, the bout caused ripples with Esparza taking particular pride in the event, even though she was not the first woman in Nevada to do so, as she claimed after winning the contest by unanimous decision.

"It's great to make history being the first woman in Nevada to do three-minute rounds," said Esparza. "I know it's been done elsewhere, but tonight it feels really special doing it in this fight. I plan on staying at three minutes and not going back to two minutes, so I know we will need to be strategic about how I train and fight."[11]

Esparza's second three-minute round fight was the following September. Fighting in a six-rounder this time as the opener for the first Golovkin–Canelo, PPV card on HBO, her opponent was a Mexican journeywoman fighting out of Denver, Aracely Palacios, who had also fought in a rare three-minute-per-round fight two years previously in Durango, Mexico. Esparza was able to outwork her, using her jab and her hand speed to great effect around the aggressive movement and fighting style of Palacios. After the fight, Esparza proudly proclaimed on Twitter, "I got the W tonight boxing 6*3 min rounds. Thank you @GoldenBoy-Boxing my coaches, sponsors and a very big thank you to all my supports [heart emoji]."[12]

Esparza's next outing in December 2017 was another six-rounder, an undercard bout fought at two-minute rounds at the Fantasy Springs Casino in California. Shown on ESPN, the fight included an NABF super feather men's fight, which may have accounted for the decision to keep the fight at two minutes—as the State of California Athletic Commission (SCAC) had no such prohibition for women.[13]

Golden Boy's decision to recruit and sign Estrada as their second women's boxing fighter was yet one more shining opportunity for women to contest in professional boxing on recognized fight cards. Oscar De La Hoya himself, in his days as a Top Rank champion fighter, was accompanied on his fight cards from 1998–2000 by the likes of Mia St. John. Choosing to put women on cards some twenty years later had a certain symmetry to it, and while Esparza was the only female on the roster for her first year with Golden Boy, her success in the ring, and willingness to push the sport, certainly opened the door for Estrada, a fighter who had nonetheless persevered in a sport that was perhaps beginning to reopen a tiny bit of daylight.

GLASS CEILINGS

At 32–0 with nine wins by knockout, and in May 2018, the sole undisputed female fighter in the eleventh year of the four-belt era, Cecilia

Braekhus had accomplished extraordinary firsts in the sport—not the least of which was being instrumental in legalizing boxing, period, in her home country of Norway.

When it came to knocking down the "glass ceilings" in the sport, however, the one that had always seemed insurmountable was the appearance of a female bout on the premiere American media outlet, HBO Boxing. Sure, Braekhus had been the main event on countless cards in her career and a boxing star in Europe who inspired successive generations of fighters. But who had heard of her in America? Without broadcasting she was virtually unknown except in the tight boxing circles that appreciated her brilliance as a fighter at the top of the pound-for-pound list in women's boxing. Still, it was women's boxing, not boxing. And yes, Shields, Esparza, Taylor, Serrano, and Hardy were appearing on American outlets from time to time and winning big-four titles, but they were still seeming "one offs" and hadn't crashed through the crucible that was HBO.

And then it happened. HBO had agreed to televise the first female bout in its forty-five-year history: the undisputed and undefeated welterweight Cecilia Braekhus versus the always game Kali Reis (13–6–1, 4-KOs) on the Gennadiy Golovkin–Vanes Martirosyan card set for the StubHub Center in Carson, California. It was to be Braekhus's twenty-second title defense. They could not have chosen better—though some boxing pundits were quick to ask why it had taken so long.

Despite the hoopla of being televised, the Braekhus–Reis fight had originally been scheduled to appear on the non-televised portion of the undercard. That changed at the end of April, when it was announced that boxer Roman "Chocolatito" Gonzalez, whose fight had been slated to open the televised portion of the card, was forced to cancel his appearance due to last-minute visa issues in his native Nicaragua. Left with a huge gap in the short six-fight card, HBO quickly switched gears to elevate the appearance of the two women.

Asked about it, Braekhus said, "Outside of America in Europe, Norway, Germany . . . there are girls selling out arenas and being put on television. It's doing well in Latin America, Japan, it's all over the world that female boxing has become very popular. Why it isn't catching on in the U.S., I really don't have an answer for that.

"It's funny, because the U.S. is normally the one who sets the trends and the rest of the world kind of follows. In this case, it's the complete opposite."[14]

HBO Sports' executive vice president Peter Nelson, who had joined the network in 2013, put it this way: "Cecilia is one of the best fighters in the world. Period. She deserves to be seen by as large an audience as possible. We are privileged that her debut on HBO coincides with ours in women's boxing."[15]

As the promoter for the bout, Tom Loeffler was particularly effusive: "I am so proud to help present the first female bout to be televised live on HBO. Undefeated world female welterweight champion Cecilia Braekhus, [women's] boxing's only undisputed world champion, will have her hands full against former WBC world female middleweight champion Kali Reis."

There was also a legacy component to the event. Braekhus had chosen to train with legendary women's boxing great Lucia Rijker during her LA-based camp. Asked about the experience, Rijker said, "It's been great working with Cecilia. She is so talented, and even more, so very dedicated to working hard and continuing to learn every day. We can't wait to show boxing fans at the StubHub Center and those watching all over the world what we've been working on."

Reis, no stranger to big fight nights and a former middleweight titlist herself, said, "I am very excited for this opportunity. I'd like to thank Cecilia and her team for this once in a lifetime chance to fight the No. 1 pound-for-pound undisputed champion. My team and I have been hard at work knowing she will bring her A-game. So will we. This is such a great card and I am grateful to be a part of it."[16]

Claiming "we will go for it, 100%,"[17] Braekhus and Reis put on a spectacular show, although for reasons not publicly divulged, Braekhus replaced Rijker in her corner with former trainer Johnathan Banks the day before the bout.

Reis had a lot on the line as well. She had always fought up, choosing to be in the big fights, and for this one had even come down two divisions to contest at welterweight. Whether it was nerves for such a big occasion, or adjusting to fighting lighter, she had a bit of a slow start, but picking up in the sixth, she was able to set up Braekhus for a straight right hand, which dropped the undisputed champion to one knee and the humbling eight-count for the first time in her career. Reis buckled Braekhus with a right hand just before the bell at the end of the eighth round as well, but Braekhus was able to keep Reis at bay with some excellent shots of her own to take the unanimous decision win. As the cards were read, the crowd, firmly behind Reis, booed the results, but a win was a win was a win, and Braekhus had successfully come out on top, even as she showed her vulnerability in the ring.

Another big first for women's boxing was the creation of the Christy Martin Award—Female Fighter of the Year, by the vaulted Boxing Writers Association of American (BWAA). Named for the champion Christy Martin, whose achievements in women's boxing were unparalleled in the sport, Cecilia "Braekhus [became] the first woman to be named Female Fighter of the Year in the 92-year history of the BWAA."

Boxing writer and longtime proponent of women's boxing Thomas Gerbasi, in his role as chair of the BWAA selection committee, said, "When we looked at Cecilia [and her record in 2017, we noted] she fought two former world champions and . . . one current world champion . . . making it a super fight between two of the pound-for-pound best. Cecilia did all of this with a target on her back, because she had five world titles to defend."

Learning that she had been selected for the singular honor of receiving the newly created award, Braekhus said, "This is important to me. It's part of boxing history and it's very big for me because of the young girls that may think about boxing in their future.

"I think also of all the girls whose name should be on this that are a huge part of this; the girls who went to the gym and trained hard twice a day, only because they loved the sport of boxing. They gave everything and didn't get anything back: money, fame or anything. They did it because they loved it and wanted to compete and represent their country. It's been a long road for women's boxing, so it's great for the BWAA to recognize a female fighter of the year. I'm very proud to be the first, but there a lot of women that came before me that made this possible."[18]

At the ceremony in New York City, resplendent in white and clearly moved by the honor of being the first recipient of the award, she acknowledged the challenges women face in the sport, stating, "My hope is this award will bring us one step closer to the recognition female boxing deserves."[19]

Concluding her brief remarks, Braekhus proudly held the plaque with Christy Martin at her side. The two women shared the moment, receiving the applause of those who understood what each had sacrificed to be there.

MAKING THINGS HAPPEN

Amid Shields and Taylor's campaigns for recognition and opportunity, in September 2018, HBO Boxing made a momentous announcement, telling the world it would cease its boxing operations at the end of 2018.

From the lens of the Braekhus–Reis bout in May and what it portended for women going forward, the demise of HBO was a huge blow for the growth of women's boxing. With one less mainstream outlet in the mix, the opportunities to build the kind of fan base necessary to prove the worth of the sport was, it seemed, having yet another hard-stop moment. Yes, Showtime's seeming commitment to put women's fights on their cards was positive, as was the new streaming upstart, DAZN Boxing's support, but having finally made traction with HBO, it was unsettling.

With their operations curtailing, however, there were plans to put on one more fight card: the Daniel Jacobs–Sergiy Derevyanchenko battle for the vacant IBF world middle title scheduled for October 27, 2018, at the Madison Square Garden (MSG) Theater. There was something wistful about what seemed to be the network's swan song, but for those on the undercard of the fairly put together evening of boxing, there was the opportunity of having a lot of eyes on their fights. One such contest was the long-awaited Heather Hardy–Shelly Vincent rematch being billed as HardyVincent2 for the vacant WBO world feather championship. For all of that, the fight was listed as the fourth on the card, though it was one of three world title fights on the bout sheet.

The first outing between Hardy and Vincent had been positively compared to a Gatti–Ward throwdown—with the second bout being touted as the female version of GattiWard2. Even so, it was also still colloquially called the "Barbie doll versus Mohawk" clash—never mind that they both could really fight, were entertaining, and sold a lot of tickets.

Of the first fight, Hardy had said, "I just felt like I was part of something that I worked hard for, and it became a part of me."

Given all of that—and the significance that had been attributed to broadcasting the Braekhus–Reis fight the previous May—HBO had not even considered putting HardyVincent2 on the televised portion of the card.

As Hardy put it, "They were announcing it as a triple header, and yeah, I was happy to be on the show, boxing at the Garden, doing the rematch . . . [but] I was really annoyed that they were announcing it. Like, how dare you announce it as a triple header, knowing that me and Shelly are going to sell out the little Hulu Theater, and for weeks I mean, I was tweeting HBO and articles, and one night . . . I was so mad . . . I called [HBO's] Peter Nelson and left a message. . . ."

The gist was to complain about not being on the broadcast portion of the card and, as Hardy later related, her promoter Lou DiBella called her the next morning asking if she'd called him. Hardy told him that she had, but only after taking a gulp and expecting an explosive reaction. Letting the silence permeate the air, DiBella finally broke it, saying, "it . . . worked." Peter Nelson had agreed to broadcast the HardyVincent2 fight, adding that there was no money in the budget for it but that he'd do it anyway.[20]

Hardy couldn't quite believe it but plowed forward, her insides awash in smiles and glee. Vincent was also excited by the opportunity—perhaps best expressed by her trainer, Peter Manfredo Sr., who said, "Shelly is really focused for this fight, the most focused I've ever seen her."

Vincent added, "To tell you the truth, I haven't been focused on anything but training, I don't care about the promotion, I don't care about nothing this time, and usually I'm the opposite."

She was of the firm opinion that she won the first bout, so the focus was important to ensure her vindication and, of course, the title. Still, at the heart of it all was a palpable and deep understanding of what the fight meant to both women—an acknowledgment of the sisterhood of the ring Vincent and Hardy had to share "as survivors, as activists in the sport, and as individuals who have figured out the best way forward is to come at life on their own terms as fighters."[21]

The fight itself was a rough and tumble of back-and-forth excitement. Hardy took the bout by unanimous decision 97–93, 97–93, 99–91, but the deeper significance of winning the title on an HBO Boxing broadcast was not lost on her—something akin to an unobtainable brass ring until Braekhus had broken the spell, but still seemingly impossible.

"If I have to pick one of my top five career moments," she said, "it was sitting on the stool in the corner between rounds of that fight and looking at Max Kellerman and realizing at that moment [he] is calling my fight.

"I had this out of body feeling," she continued. "Max Kellerman is calling my fight in Madison Square Garden on HBO, and it was just . . . surreal."

The fight was also a $20,000 payday—a career high in boxing for Hardy, but still nothing more than a break-even night with fully "30% going to the corner, off the bat," plus all the other expenses and lost revenue for working less during camp. She added, "I understood the business side of how to make money in this industry" by working hard to market herself, but that savvy still wasn't translating into a six-figure fee for fighting for a title, no matter how much she and Vincent brought to gate in ticket sales.[22]

The other high-profile female bouts at the close of 2018 had historic overtones even as they helped build the brands of the fighters.

The first was certainly the most momentous. HBO Boxing's truly last evening of programming was announced for December 8, 2018. It was to be broadcast under HBO's Boxing After Dark brand, at the StubHub Center, site of so many legendary fight nights, and promoted by Tom Loeffler's 360 Promotions.

The surprise was that the fight card was to be headed by none other than Cecilia Braekhus—shattering yet another glass ceiling as the first women to be the featured star of an HBO Boxing show.

Mike Coppinger, writing for *The Ring*, opined: "It's a step forward for women's boxing, and Braekhus, *The Ring's* No. 1 female fighter, deserves to headline her own shows. But for HBO to go out this way, with no investment in the women beforehand, is an uninspired choice. Naturally, the female fights cost far less money."[23]

The slap was firmly felt—acknowledging the necessity of the step for women in boxing on the one hand and besmirching the moment on the other, though the comment on the economics of boxing was certainly true. Eschewing any potential for negatively, Braekhus said, "It's an honor to be in this position right now. It's truly a validation for the great year it's been for women's boxing all over the world, and how strong the future is. We have come a long way in the sport, and I believe there are even more opportunities to come our way."[24]

As the sport's only undisputed fighter, it did seem fitting that Cecilia Braekhus was chosen to lead the card. She would enter the ring looking for her thirty-fifth win fighting the Polish boxer Aleksandra Magdziak Lopes (18–4-3, 1-KO), and giving what she hoped would be a stellar performance.

In another fitting choice, the opener of the three-bout HBO Boxing broadcast featured Claressa Shields (7–0, 2-KOs) in her HBO Boxing television debut looking to defend her unified middle titles against Belgian fighter Femke Hermans (9–1, 3-KOs), whose only loss to date had been earlier in the year to Alicia Napoleon for the vacant WBA world super middle title.

As fight nights go, not much happened that wasn't expected; Shields enjoyed a rout of her opponent with a 100–90 wipeout on all three cards. She herself rated the fight a "B," stating, "there's still things I need to work on but I'm happy with my performance."

It proved to be much the same for Braekhus, who finished the night with similar scores. "It was an honor to fight for the second time this year on HBO and to be chosen for the main event on their final boxing telecast," she said. "I thank them very much for their support of my career. This was a great night for women's boxing."[25]

The veteran announcers on the show, Jim Lampley, Max Kellerman, and Roy Jones Jr., with a surprise reminiscence between Lampley and the venerable Larry Merchant, did their best to infuse enthusiasm, but if their hearts were anywhere, it was in looking backward, rather than at what lay ahead. That HBO Boxing had chosen those two fights for their actual "swan song" was something else again, for whatever the motives were, its place in the pantheon of women's fight nights was important and a marker for the future despite the funereal exhibition that it otherwise seemed to be with gaps in the stadium and plunging temperatures as the night wore on.

Katie Taylor's final bout of 2018 was set for December 15 at Madison Square Garden on the undercard of the Canelo–Fielding fight for the WBA world super middleweight title broadcast on DAZN Boxing. She was slated to do battle with the Finnish boxer Eva Wahlström (22–0–1, 3-KOs), who'd arguably lost her mixed-decision win for the WBC world super feather title bout against the always scrappy American fighter, Melissa St. Vil, in her last outing.

Defending her unified titles in her Madison Square Garden debut, the hope was that Taylor would gain a decisive win that would in turn bring about a shot at contesting for the other two parts of the undisputed lightweight prize: the WBO and WBC championships. For those, she hoped to target the Brazilian fighter Rose Volante, who'd won the WBO world title in September and the always fearsome Delfine Persoon, the WBC world champion since 2014.

Taylor fought with her usual speed, aggression, footwork, and guts, not afraid to mix it up in close quarters with Wahlström. Following an exciting bout, Taylor was quick to praise her opponent after gaining the blowout unanimous decision win in front of the partisan Irish New York crowd: "I thought it was a very good performance. She's obviously a fantastic champion and a great, great fighter. I knew it was going to be a great showcase for women's boxing."

Speaking of the future, she was clear in outlining her next steps: "The goal is to be the undisputed lightweight champion of the world. Obviously one of the biggest fighters out there is Amanda Serrano, and that's a huge, huge fight."[26]

CHAPTER SIX

Boxing Queens

WHILE CECILIA BRAEKHUS REMAINED THE ULTIMATE QUEEN OF BOX-
ing, with the advent of Shields and Taylor, mainstream media companies
in the United States in league with promoters began to map out a new
future with women on "main" boxing shows—and as the main event. The
groundwork had been laid out in the pivotal transition year of 2018 with
all of the ingredients set for the prospect of crowning two new undisputed female champions in 2019. Even amid these extraordinary changes
in opportunities for women's boxing, some promotional companies
remained resistant to adding women's bouts on their fight cards—or, as
in the case of PBC, began to pull back from offering opportunities. The
primary reason cited was the alleged lack of financial return in female
fights, and the belief, however mistaken, that there is not enough talent
to anchor such cards—with the obvious "chicken-and-egg" dilemma of
which came first, women on cards to grow the sport, or not having them
at all because they don't bring in money.

Boxers seeking a way out took to social media to interact directly
with fans and to help build the momentum for women's boxing through
nontraditional channels of communication. The period also saw the
rise of such boxing talents as the United States' Jessica McCaskill who,
though she lost to Katie Taylor in 2017, went on to become a super
lightweight champion with her 2018 win over Argentina's Erica Anabel
Farias, thus catapulting her toward the elite ranks of professional boxing
through effective promotion and social media savvy—a necessary component for the era.

Even the world-renowned International Boxing Hall of Fame voted to begin inducting women into its august world of elite fighters beginning in 2020 with the inclusion of two women's divisions: trailblazers and modern. In all, a momentous year in women's boxing.

QUEENS OF BOXING

At the start of 2019, Cecilia Braekhus remained the pathfinder for women to achieve undisputed greatness in the sport. She had not only won the four major welterweight belts but the support of the sanctioning bodies to allow her to contest for them in the first place. As the undisputed champion she had had to defend her belts. This brought about the always thorny issue of choosing opponents.

Determining the "mandatory" challengers, and the fair and equitable ranking of female fighters in individual weight classes, is part of the work of sanctioning organizations. They must also accept opponents for title fights who may not have been strictly ranked. Since many of Braekhus's defenses had been in Europe, upcoming fight dates and the pool of talent were not generally on the radar of American boxers, per se. With her higher visibility in the United States, however, came greater scrutiny for future opponents.

One boxer who felt very slighted was Layla McCarter, a perennially highly ranked fighter at welterweight during Braekhus's reign, number three on the 2018 BWAA list of pound-for-pound women's fighters, and number one at welterweight on some sanctioning body lists. McCarter had been vocal in calling out Braekhus even before she had won the undisputed mantle, and, with Braekhus's growing prominence in the United States, was not shying away from expressing her frustration at not being offered an opportunity.

"It looks like they (Team Braekhus) just don't want to do it, and it's the same old story. They're probably gonna fight some easy opponent for cheap money. It's very sad because this is THE fight in women's boxing, and you know, at some point the best have to fight the best."

Braekhus had her own opinions on the potential bout, telling an interviewer, "Layla cannot just ask for a lot of money, and [expect] we will just cave into that. That's not how it works, considering I'm coming in with the belts, with the TV deal, with the audience, with everything. She also needs to start working a little bit on her side, with promotion. This is a tough game, this is brutal, unfortunately it's not only what you do in the ring, it's what you do outside. . . . [N]ow that she's signed with Mayweather promotions, hopefully they will launch her a little bit more, push her forward, and then maybe we could do two fights on Showtime."[1]

A recurrent issue in boxing, never mind women's boxing with its fewer opportunities for high-level fights, compounded by the need to go up and down in weight; the pursuit of sanctioned belts was a complex process with fighters doing their best to negotiate the myriad of traps that many had to face due to their lack of promotional deals, money, and opportunity. These were hard lessons learned by fighters in the early part of the decade, but continued to echo even as fighters with more elite pedigrees were pushing at the status quo.

For Claressa Shields and Katie Taylor, who'd entered the field of play at the top of the heap, pushing forward to win all the belts was a mark of boxing excellence they were determined to attain. Both were eager, had promotional support, and based on their self-assurance, saw winning all the belts as the next step for themselves and the sport they were determined to elevate. Their achievements in 2018 were steps toward the goal—but it was now up to them to deliver.

Claressa Shields was the first to contest for the undisputed crown. With the "band" back together, an April 13, 2019, fight date was announced in mid-February for the much-anticipated Claressa Shields–Christina Hammer showdown at Boardwalk Hall in Atlantic City, New Jersey, set to be broadcast on Showtime Boxing: Special Edition.

Both fighters were undefeated, but with very different trajectories as professional boxers. Hammer had started to train at age thirteen, competing in amateur bouts before turning pro in 2009 under the tutelage of Dimitri Kirnos, who became her long-term trainer. She had her first professional bout a couple of months after her nineteenth birthday, winning by TKO in the second round. With a muscular, 5'11" frame, Hammer was both statuesque and athletic, a winning combination in the ring. She rose quickly in the sport, with a succession of wins mostly in Germany, where she had emigrated from Kazakhstan as a baby.

With that success behind her, Hammer earned her first major title, the WBO world middle belt in October of 2010 at the age of twenty—successfully defending it eleven times prior to her fight with Shields. Those wins included the two bouts against Kali Reis. She picked up the WBC belt after defeating Reis in their second meeting.

Speaking about boxing, Hammer said, "I do love boxing because I fight for my dreams, literally and figuratively. As a woman, success, specifically in the ring, on an elite level, I know is empowering, not only for me but for women from all over the world who watch me perform in the ring, in prime venues televised on major networks all over the world."[2]

On paper, at least, Hammer was bringing a lot to the table. She had an undefeated record, and from her perch in Germany enjoyed enormous success and recognition. Her fighting style was the question. She was less versatile than Shields, generally leading with her jab and fighting tall from the outside, which if Shields was on her game would be "red meat" for her aggression and quickness.

Ahead of the battle, Shields was eager to press her case. "I always seek the biggest challenges and set the highest goals. I will be ready like never before. . . . Nothing will stop me from becoming undisputed champion and continuing my journey to carry women's boxing to never-before-seen heights. I want to be the greatest of all-time and change the game forever for all women in sports, and April 13 is an important step on that road to history."[3]

And it was a big deal. *The Ring* magazine had offered up their inaugural female middleweight belt to add additional heft to the contest, noting "[it's] the first time the magazine recognizes a women's boxing match as a Ring championship bout."[4]

The winner would not only be the second female to achieving undisputed status, but only the sixth fighter in history, male or female, in the four-belt era—a veritable EGOT (Emmy, Grammy, Oscar, Tony) of boxing.

Ahead of the bout, the trash talk began to fly, but at the root of it was a desire to push the hype for the battle to increase the number of viewers for the fight. There was also an important statement to be made. The fight was a big deal to the sport, offering the chance to demonstrate the increasing value of women's boxing. In so doing, it was attracting the attention not only of boxing media, but the sports world.

As the main driver, Shields was not shy about it or her place in the contest, nor was she afraid to ruffle feathers in the process.

"I think it's the biggest women's boxing match to date because you know who both of us are. Just the flame that women's boxing has with me being in the Olympics twice, me winning world titles and becoming the first woman to main event on Showtime on premium cable and me fighting on HBO and DAZN co-main events, it just shows how much women's boxing has grown."[5]

Fight night was loud and excited at Boardwalk Hall, with veteran referee Sparkle Lee in attendance as the third woman in the ring. The first round saw Shields fighting in a subdued manner, quick in her counterpunching and defensive postures but measured in her offensive output as Hammer fought from the outside and threw her successive jabs and combinations with growing confidence. Trainer John David Jackson, for his part, praised Shields's first-round efforts, calling out her head movement and reminding her to take her time and step back from the jab before going to the body—clearly showing the strategy had been precisely to lay back in the first round to feel out her opponent.

Quickening her pace in the second round, Shields had the crowd behind her as she snuck up from weaving under a jab to return with a solid right hand, and with increasing forward momentum used her own jab to great effect. By the fifth round, Shields found a home for her right hand, along with her double and triple jabs, and as she came inside, dominated Hammer through most of their exchanges. The eighth round pushed the fight even further in Shields's favor. She threw a battering series of lefts and rights that caused Hammer's mouthpiece to fall out, before continuing to retreat from Shields's onslaught across the rest of the round. Sparkle Lee, renowned for letting fighters work out their tussles, let the fight continue into the ninth, though it seemed Hammer's corner was uncertain if the fight would continue, as were some of the announcers. For Shields's part, she began to put on a clinic in the ninth and tenth rounds, demonstrating great head movement, effective footwork, and importantly, remaining relaxed, loose, and continuing to sit down on her punches: a testament to her work with her trainer.

Shields's win was as momentous as it was decisive, taking the bout by a 98–92 unanimous decision across all three judges' scorecards. Almost anticlimactic after her stellar performance, Shields was pumped with emotion as she realized she had captured the undisputed middleweight crown. Joking the day before the fight, Shields had exhorted the press to use her headline, "Shields Nails The Hammer." She had, in fact, done just that, not only by dominating in the ring, but by offering her most mature outing as a fighter.

Calming a bit from the elation of the moment but still clearly ecstatic, the newest member of the undisputed club said, "I am the greatest woman of all time. I did it. She didn't win a round. I almost knocked her ass out. I swear, I feel like I'm dreaming right now. Thanks to Christina Hammer and her team. They said she had a hard jab, and they weren't lying. Her jab is off the chain."

Hammer, exhausted by her efforts, said, "I didn't fight very good or fast. That's boxing—anything can happen. I wanted this fight. She won, respect to her. She's a tough, strong woman, and that's all I can say. She's fast, she comes forward, she has fast hands. I couldn't land my jab as good as I expected. That's boxing. I'll come back, and I'll be back stronger."[6]

Going back to Germany after the fight, she met with success in the ring, but not at the level of the stage she'd had with Shields, as if to say again, "that's boxing."

Katie Taylor was up next. Having dispatched Rose Volante with a ninth-round TKO win to pick up the WBO world light title in March, she was ready to challenge for the vaunted WBC green belt and the honors that went with being an undisputed champion.

"Now we can start talking about that fight, Persoon," she said. "That name's been coming up over the last two years. I've got the three belts, she's got the WBC belt, so we have to get that fight on next."

Acknowledging that she was also looking at other big fights, she added, "My goal is to become the undisputed [lightweight] champion first and foremost. The fights with Amanda [Serrano] and Cecilia [Braekhus at a catch weight] are a lot bigger when I have got the four belts. So that fight with Persoon is a fantastic chance. She's been a long-reigning champion for many years. That's going to be a fantastic fight."[7]

Taylor was right.

Persoon was 43–1 with eighteen wins by knockout, and just a week before Taylor defeated Volante, she had easily defeated Melissa St. Vil by leaving her on her stool at the end of the seventh round. Fighting almost exclusively from her perch in her native Belgium (with one exception in Switzerland), Persoon attracted fighters from all over the world. One such battle was in 2014, when Argentina's Erica Anabella Farias came to Belgium for her eighth WBC light title defense. In a fearsome brawl where both had lost points for headbutts, Persoon captured the belt by unanimous decision. She went on to pursue her title defenses with a vengeance, crushing such luminaries as Christina Linardatou, Maiva Hamadouche, and Diana Prazak, among others. Despite her prowess in the ring, she'd been virtually unknown outside of the close boxing circle at home. She was also unable to earn a living as a professional fighter and had been balancing her career in law enforcement as a federal police-woman with boxing since she'd first turned professional in 2009.

The Taylor–Persoon undisputed matchup was a highly competitive outing with risks for Taylor, who though a scrappy fighter in addition to having the skills of a boxer, would be facing a come-forward machine who breezed through frontal assaults with barely a deepening of her breath. The bout was also going to be distinctively different than the Shields–Hammer fight in that it would not be the main event. Rather, it was to be contested on the Anthony Joshua–Andy Ruiz heavyweight unification card and broadcast on the DAZN Boxing new subscription-based streaming service in the United States and Sky Sports in the United Kingdom.

The card was set to be contested in the main arena at Madison Square Garden. This was good news for Taylor, who lived and trained in Connecticut. That aside, boxing in New York City always felt a bit like a homecoming. The supportive Irish community not only bought tickets in droves, but loudly cheered her on. If that weren't enough, the location offered an easy plane ride for any fans from her native Ireland who wanted to jump over the pond to see her fight.

With the bout offering a large, but undisclosed, payday for Persoon, and a guarantee for Taylor's largest purse earnings, the fight was set for the June 1 card. In the run-up to the bout, Persoon was quick to point out that as a policewoman she was looking for a "once-in-a-lifetime" opportunity, not so much to play spoiler to Taylor's trajectory, but to make a statement as to her own abilities as a fighter. She told the press, "My trainer has been busy looking at this fight for two years, hoping I may get a chance. We did not think we would but I thought: If I just keep my WBC title, maybe one day she would want it."[8]

In readying for the fight, Persoon noted she was using the overtime she had banked so that she could have an uninterrupted camp and not the usual extra end-of-shift hours she usually dedicated to getting ready—something Heather Hardy knew all too well.

Talking about it further, she made the distinction even clearer, making note that Taylor was supported in her boxing even as an amateur. "I go working and don't get that kind of money. That's the difference in the fight. For her, it's a job. For me, it's my passion."[9]

To sweeten the pot for the fight, *The Ring* magazine's ratings committee voted to bestow their first female lightweight title on the winner—a continuation of their commitment to women in boxing as well as their advocacy for equity.

With all the preparations set, fight night seemed to come upon them quickly.

Taylor wore purple and gold with her signature "KT" logo sewn in the center of her top facing across to Persoon, decked out in black, yellow, and red, the colors of the Belgian flag and festooned with the logos of her sponsors. The two women were ready to do battle, and once again, as a solid refrain, Sparkle Lee, who'd been given the honor of refereeing her second undisputed bout, called the pair to the center of the ring for their last instructions.

The bell for the first round brought both women back to the center, this time in their boxers' stances. Taylor's jab was the first to land as they warily circled each other. Some seconds later, Taylor let a double jab fly followed by a step back and a quick cuffing left hook that landed on Persoon's right ear as she spun around. By the middle of the stanza,

Persoon began to aggressively move forward with lefts and rights flying. Though she was missing the target, she caught Taylor close to the ropes and let loose with a rapid volley. Taylor was able to fight back, catching Persoon with a hard check left hook before they were pulled apart by Lee. The women resumed at a fast pace and similar action for the remaining time left.

With the crowd firmly behind her yelling, "Katie, Katie!" the action picked up even more in the second round with Taylor demonstrating her boxing acumen, but with Persoon showing a fearlessness as she threw her punches moving forward. She caught Taylor with a sharp thudding right hand toward the latter part of the second round, and then landed a series of lefts and rights at the end of the stanza, punctuated by another straight right to Taylor's face as the bell tolled.

With her corner telling her to stay out of the pocket by side stepping after her work was done, Taylor made her way toward her opponent in the third round with a reset to her stance and a determination to hold the center of the ring even as the hallmarks of a rough and tumble bout started to clearly emerge.

Awkward, hard hitting, and unrelenting, Persoon followed a game plan across the bout to disrupt the boxer in Taylor. She did so by forcing her into a dog fight of close clinches and smothered shots in between Persoon's battering, and even more clinches whenever Taylor was able to reset and let loose with her cleaner shots. Sparkle Lee also had her hands full measuring the calculus of when to intervene to pull the two combatants apart.

The marks on their faces gave evidence as to the intensity of the brawl. The fourth round saw Persoon with a pronounced swelling on her left cheek and the beginnings of a shiner on her left eye, while as they entered the fifth round, Taylor's face was showing bruising under her right eye and a cut on the bridge of her nose.

It was evident that Persoon's unorthodox fighting style was goading Taylor to lose sight of her crisp, sharply thrown accuracy. What she failed to see, though, was that the girl from Bray, Ireland, also loved to mix it up, sometimes—to the consternation of her corner. This was best exemplified when toward the end of the fifth frame Taylor stood along the ropes, the blood dripping from a cut on her hairline, and egging Persoon on, waved for her to come in as she slipped underneath Persoon's winging shots to return fire.

The ebb and flow set in the early part of the battle became the road-map for the full ten rounds of the championship match. Each stanza ended with a slight edge to either fighter depending upon how one saw the bout, giving advantage to output and aggression or cleaner, clearer punches that landed convincingly.

The pair also adjusted and readjusted as the fight wore on. Taylor was at times looser on her feet and more confident moving backwards and laterally to motor out of harm's way until she saw an opening to tag Persoon's ever swelling left eye or pummel her with body shots. On Persoon's part, she was unrelenting in pushing forward, defying Taylor's sense of her boxing omnipotence by throwing yet more barrages that by the eighth round began to tell the story on Taylor's right eye.

The ninth and tenth rounds would decide the fight.

Both Taylor and Persoon dug deep to stay in the moment and gain advantage. Taylor succeeded in the ninth round, fighting cleanly and with a bit of a bounce. On Persoon's part, the tenth round was her crucible, throwing down to disrupt her opponent's game plan yet again with all the sensibilities of one who would not be denied.

As the tenth round began, the crowd was on their feet. The two champions touched gloves at the start of it and then fought nonstop, gutting through their exhaustion and hopes and dreams as they kept throwing punches through the final bell. Persoon had landed the cleaner shots in the round and walked back to her corner clearly elated. Taylor's walk was less assured, but she smiled through it.

With all the belts on the line, the fighters waited to be called to the center of their battleground to hear the results. Taylor showed a nervous demeaner, while Persoon exuded the confidence of a winner. The crowd was still on their feet waiting as well in anticipation of the outcome.

The scorecards were read out, 95–95, 96–94, 96–94, a majority decision in favor of the new undisputed lightweight champion of the world, Katie Taylor, who stood with her eyes gazing upward as she raised both of her arms in the air.

For her part, Delfine Persoon was stunned, her head shaking from side to side as she edged her way toward the ring apron. After a beat, she and her trainer left the ring clearly disgusted by the outcome. A camera was ahead of Persoon as she walked through the tunnel out of the arena, by now with tears streaming from her eyes as she tried to avert her gaze by dipping down under her peaked cap, the loss hurting her deeply because she felt she had done enough to win.

In the aftermath, Taylor was shown to have been the more accurate of the pair, with Persoon throwing more. Speaking of her performance, Taylor said, "That's my problem sometimes. I like a fight a bit too much. . . . I probably should've fought on the outside a bit more. . . . But then I just needed to dig deep and get that win."[10]

The fight had been very close. Some scored it for Taylor, some had it even, and others gave the majority decision to Persoon. Those who saw it, though, knew they had witnessed greatness, which eventuated in a rematch over a year later in August 2020, held under the conditions of the COVID-19 pandemic at the Matchroom HQ Garden in Brentwood, England.

THAT FEELING OF INVINCIBILITY

The latter part of 2019 had an air of invincibility about it when it came to women's boxing—even with the inevitable blips. Heather Hardy started the fall 2019 boxing season fighting her first WBO feather title defense against Amanda Serrano at Madison Square Garden. A hard scrap with Hardy almost out in the first round, she dug deep against Serrano, managing to end the bout still standing. Serrano's triumph had also awarded her the WBC interim title—and much more serious talk of fighting Katie Taylor with her promoter, Lou DiBella, already having occasional calls with Eddie Hearn at Matchroom Boxing.

The Heather Hardy–Amanda Serrano fight in September 2019 had also been the first bout to sign on to the WBC Clean Boxing Program (WBC CBP) protocols. In a surprise, Hardy had been found to test positive for Lasix, a diuretic and banned substance under VADA. In a statement on social media, Hardy said, "My VADA test results just came back, negative for performance-enhancing drugs, but detected a prescription drug used to treat kidney and heart problems. I told the testing and (medical) professionals what I took heading into the fight, a prescription (medication) for period symptoms. They acknowledge this, and my . . . team is getting to the bottom of the findings."[11]

Hardy was eventually fined $10,000 and received a six-month suspension by the New York State Athletic Commission. Having requested an administrative hearing, Hardy's suspension was cut back to four months. In a statement after the hearing, Hardy said in part, "I never took a PED [performance enhancing drug] and never will—they are dangerous to the user, opponents, sparring partners, while also compromising the sport. Ignorance is no excuse, which is why I volunteered to work with the WBC to bring greater awareness to all aspects of the rules, including those pertaining to prescription meds."[12]

"Doping" with PEDs is not unique to boxing, and some big names on the male side of the sport have been ensnared, facing hefty fines, suspension, and being banned from the sport for varying periods of time. In women's boxing, there had been infrequent publicized incidences. Pioneer boxer Mia St. John entered the fray of controversy swirling around Canelo Alvarez when he was found to have a positive drug test ahead of his showdown with Gennady Golovkin in 2018. Feeling as if the boxing community was being a little bit sanctimonious, she had tweeted out, "Everyone does it & everyone in boxing knows it."

The firestorm aside, Mia St. John went on to admit to using banned substances during her career, telling the *Los Angeles Times*,

> I was tested many times. There's many methods to get around it. Just because you didn't get caught doesn't mean you weren't doing it. It just meant you didn't get caught.
>
> I did my homework. They gave us a whole list of what not to do and I knew a lot of stuff I was doing was on that list. I did everything I could to mask it—masking drugs, catheters with other people's urine—and then the rest is up to luck.
>
> I would leave the bathroom shaking, praying and sweating bullets. You cross your fingers. Crazy enough, I didn't get caught. Some girls did and I felt so awful and ashamed, like what a hypocrite . . . in many ways, yes, I was protected.[13]

In another interview with boxing writer Michael Woods, St. John admitted that her drug use had a dark side: "I have irreversible damage and if I could take it back, do it over again, I would never (have taken PEDs)," she stated. "It's not worth it. The damage could be with you for the rest of your life."[14]

The darker strands and stresses of boxing aside, Jessica McCaskill was also entering the conversation. She'd fought Taylor back in 2017 and though she'd sustained a loss, Taylor had called her a tough opponent. With that golden ticket in her pocket, McCaskill went on to capture the WBC super light title in October 2018 against Erica Anabella Farias and unify with the WBA super light title in May 2019 by defeating another Argentinian champion, Anahi Ester Sanchez. Her successful rematch against Farias in October saw her stock rise further, exemplified by her appearances as a guest commentator on DAZN Boxing. With Chicago as her homebase, and still working her day job as a regulatory reporting analyst for a brokerage firm, she'd had a limited amateur career before turning pro in 2015 in the wake of the Olympics—and was determined to push her career in the pros toward bigger opportunities.

Mikaela Mayer had been enjoying a steady rise with three fights in 2017, and six in 2018—having captured her first belt, the NABF super feather title by unanimous decision over the Colombian journeywoman Calista Silgado. The year 2019 saw Mayer defend her belt three times, even appearing on the main ESPN card during her October defense against Argentina's Alejandra Soledad Zamora, which netted Mayer the win when the fight was called at the end of the sixth round.

Along with Alycia Baumgardner, an Ohio transplant fighting out of Michigan who was beginning to make noise, the Greek–Dominican powerhouse Christina Linardatou, who'd defeated Baumgardner in 2018, captured the WBO super light title in March 2019 with a definitive sixth-round TKO win over Kandi Wyatt. Linardatou successfully defended the belt in June by unanimous decision before facing Katie Taylor, who'd challenged herself to become a two-weight champion after having captured the undisputed crown at light weight.

The Linardatou–Taylor contest in November 2019 was very hard fought, and while Taylor came out with a solid win on the cards, fighting smartly on the back foot and refusing to enter into a fire fight, the former kickboxer Linardatou established herself as a serious contender in front of the crowd at the Manchester Arena and the watching audience on Sky Sports. Taylor, satisfied to have become a two-weight champion, returned it shortly thereafter.

THE CHALLENGE OF BEING THE CHANGE
Even with her extraordinary effort to become the undisputed middle-weight champion, Shields was not content to rest on those laurels. She wanted to solidify her self-proclaimed status as boxing's "GWOAT"—the greatest woman of all time—by demonstrating to the world that she deserved the title. To do so, Shields set out to battle for the vacant women's WBO junior middle and WBC super welter championship belts against the Croatian boxer and former IBF world welter champion Ivana Habazin (20–3, 7-KOs), rated the number one fighter at 154 pounds by the WBO.

Shields's intention was historic. In winning the fight, she would become the youngest fighter, male or female, ever to win major titles in three weight classes. Her cause was also in service to her larger, more far-reaching goals. "It's another big step forward in lifting women's boxing on the road to equality," she said.

Promoter Dmitry Salita concurred, but also stood firmly in support of his fighter's importance to the sport. "We're continuing our goal of advancing the state of women's sports to new heights and Claressa's greatness helps make this happen."[15]

The fight was set for August 17, 2019, in Shields's hometown of Flint at the Dort Federal Event Center, and to be broadcast on Showtime. A knee injury suffered shortly after the announcement sidelined Shields, but there was no sense that it was in any way serious. Fully mended, a new fight day was announced in early August. Both fighters had agreed to face each other on October 5 at the same venue in Flint with Show-time still on board as the broadcast partner.

The run-up to the bout had all the usual posturing of most Shields bouts—lots of bluster and talk of KO wins by each fighter in turn. At one press conference in September, Habazin had said, "I feel strong. I feel I have power to knock people out. For this fight, this is my goal because I don't believe judges' scorecards. When you knock somebody out, that's the only way you can win (for sure)."

Shields for her part retorted, "She's going to say a whole lot of stuff. She called me fat. I think she's just trying to say stuff. I do have a helluva chin and I like to go in there and test people's chins. I respect that she thinks she's going to knock me out."[16]

The fight itself was on track, until the weigh-in.

There had apparently been a heated discussion between Habazin's trainer, James Ali Bashir, and some of Shields's entourage, during which time Claressa Shields left the stage area and Bashir walked off in the opposite direction.

Claressa Shields's manager, Mark Taffet, related the incident to the press, noting, "Claressa was stepping on the scales before the weigh-in to check her weight. There may have been confusion about whether the real weigh-in was taking place. [James Ali Bashir, Habazin's trainer] was trying to get close to the scales to verify Claressa's actual weight, and then words were exchanged."

Some time later, Bashir was sucker punched in the back of his head by a man, later identified as Shields's brother, Artis Jaquel Mack, who ran from the scene but was subsequently apprehended by an officer nearby.

The sixty-eight-year-old Bashir immediately fell face down onto the concrete floor and was reportedly unconscious for approximately twenty minutes before being rushed to the hospital, where treatment included emergency surgery for the facial injuries he sustained. Habazin was at his side, visibly sobbing as she sat with him on the ground. Establishing control over her emotions as he was lifted on to the stretcher, she accompanied him to the hospital.

Shields's promoter, Dmitry Salita, and manager, Mark Taffet, both went to the hospital as well. Just prior to departing the venue, Taffet made a preliminary statement to the press: "Right now, I am on my way to the hospital to visit Ivana Habazin and her team and her trainer."

He continued: "I want to make sure they're okay. We want to make sure they get the best proper treatment and it's unfair to assess or address anything until we make sure first that her trainer is fine and that's she's calm and comfortable. After that, we will the address the situation."

Left in the air at that moment was whether the fight would continue as scheduled the following day, with Shields stating, "nothing is canceled from what we know. I don't condone stuff like that. It's unfortunate it happened here."[17]

In the aftermath, it was determined that the fight could not go on, although the card, minus the Shields–Habazin fight, was broadcast as scheduled with refunds offered to ticket holders in the aftermath of the cancellation of the main event.

Shields's initial comments on social media appeared to many to be somewhat "tone deaf," saying, "Her name is Ivana 'No Excuses,' so I'm hoping we don't have none."

In fairness, her comments were made live shortly after the incident, and without having learned of the true extent of Bashir's injuries. She also said, "I don't condone that kinda stuff, and I don't tell nobody to do that kinda crap. . . . I wish him a speedy recovery, I hope that Ivana is in good spirts . . . and I hope 'no excuses,' she comes to the fight, and no way in hell I want to give this fight up, and even for her, just for what happened to her coach, she should be mad as hell."[18]

By the next day, with the fight canceled and with a much fuller picture of the extent to Bashir's injuries having become known, Shields expressed sorrow on Facebook: "I did not see what happened and am relying, like so many of you, on what I have heard. Despite the videos that are out, the actions that took place against Coach Ali was not right. I do not stand for that and do not in any way justify what happened no matter what he said! I stand with Coach Ali and Ivana Habazin and I also understand their stand on our fight."

She further stated, "My heart is with coach Ali, a coach who has given his heart to this sport and to so many fighters over a long career. My heart is with Ivana Habazin, whose courage, discipline and heart were evident in the way she trained for this day and traveled a long distance to realize my dream of fighting in my hometown of Flint."[19]

Habazin was clearly angry and affected by what had happened. The following day, after she'd been at the hospital with Bashir until he was stabilized—and having left after midnight—she was still upset. Writing in Facebook, her tone remained defiant:

> With deep regret my trainer James Ali Bashir was punched in the back of his neck by someone in Shields entourage. Bashir was taken to a local hospital and has now been moved to Henry Ford Hospital because delicate facial reconstruction surgery must be performed. . . . During the pre weigh-in my coach wanted to look at Clarissa's weight and her sister and Bashir exchanged words. Her family and friends should have never been allowed on the stage.[20]

Within days, it had seemed that Bashir was on the mend and had even been released from the hospital, only to be rushed back with a bleed in his brain. Luckily, his medical team was able to address the issues as well as complete the necessary facial reconstruction. Artis Mack, the alleged perpetrator, was also arrested and charged with assault for the brutal attack.

Addressing reporters on the likelihood of rescheduling the fight, promoter Dmitry Salita addressed the matter, stating, "We're working to make it happen. It's not totally off. Both the fighters want the opportunity for this fight and both are prepared. Both wanted it and both deserve it. They were ready."[21]

The reaction of the public was less forgiving, either way, with the boxing pundits and fans doing a lot of "trash talking" of their own across the social media ecosystem—but ultimately leaving the topic for the next big thing in boxing.

In mid-November, with terms finally agreed upon, the much-anticipated match between Shields and Habazin was rescheduled for January 10, 2020, at the Ocean Casino Resort in Atlantic City, New Jersey, and to be broadcast as the main event on Showtime: Special Edition.

In the press release for the bout, Habazin stated, "I've been thinking about this since October, and I have more of an incentive now given what happened. I feel like I'm fighting for James Ali Bashir, as well as for my own pride and respect."

Habazin also dedicated the fight to her trainer.

Acknowledging that her goal of becoming the fastest three-division champion, male or female, in history was still foremost on her mind, Shields said, "This is a very significant fight for both of us."

"We have both trained really hard twice," she added, referring to both their August and October fight dates. "Great opportunities await the winner, so hopefully, three times is the charm."[22]

Their next weigh-in went off without incident, despite a flare-up of insinuations at the press conference earlier in the week. On fight night, it was apparent that both fighters were keyed up and ready to put on a stellar performance. Shields seemed to pick up quite effortlessly from where she had left off in her bout with Hammer, fighting with patience and acumen and shooting off repetitive jabs that hurt just to listen to. Overpowering Habazin across the bout, she felled her to one knee after throwing a series of body shots. Shields went on to win the bout by unanimous decision, 99–89, 100–90, 100–89, reaching her goal of winning championships in three divisions with a 9–0 record as she captured the WBO and WBC 154-pound belts. Uncharacteristically subdued in the ring in the aftermath of the bout, she said, "This feels great—I did it in 10 fights. Now I'm No. 1, the fastest boxer in history to become a three-division world champion. . . . I wanted victory."[23]

The undercard also included a bout between Alicia Napoleon and Elin Cederroos for the unified IBF and WBA super middle titles. Napoleon was down in the second round and lost by a close unanimous decision. Shields had previously spoken of a possible middleweight undisputed defense against Napoleon, but with the loss, that was off the cards.

What the saga also showed was that boxing has its own rules and rhythms inside and outside the ring. The lesson for Shields was not only how to manage adversity, but to channel the emotions of the moment into something greater.

THE INTERNATIONAL BOXING HALL OF FAME

The success or failure of any endeavor has many ingredients. When it comes to women's boxing, institutional support whether in the form of boxing commissions, sanctioning bodies, media organizations, or even boxing halls of fame, provides a legitimacy that ultimately helps propel success.

Perhaps the biggest change in institutional support occurred in 2019, when the International Boxing Hall of Fame board of directors voted to add two categories for female boxers.

Long the brainchild of the Hall's executive director, Ed Brophy, he demonstrated a long-term commitment to the idea of recognizing women, noting:

Women's boxing has spanned many generations, but since the establishment of the International Boxing Hall of Fame in 1989, this section of the sport has made tremendous strides in many quarters. The talent pool has expanded in terms of numbers, achievements and global impact. The Hall has been tracking that progress throughout the last three plus decades and in recognition of their success, the International Boxing Hall of Fame decided in July 2019 to recognize the women who have excelled at the highest level with the opportunity for enshrinement beginning with the Class of 2020.[24]

The categories included a "trailblazer" designation for boxers who had had their last competition no later than 1988, and a "modern" division for fighters who had started in the sport no earlier than 1989. The other requirement was that modern fighters must have retired no later than three years prior to the voting year—a condition for male and female boxers. The amendment to the voting process read, in part: "In recognition of their success, the International Boxing Hall of Fame will recognize the women who have excelled at the highest level with the opportunity for enshrinement."[25]

The first ever women's modern ballot was a "who's who" of female boxing and included Laila Ali (United States), Sumya Amani (United States), Regina Halmich (Germany), Holly Holm (United States), Susi Kentikian (Germany), Christy Martin (United States), Lucia Rijker (Netherlands), Gisselle Salandy (Trinidad), Mary Jo Sanders (United States), Laura Serrano (Mexico), Ana Maria Torres (Mexico), and Ann Wolfe (United States). In compiling the list, Brophy stated, "The Hall of Fame conferred with leading historians and journalists to compile the initial female boxer ballots (Modern and Trailblazer) to ensure the best possible representation of boxers from around the world. Also, knowledgeable historians and journalists were added to the voting panel to cast votes on eligible candidates."

The first women to be inducted into the class of 2020 were Christy Martin and Lucia Rijker, a fitting tribute to arguably two of the best pound-for-pound female boxers of all time. It was also particularly appropriate that the first trailblazer inductee was Barbara Buttrick, whose contributions in and out of the ring were the very definition of a trailblazer.

The first ceremony had been set for June 2020, but as with so many other events, it was canceled due to the COVID-19 pandemic. The International Boxing Hall of Fame (IBHOF) was finally able to celebrate the 2020, 2021, and 2022 inductions as an induction trilogy in June 2022. It not only celebrated Martin and Rijker, but the 2021 inductees Laila Ali and Ann Wolfe, along with trailblazer Marian Trimiar and the 2022 inductees Regina Halmich and Holly Holm.

Many of the inductees were in attendance standing alongside their male counterparts—their fists out, proudly displaying their Hall of Fame rings. For supporters of women's boxing and for the inductees themselves, those moments not only celebrated the legacy of the past but foretold a greatness for the future.

"We went to great lengths to be accurate in showing the depth and breadth of the history," Ed Brophy said. "In addition to the women inducted in the Hall, we are actively showcasing memorabilia from today's top female stars such as Claressa Shields, Amanda Serrano and Seniesa Estrada as today's ring action becomes tomorrow's history."

He added, "One truly incredible thing has been seeing men and women of all ages, but particularly young kids—looking at the Hall of Fame Wall and commenting how inspiring it is to see female boxers represented."[26]

Part III

2020–2022 (and Beyond)

Perhaps better titled "Women's Boxing: The Rise, Fall, and Rise Again," the years 2020–2022, though indelibly marked by the tragedy of the global pandemic, also saw a tremendous gain in the sport due to the first ever main-event bout in the storied Madison Square Garden main arena. A lot of the momentum that had been gained from the success of women's boxing in 2019 was affected by the global pandemic, and as plans had been scrambled, some women saw their career opportunities sidelined or disappear entirely while others saw them blossom. Boxing, not immune from the shock of the shutdowns, had to contend with the fallout of the pandemic along with other major sports. A few promoters created "isolated" boxing bubbles wherein fighters, their trainers, staff, and crew agreed to live in isolation for a "season" of boxing contests. These short-lived boxing series included first-time main events by female boxers.

With the worst of the pandemic over, and the delayed 2020 Olympics finally contested in 2021 with five weight classes for women, female boxing began an ascendency with new promotional opportunities centered in the UK by the likes of Eddie Hearn and newcomer BOXXER, under the auspices of Sky Sports. With the new signings of female boxers came better paydays, and opportunities for older champions who were contracted to fight this newer generation of boxers as opponents. The enlargement of the rosters has also meant that elite female fighters have finally entered an era of seven-figure deals, along with a greater say in their promotion and the chance to sit at ringside to give commentary, much like their male counterparts. It's also given rise to real women's ratings, including *The Ring* magazine, which began a women's ratings panel in 2021 with all the care and attention of its men's boxing counterpart. Such recognition has further legitimized the efforts of the sport's practitioners and, as with the Olympics, has provided markers for high achievement in the sport.

CHAPTER SEVEN

Pandemic Fighters and Champions

IN 2020, MIKAELA MAYER WAS ON HER MARCH, IN EARNEST, TO BECOME a world title holder. With her NABF "baby belt" in hand, savvy boxing prowess, and an Olympic pedigree, she was ready. The next step was a fight against a former champion—and to that end, a fight had been set against Melissa Hernandez, who was on a comeback of sorts due to the renewed interest in the sport and improved prospects for a decent payday. All had been set for a March 17 bout at Madison Square Garden, a traditionally great day for boxing in New York City, and slated to be live streamed on ESPN+, the vaulted sport network's new streaming service. But such was not to be as the pandemic hit, and while Hernandez was not able to get another opportunity until her 2021 super lightweight title bout against Great Britain's brilliant Chantelle Cameron, Mayer was able to fight journeywoman Helen Joseph in "The Bubble" on July 14. Such was the difference between signed elites and women who'd entered the opponent status. Still, the paydays had increased substantively with higher visibility and with chances for more bouts.

Another great fight during the pandemic summer was British boxer Terri Harper's title defense of her IBO and IBF super featherweight titles against Olympian Natasha Jonas at the Matchroom HQ Garden. Arguably considered the best fight of the pandemic summer season, male or female, the slugfest ended in a split-decision draw, allowing Harper to retain her titles.

On the strength of her demonstrated ability, Jonas went on to acquit herself well in a bout against Katie Taylor at lightweight in 2021, and then went on to defeat Uruguayan boxer Chris Namus by stoppage in the second round to capture the WBO super welterweight title in 2022 after signing with upstart Boxxer. Still, with fighting and even training at a standstill in many locales, the pandemic period added additional strain to an already fragile renaissance for women's boxing. One other fallout of the pandemic was the postponement of the 2020 Olympics—truly heartbreaking for the athletes who'd worked so hard to win their places on the team.

THE TRIPLE CROWN
The Triple Crown International Showdown card was the brainchild of boxer Mary McGee. A homecoming for Indiana's favorite boxing daughter, and now champion, the card was promoted by her own in-house McGee House of Champions in association with DiBella Entertainment, Team Empire Management, and 4 Champs Promotions, with the broadcast to be provided by the local LRP Network.

McGee had first turned professional in 2005, mostly fighting in venues in and around her native Gary, Indiana. She was likely unaware of the early history of the sport an hour or so to the east from Gary in South Bend, where boxers JoAnn Hagan and Pat Emerick first fought beginning in the late 1940s.

McGee captured the WBC international light championship in 2009, and other than a loss against the hard-fighting Brooke Dierdorff in a close six-round non-title bout in 2010, McGee fought successfully until getting back-to-back title shots in 2013. For the first bout, McGee traveled to Albuquerque to battle Holly Holm for the IBA and WBF world super light titles. McGee showed aggression throughout, but Holm was able to make liberal use of the large ring, motoring out of harm's way. Holm fought more offensively in the later rounds, scoring shots, but even though McGee had acquitted herself well, she lost 90–100 on all three cards. For her next opportunity in October 2013, she faced Erica Anabella Farias for the WBC world light title in Argentina. Farias threw sharp stinging punches with McGee returning fire, but Farias was able to fight equally well at distance and in the clinches. Both fighters threw bombs, but Farias seemed to score more. The hometown advantage aside,

McGee was able to capture a couple of rounds with her clean punching, but took a unanimous decision loss, 90–100, 91–98, 90–98.

McGee came back home winning a series of four- and six-rounders. Despite this, McGee was only offered another shot at a title in December 2019 for the vacant IBF super light belt. McGee had waited too long to let the opportunity slip past her, and besides having a tremendous camp to get into shape, she fought a blistering offense against Argentina's Ana Laura Esteche to capture the belt by a tenth-round TKO win. The fight card itself had been promoted by Lou DiBella in New York City featuring DiBella Entertainment fighters and was broadcast on one of the new crop of streaming services featuring combat sports—UFC Fight Pass. This development was in part a reaction to the loss of HBO Boxing and the reordering of priorities on other mainstream broadcasting outlets that were making it harder and harder for independent promoters to put shows on networks or even add their fighters to the cards.

With the title strapped around her waist, McGee's record was an impressive 26–3, with fourteen knockout wins. The question for her was how to keep the momentum of her win going. Assessing herself and her options and feeling confident that she was in great shape from her win in December, she decided to go her own way to put on a momentous fight card on February 8, 2020, in her hometown of Gary. As her manager, Brian Cohen, put it, "I want to talk about Mary's unselfishness. She did just win the title and could have hogged the spotlight and said 'Just put me on the card, I'll carry the card. I'll do whatever,' but she wanted her teammates."

Cohen continued: "She is a single mother and I just want the best for Mary. I want to thank you from my heart, for bringing your team to fight on your card."[1]

As the CEO of Team Empire Boxing, and based in Philadelphia, Cohen had begun managing female fighters in 2009 as his own professional boxing career wound down. Starting with Melissa Hernandez, he added Ronica Jeffries shortly thereafter and worked to add boxers as time went on. In an interview with Felipe Leon, Cohen said, "I just enjoy managing women boxers, sometimes they are much easier to deal with than the men. I enjoy their fights a bit more with all honesty. With the two-minute round, they are all business."

He also talked about his experiences early on trying to place his fighters on cards: "Some of the questions you get from promoters and TV folk are do they look like boys . . . I guess some promoters saw them as a sideshow at one point, some kind of special attraction."

Paydays were also an issue. As Cohen put it, "It was very disrespectful with pay but if you didn't take the pay, you didn't fight. Back then, seven, eight years ago, title fights were three-grand. You were pretty much told to be happy to take that. Times have changed."[2]

The card itself included three female title fights, three undercard female fights, and eight male fights. The co-feature for the card was set for Linardatou to contest once again for the WBO super light belt she'd lost on the cards to Katie Taylor but that had subsequently been vacated after defeating Linardatou. Hoping for a highly competitive fight, she defeated Prisca Vicot, taking the strap by unanimous decision. She subsequently relinquished the title herself, having given birth to a son in September 2021. Taking a break to be with her new baby, she found her way back to boxing, winning a six-rounder in July 2022 in her native Greece.

In addition to the two women's world titles, Melissa St. Vil (12–4–4, 1-KO) battled in a ten-rounder for the NABF light title against Jessica Camara, which she won by unanimous decision 96–94, 96–94, 97–93 in an all-action battle.

St. Vil was a former two-time all-American in the 100-meter and 400-meter high-hurdles at Mohawk Valley Community College in Utica, New York. A first-generation Haitian from Long Island, her family had sent her to in Haiti during her childhood. Her ties to the island have been important to her, and St. Vil is recognized as Haiti's first female boxing champion. She has also been no stranger to adversity or challenges. She fought briefly as an amateur before starting her professional boxing career in 2007. St. Vil has not only fought against tough opponents in the ring, but against the changes in momentum and fortune that beset female boxers in the era. She has also had to fight against her own demons of child abuse and hardship, not to mention the notoriety of her experiences fighting and living in Las Vegas when she came into the orbit of the Mayweather family early in her career.[3]

With the struggle still very present, but working hard to advance past it, she'd met with recent success and aside from a lopsided loss to Delfine Persoon in March 2019, she was very much in the mix as a substantive fighter.

Camara was also managed by Brian Cohen, coming into the fight with a 7–1 record and high hopes for the future, with her only prior loss coming from Natalie Brown, who defeated her by a third-round knockout in 2018 on a fight card in Canada.

The other Brian Cohen fighter on the undercard was Ebanie Bridges, a "firecracker" boxer with a string of amateur successes in her native Australia and a 3–0 record as a pro. She was pitted against the journeywoman Crystal Hoy. Bridges, with a lot of self-assurance and swagger, was also certain she was poised for bigger things—and won her bout against Hoy 60–54 on all three cards.

For the main event, McGee faced Deanha Hobbs (8–1, 5-KOs). Hailing from Australia, she'd lost her previous outing to Linardatou for the WBO world super light title the June before. Heading into the bout, Hobbs had told the press that she was honored to have the chance to fight McGee, whom she knew to be a tough fighter. With the stage set, McGee did not disappoint; she patiently handled Hobbs's early aggression, to put on a rough-and-tumble performance, getting the ninth-round TKO win at 1:55 into the round after pummeling Hobbs throughout the fight and knocking her down earlier in the frame.

McGee had promoted the evening of boxing to provide a showcase for herself and the other women on the card who shared her dreams of greatness in the ring. None had yet cracked the top-tier elite, but with her card, McGee had laid down a gauntlet of filling the spaces that were wide open because of the shifting landscape of mainstream promotion and broadcasting in the United States. The hope was by packaging exciting fights, there would be a chance to break through in the way American fighters Shields, Esparza, Estrada, Mayer, and McCaskill were starting to garner attention and opportunities. Time would tell.

PANDEMIC

With the best-laid plans, and fight camps in Miami, Florida, and at Brooklyn's Gleason's Gym, Melissa Hernandez (23–7–3, 7-KOs) was intent on making her St. Patrick's Day bout against Mikaela Mayer count. As a New York City–born Puerto Rican boxer, Hernandez knew firsthand how much her hometown fans loved to come out to support their fighters at Madison Square Garden on St. Patty's Day. And she was counting on that, hoping that she'd fill the house for her professional debut at the Garden, something she'd waited for across her long career. She'd also watched the rise in interest in women's boxing and figured she had nothing to lose by giving it one more try. Hernandez had been in the ring the year before and won an eight-rounder in Louisiana. She'd experienced a bit of the old magic preparing for that fight, and with the win behind her felt the confidence to do it again when the opportunity to fight Mayer came up, not to mention the chance to garner a decent payday.

As late as March 4, in response to an interviewer's question about what to expect, Hernandez smiled and coyly answered, "tune in to see what happens. It's a great fight for women's boxing. It's a good win for me."

Asked about where she thought the sport was headed, she said, "We're going from girls to women. The cool thing is women can go from [the amateur] novice to open class, to professional, which we didn't have before. . . . So watching the Mikaelas, the Claressa Shields, is a beautiful thing. And we're also getting a lot more publicity, kind of like women's boxing in the 90s."[4]

Zooming out from the lens of her insouciant brevity, the larger world she inhabited on that March 4 afternoon was something else again. Newspaper headlines, television's talking heads, and government leaders were consumed with a growing sense of foreboding about the novel coronavirus, SARS-CoV-2. CNN had by then devoted a page a day to the growing scourge, noting that the death toll had risen to 3,200 people worldwide, with "close to 95,000 global cases, and infections [being reported] in more than 70 countries and territories." In Italy, officials had ordered their first lockdowns, and two cruise ships with sick passengers were halted at sea off the coast of San Francisco and San Diego as a state of emergency was being declared in California.[5]

In New York City, cases were also starting to rise, with a quiet panic in the halls of city government as its agencies and hospitals scrambled for what they knew would be the coming onslaught.

A week later, on March 11, the World Health Organization declared the novel coronavirus outbreak, known colloquially as COVID-19, a global pandemic—and with the pronouncement, at its most essential, ordered the closure of the world.

Reading the tea leaves, Mayer's promoter, Top Rank, had no choice but to cancel the fight card set for Tuesday, March 17, and the card they were promoting on Saturday, March 14, that headlined their up-and-coming boxing phenom, Shakur Stevenson. The truth was, they'd already confronted the issue at the end of January when one of their fighters who was to have competed in China was told the fight was off due to the spread of the virus beyond Wuhan.

Releasing a statement to the press to announce the cancellations, it read in part, "After close consultation with the New York State Athletic Commission, it has been determined that Saturday's and Tuesday's events cannot proceed in light of the ongoing coronavirus crisis. Top Rank will work with the commission to reschedule the events as soon as it is safe for all involved. The health and safety of the fighters and their teams, and everyone involved in the promotion of these events, necessitated taking this step."[6]

Even with Top Rank's decision to pull their two New York cards, there were some forty plus scheduled events held that weekend in sixteen countries. By St. Patrick's Day, however, there were no shows anywhere in the world, nor did it seem there would be for the foreseeable future.

In New York City, any hope of promoting a boxing event was finally dashed the following Sunday with the closure of all non-essential businesses including the city's boxing gyms, along with all congregant gatherings. The city, seen from the perch of Madison Square Garden, was forlorn in the silence, punctuated only by the endless ambulance sirens racing up and down Seventh and Eighth Avenues, filled with victims of the virus.

The devastation of illness and death staggered the world in waves; but still, businesses had to survive. For those whose livelihood centered around the ring, the closures were devastating. A corporate worker could rely on the internet and a laptop to work—but for the business of boxing, from gym managers, to trainers, to fighters, there was no easy solution. For female boxers already on the margins economically in the fight game, it was devastating. Fighters like Heather Hardy, a single mother who earned her living as a boxing trainer, no amount of small residual checks from the tiny sponsorships she had was going to pay the bills or allow her to provide security for her daughter. With the gym closed, there was no income to be had or any hope of earning even the break-even paydays she'd received from boxing.

Hardy's story was repeated across America and the other centers of women's boxing around the world. Their careers were on hold, with no sense of what the future would portend. Such uncertainty was mind-numbing, as was the prospect of the illness that stalked people even when masked and gloved.

By the end of May, as lockdown measures were starting to push back the avalanche of illness—even as the United States was reporting nearly 1.8 million cases since February—the survival of boxing along with other professional sports was on the minds of everyone in the business. Such groups as the Ultimate Fighting Championship (UFC) and the National Basketball Association (NBA) were two of the many sports organizations engaged in figuring out how to put on athletic competitions in whatever form they could. Nonetheless, the reality of COVID-19 was similar to a stampede careening through stacked shelves of vintage bone china.

In reaction, Top Rank had cautiously, and correctly in their own judgment, continued their hiatus. What they did not do was stop thinking about how to get their fighters back into the ring—along with the people who made a boxing match possible—the trainers, referees, judges, announcers, ring doctors, broadcasting crew, boxing commission and sanctioning personnel, and a host of others.

With a mission akin to the old adage, don't mourn, organize (and admittedly having nothing to do with the kind of labor strife that gave rise to the saying), by the beginning of April, Top Rank's chief operating officer, Brad Jacobs, was working the problem. He had his team reviewing the status of pandemic closures across the country to determine what it would take to put on a boxing show—but always with a view of centering it all in Las Vegas. The city was, after all, home—an important consideration for Top Rank president Todd duBoef, not only for his organization, but as a symbol of how the country was turning a corner, as if to say, "Hey, let's get some confidence back. Las Vegas is still around."[7]

Brad Jacobs, for his part, had started to create the bare bones of Top Rank's playbook—a roadmap of what it would take to get back to promoting a series of boxing shows with a five-pronged approach that looked at everything from identifying risks to the specifics of how to put on a boxing match safely. As for the fights, it was envisioned to start off with two shows per week on Tuesday and Thursday nights; after all, there wasn't much to do otherwise, so why not offer live boxing?

With the Las Vegas MGM Grand Hotel on board as a partner, and the Nevada State Boxing Commission in receipt of "the book," the creation of what became known as "The Bubble" was born, along with ESPN's broadcasting partnership. Execution of the plan, however, was something else. The first thing was to take over the entire twelfth-floor space at the MGM Grand Hotel, which was to be used by personnel from Top Rank, ESPN, the fighters and their retinues, and all other personnel. Top Rank also took over the first-floor conference center and repurposed it for boxing training areas, a studio where the boxing matches would be held with cameras and lights in place for broadcast, plus a catering area where meals were to be provided for everyone in The Bubble, plus offices for staff and crew.

In speaking of the setup, Jacobs remarked, "your life is in between the floor you sleep at night and the conference center where everything takes place."[8]

Aside from the thought put into the facilities, strict protocols had to be put in place to ensure The Bubble would remain a safety zone from COVID-19. This included testing and quarantine pre-entry processes to guarantee that once inside The Bubble, there was a limited opportunity to catch or spread the disease. The efforts were no doubt stringent, but necessary. With no vaccines or targeted antiviral medicines, catching the virus still meant there was the potential for serious illness and weeks of hospitalization, even for the young and healthy.

Confident that all would be in readiness, a June 9, 2020, launch was announced featuring Shakur Stevenson fighting in a ten-round bout against Felix Caraballo. Mikaela Mayer was also announced for the card, though she would not be fighting Melissa Hernandez as originally scheduled in March. As an alternative, Mayer was to fight the Nigerian-born Helen Joseph (17–4–2, 10-KOs), who boxed out of New York City's Mendez Gym. Joseph debuted as a professional in 2004, and though she had competed for major titles, the wins had eluded her, though she did hold a WIBF belt. Her last outing had been a ten-round bout against Delfine Persoon the previous November, which she lost on the cards.

Mayer felt she had been in top form coming into the fight with Hernandez. She had gone back to Colorado immediately after her fight was canceled in March, but after a period of aimlessness wanted to ensure she was fight-ready. Determined to stay in shape so that she could jump at an opportunity to be on the first card once the restrictions were lifted, Mayer drove across country from her home in Colorado with her former Olympic teammate Ginny Fuchs and her two dogs, to train and live with her coach, Kay Koroma, in Washington, DC.

Speaking of that time, she said, "We didn't even have the lights on in the gym. There was no electricity running while there was quarantine, they shut that all off. . . . Coach Kay had a friend there who opened it up for us, and we would bring one or two people in for sparring while we were there. It was just us, four or five people in the gym."[9]

As the time passed, and Top Rank began to put together the card for June, Mayer traveled back west to Houston, Texas, where she finished up her camp at Main Street Boxing.

During her training, the gym reopened to the public.

It was "super weird and a little nerve-wracking," she said of the experience, "because all of a sudden the gym is packed with younger people, and I'm like, 'How safe are these young people being before they come into this gym?' Even though I wasn't quarantined at home like a lot of people were, locked in their house . . . I was very cautious."

Coming into Las Vegas two days before the fight, she and her team came to the testing area at the MGM Grand Hotel to begin the pandemic protocols put in place to ensure the safety of The Bubble. While Mayer's team breezed through with negative tests, Mayer herself received the devastating news: she was positive.

"It came as a complete surprise," Mayer wrote in an Instagram post. "I am currently asymptomatic and am quarantining at an off-site location per recommended guidelines. The rest of my team tested negative and they are all in good health."

Asymptomatic or not, her co-feature bout had to be called off. As Brad Jacobs had previously stated, "The bottom line is if someone comes up positive on their test, there's no retest. . . . You're done. Very simple."

Writing further on her post, Mayer told her fans, "I was really looking forward to bringing back boxing for all of you and I'm disappointed for myself, my team, my supporters and for my opponent, Helen Joseph, who worked just as hard to be here this week and put on a show for everyone."[10]

With the fight off again, Mayer's team had already begun working with Top Rank to find the earliest possible date for the fight to go forward. In a coup for Mayer, the fight was rescheduled as the main event on the Tuesday, July 14, show—a first for her, and for Top Rank.

The Main Event

Coming into fight night as the featured attraction, Mayer entered the ring with a significant height and reach advantage over Joseph. Sure, there were no fans, and everyone was masked and gloved, but her fight was still the main event of the evening.

Prior to her big night, Mayer had engaged in yet more training, this time at altitude, and came into the fight with a lot of confidence. Joseph also had worked very hard—something she did nearly every day in case she got the call for a fight. A journeywoman, she was dedicated to her own chance at greatness.

"I love this game so much," she had said several months before, "and I am ready to fight every month, every week, I love boxing more than everything else apart from my God. . . . And here I am today, and I never gave up on my dream."[11]

Appearing fresh and ready to go, Joseph came forward with the intention of powering through Mayer to take the fight inside, while throwing wide-looping overhand rights to get Mayer's attention. For Mayer's part, she fought smartly as the taller fighter, and playing the veteran's trick, wisely grabbed hold of Joseph when she did get inside. The flow of the fight stayed pretty much the same from the opening bell, with Joseph able to land some decent shots, but with nothing Mayer couldn't handle as she peppered Joseph throughout, winning by unanimous decision 100–90.

While Mayer's main-event feature had been the first female bout in the United States since the lockdown, Mexico's former interim WBA fly champion Yesica Nery Plata had fought in an eight-round contest. She had appeared on the first show broadcast from the Gimnasio Azteca TV studio on June 20 in Mexico City, a setup modeled in part on the Top Rank bubble. In Azteca TV's third show, the great Mexican fighter Jackie Nava was the main event in a non-title ten-round bout, and later in the summer, on August 22, they featured the up-and-coming bantam fighter Paulette Valenzuela in an eight-round undercard bout.

Boxing was very slow to start worldwide, and in the United States, in June and July, aside from The Bubble, the shows were primarily in small venues with a few shown on the FITE TV streaming service. None of those fight cards featured female bouts, with the exception of the Golden Boy card later in July.

Around the world, as events started to be put on, women began to appear, including a show in the Czech Republic that featured 2 four-round female bouts at the end of June. And on July 18, three of four fight cards in Germany featured a female bout with one of them broadcasting an eight-round battle between the feather boxing prospect Nina Meinke and journeywoman boxer Edina Kiss, whose long record included battles against a slew of American fighters. The three cards in the United States that evening, however, did not have any female fights.

The following week, on Tuesday, July 21, The Bubble featured a second female attraction between the undefeated flyweight Canadian boxer

Kim Clavel and American Natalie Gonzalez in an eight-rounder. Both fighters demonstrated a high caliber of skill, showing the depth of the women in the sport with the thudding of the shots punctuating the fight throughout in the otherwise empty studio. Clavel won by 80–72 on all three cards, having thrown the sharper and cleaner punches across all eight rounds.

The next marquee American fighter to box during the first summer of the pandemic was Seniesa Estrada. She appeared in an eight-rounder at the first Golden Boy Promotions "bubble" event on July 24 set up at the Fantasy Springs Casino in Indio, California. Broadcast on DAZN Boxing, she was supposed to have fought the Mexican champion Jacky Calvo in a rescheduled bout from their original fight date on March 20 that had been among the first wave of canceled events. Calvo, however, had suffered an injury just days before the new July fight date and had to withdraw. In her place, a game Miranda Adkins (5–0, 5-KOs) agreed to step into the ring against Estrada. Adkins had started her career in amateur kickboxing and, switching to professional boxing, had only fought eight actual rounds to date, even though her unbeaten record may have implied otherwise.

For Estrada's part, she was in it to win, striding across the ring to begin her work with the bell. All it took was seven punches thrown in two rapid-fire spurts to gain the fastest knockout in women's boxing history just seven seconds into the first round. Adkins lay under the ropes on the apron for some time before being helped to the center of the ring, with Estrada briefly resting her gloved hand on Adkins's shoulder and warmly embracing her when she was announced the winner along with being awarded the WBC silver light fly belt. Estrada had last fought in November at the MGM Grand Hotel on the undercard of the Alvarez–Kovalev card shown on DAZN Boxing. Facing her Golden Boy Promotions teammate Marlen Esparza for the WBA interim world fly, the fight had been contested with three-minute rounds. The pair fought an all-out war, with Esparza sustaining a deep cut at the hairline from a clash of heads in the middle of the fifth stanza, a not uncommon circumstance between a southpaw and an orthodox fighter. Esparza fought heroically, with her vision obscured, but by the ninth round, the referee had seen enough and stopped the fight. In accordance with the rules, since it had gone past the fourth frame, it went to the score cards with Estrada winning on points to gain the interim title.

The only other female fight the weekend of Estrada's seven-second knockout wonder was in Mexico. American fighter Shadasia Green (4–0, 3-KOs), who previously fought in Mexico on March 14 in one of the last cards before the shutdown, appeared in an eight-round bout, defeating her opponent Marcela Garcia Mendoza by TKO in the sixth round. Green had managed to fly in and out of Mexico for both fights, having traveled with precautions and the necessary steps to stay COVID-free.

Great Britain began their pandemic summer season of boxing events on July 10. Promoted by Frank Warren's Queensberry Promotions, the first broadcast of a "bubble" fight was from the BT Sport Studio on what would become a seven-event series carried through mid-November, but with none of the cards featuring a female bout.

British promoter Eddie Hearn had also been working on a bubble setup. Using the garden at the Matchroom Headquarters in Brentwood, Essex—the back of Hearn's actual childhood home—the Matchroom HQ Garden, known as "Fight Camp," held a series of four events in August 2020. While the first card held, on August 1, did not include a female bout, the next three did.

The second event at Fight Camp was broadcast live on August 7. Hearn had planned a doozy—a history-making main event with the first world title fight between two British women. Originally scheduled for April 24 but caught in the maelstrom of the pandemic, WBC and IBO world super feather title holder Terri Harper (10–0, 5-KOs) was paired with British Olympian Natashia Jonas (9–1, 7-KOs): a test for both women, and as executed arguably the best scrap, bar none, of the pandemic summer, male or female.

Jonas had suffered a shocking loss at super feather against the Brazilian fighter Viviane Obenauf (12–4, 6-KOs) two years earlier in a ten-round battle in Cardiff. Down twice in the third round and once in the fourth, her corner had thrown in the towel to give Obenauf the TKO win. Jonas had three wins after that in a four-rounder and 2 six-round bouts, so her appearance in the title fight against Harper signified an opportunity to get her career fully back on track. For Harper's part, she'd defeated fellow British boxer Nina Bradley (7–0) to pick up the WBC international light weight title in March 2019, and won the IBO world super feather belt in July against South African Nozipho Bell (9–2–1, 3-KOs), by TKO in the eighth round.

Harper's next achievement was to defeat the WBC world super feather title holder, Eva Wahlström, on the cards to capture her second title. Facing Jonas, Harper would arguably be competing against her toughest opponent as she defended her green belt for the first time.

Both fighters were intent on winning as they entered the first frame at a fast clip. Jonas, coming out hard and exhibiting beautiful boxing, cleanly won the first round, but having suffered a cut over her right eye from what looked to be a left hook, Jonas came out with lethal intentions in the third round, only to be outboxed by Harper. Fiercely determined, Jonas grabbed the fourth with perfect execution offensively and defensively. And so the fight went, round by round, both fighters taut, showing off beautiful skills and fierce determination. Jonas had a big performance in the eighth, with sharp accurate shots, and stunned Harper with a sharp right hook. Jonas seemingly pulled out the ninth as well, continuing her great inside game and clean short right hooks, while Harper gained the advantage in the tenth, driving Jonas to the ropes before she was able to push off. Feeling she had done enough, Jonas's trainer, Joe Gallagher, lifted her up at the end of the bout, as the announcer proclaimed the bout a terrific advertisement for women's boxing. The scores at the end of the battle were 96–95, 95–96, 95–95—a split-draw, allowing Harper to retain her titles.

At the end of the fight, perhaps surprised at the draw, Harper noted she was disappointed with her performance, but was also quick to point out that at twenty-three years of age there was still a lot she needed to learn. At the end, she thanked Jonas for the great fight and learning experience, promising to get back to the gym. Jonas thought the fight had been even coming into the eighth round, and that she had not only won the ninth cleanly but had done enough in the tenth to edge out Harper. Taking it in stride, she did get excited at the notion of a rematch.

Fight Club's third card broadcast on August 14 included an eight-rounder with the undefeated British boxer Shannon Courtney (5–0, 1-KO) losing on points to Rachell Bell (5–1).

It was Eddie Hearn's next promotion, however, that solidified his place as the chief proponent of women's boxing during the pandemic period when he featured another blockbuster female main event between the defending undisputed welterweight champion Cecilia Braekhus (36–0, 9-KOs) and Jessica McCaskill (8–2, 3-KOs).

The fight had originally been set for April 17, yet another fight postponed due to the pandemic. Braekhus had been training at the Summit camp located in Big Bear, California, where she had signed on to train with one of the best trainers in the business, Abel Sanchez. Not wanting to risk the flight home to Norway, where she could possibly infect her elderly parents, Braekhus stayed in Big Bear and continued to train, noting it had "given me new life in boxing."

Sanchez opined, "In an odd way due to COVID, she's actually been able to isolate herself and we get to work on so many other things that maybe without this lockdown we wouldn't have. The progression has been a lot quicker because of that. It's just her and me. You get to work one-on-one," and added, "She is really special."[12]

For the first Matchroom bout in the United States during the pandemic, a ring was set up at the intersection of E. 5th Street and S. Boston Avenue in Tulsa, Oklahoma, flooding the otherwise eerily empty downtown area with light as the fight began. Braekhus was looking to win her twenty-sixth consecutive title defense win and the chance to break Joe Louis's long-standing record of twenty-five defenses. McCaskill, however, had other ideas and came out blazing with hard overhand rights and lefts as Braekhus kept McCaskill on the outside as she returned fire and swatted off punches. By the third round McCaskill's disruptive style showed versatility in the ring, throwing in between Braekhus's shots and counterpunching effectively from odd angles to break the rhythm of her opponent. She also worked to force her into a close inside brawl rather than Braekhus's consistent outside style that relied on the jab as the arbiter of her game as well as her clean punches.

McCaskill was having none of it, roughing her up at every turn, even as Braekhus continued to block some of the incoming fire to get off good shots of her own. As the fight progressed, McCaskill continued to fight aggressively, though Braekhus returned to her fighting style relying on the jab, right hand, with a new left hook added to her repertoire. With that in play beginning in the seventh round, she was better able to keep McCaskill at distance, seemingly taking the momentum of the fight coming into the tenth round. McCaskill, not willing to cede anything, gained ground whenever she was able to muscle through Braekhus's defenses to get inside.

Scored a majority decision, 95–95, 97–93, 97–94, the newest member of the undisputed club was Jessica McCaskill. Speaking after her win McCaskill, quite overcome with emotion, said, "This is for the fourth grade homeless Jessica," and when asked about the fight added, "I just didn't stop. I didn't expect her to be as rough as she was, but I was prepared to be as rough as I had to be."

Braekhus, seemingly unphased by the loss, congratulated her opponent and said somewhat wistfully, "I don't know what's going to happen right now, but I'm so proud to be a part of women's boxing right now. If this is my last fight, I can leave women's boxing and say I was a part of this, I was a part of taking it to this level. That will be my biggest achievement of all."[13]

Having put on two great title fights on consecutive weekends, Fight Camp's last card of the summer schedule for August 22 featured the highly anticipated rematch for lightweight undisputed honors between Katie Taylor and Delfine Persoon.

Prior to locking in the rematch fight with Persoon, however, Taylor had been matched with Amanda Serrano for a super fight to be contested in Manchester on May 2, 2020, with the undisputed belts on the line. Unfortunately, the highly anticipated showdown was canceled due to the pandemic. Searching for a date to reschedule proved elusive, at first. Serrano's camps were usually in New York City, but with the lockdown and bans on sparring, there were purportedly concerns about finding a suitable and safe location. When the call did come through from the Serrano team to cancel entirely, the reason given was reportedly the low purse size, although Eddie Hearn had maintained that she had been provided with advances and that the fees for the fight were more than fair.

Taylor had begun her preparation for the Serrano fight back in January 2020 coming over from Ireland to train in Connecticut—with Serrano choosing to take an eight-round tune-up fight in Miami on January 30 as part of her preparation. With the fight postponed due to COVID-19 in late March, Taylor decided to quarantine in place while continuing to train to await the new fight date, much as Braekhus had. When the Serrano fight finally fell through, and the Persoon fight came on the schedule, Taylor stayed on to prepare for that new challenge.

With a parallel to Braekhus, Taylor said, "it was a great opportunity for me to actually build . . . and to improve on a few things . . . I definitely feel like I've gotten a lot stronger over these last few months. That's one of the things I . . . worked on and improved."[14]

Serrano did not fight again until December 12, when she fought in a non-title eight-rounder against Dahianna Santana in the Dominican Republic. She did, however, still retain the WBO world feather title she had won in 2019.

The much-ballyhooed TaylorPersoon2 bout was a great way to end Fight Camp. Taylor was able to achieve victory, demonstrating to the viewers her disciplined approach to her second outing against Persoon that left in no doubt that she had dominated the fight.

Persoon said, "This time, I respect the result. I couldn't hurt her this time."[15]

Taylor noted in the postfight interview that the two hard-fought battles with Persoon were great for the sport.

Speaking about the summer of boxing, Taylor said, "It's amazing, just over the last few weeks alone, [we] have [had] . . . four incredible fights for women's boxing." She added: "We're definitively, bridging the gap between male and female boxing. The interest is definitely there for female boxing. That's amazing to see and it's great to be a part of."[16]

THE FALL SEASON

With their hiatus until August 21 and a switch to fights on Saturday nights, The Bubble featured their third and last women's bout of 2020 on

October 31, when Mikaela Mayer fought for her first championship at junior lightweight. Coming as the opponent against the undefeated Polish titlist, Ewa Brodnicka (19–0, 1-KO), the bout was the co-feature on the Naoya Inoue–Jason Maloney card. Unfortunately, Brodnicka came in overweight after trying twice on the scales, which meant she lost her title before ever stepping into the ring. The WBO gave Mayer the go-ahead to fight for the belt regardless.

Excited by the prospect of finally gaining her title shot, Mayer worked hard to cut off the ring to engage with her crafty opponent, using her right hand to great advantage as well as her sharp jab that landed with precision. Working around Brodnicka's ploy to hold her, even after she'd had two points deducted, Mayer was able to impose her will, winning the contest 99–89, 100–88, 100–88. After the fight she offered that her movement and her holding were a little tricky to catch on to and felt there were some things she could have done "a little bit better," but that it was a "good learning fight" and one she could be proud of.

Marlen Esparza had an opportunity to fight on October 30. Boxing in an eight-round bout a few days shy of the one-year anniversary of her battle with Seniesa Estrada, Esparza fought the undefeated Mexican fighter Sulem Urbina (12–0, 2-KOs) at the Fantasy Springs Casino. Esparza won handily, scoring an across-the-board, 80–72, unanimous decision. While not a title bout, it was keeping Esparza in the game until she could contest for a title again in the coming year.

The main event for WBC bantam title was also fought on October 31. The powerhouse long-term belt holder, Mariana Juárez, ended up losing her title ninth defense to Yulihan Luna Avila. Fighting with precision at the end of her punches, Avila was able to take the belt by unanimous decision from the long-term title holder—the second women's boxing icon to fall in as many months to a hungry upstart.

In the UK, on October 31, Savannah Marshall began her world title quest by winning the vacant WBO world middle title against Hannah Rankin by TKO in the seventh round. Fought at the Wembley Arena, the card also featured two other female bouts. Britisher Amy Timlin (4–0) contested in a ten-round title bout against fellow Briton Carly Skelly (3–0) for a commonwealth boxing council super-bantam title—having fought to a draw. And the debut of a new Matchroom fighter, Ramla Ali, with potential for stardom. Ali was a Somalian refugee who had already made a name for herself as the first British Muslim woman to win national amateur titles. She also had a presence in the wider world as a Nike spokesperson, a self-defense guru through her Sisters Club, and as a UNICEF ambassador. The card itself was emblematic of the continued growth of women's boxing in the United Kingdom's mainstream boxing world, as well as the range of talent—even in the midst of a pandemic.

Earlier in the month, again demonstrating the depth of British women's boxing, Chantelle Cameron (12–0, 7-KOs), who been Natasha Jonas's sparring partner as she readied to face Terri Harper, fought in her own title fight for the WBC world super light green belt vacated by Jessica McCaskill. Cameron's opponent was Brazilian boxer Adriana dos Santos Araujo (6–1, 1-KO). As she had failed to make weight, only Cameron was eligible for the title. The fight was held at the Manchester Arena as the co-feature and broadcast on DAZN Boxing. Cameron breezed through the bout for an easy 100–90 victory and, looking past it, hoped to be able to begin to unify the titles.

McCaskill's other vacant belt, the WBA world super light, did not go wanting for long. Kali Reis (16–7–1, 5-KOs), who'd last fought in a six-rounder the previous August 2019, was grateful for the opportunity to try for another title, especially one that would be contested as the main event. Her opponent was Canadian fighter Kandi Wyatt (10–1, 3-KOs). The match was held in St. Petersburg, Florida, at the St. Petersburg Marriott Clearwater. The fight card was also held in conjunction with the Florida Boxing Hall of Fame's annual induction weekend—and in a first for the Hall, with a women's bout as the featured attraction. The broadcasting rights were given to another new player in boxing, the Impact Network's Impact Boxing Championship series, with promotion by several groups including DiBella Entertainment. With all of that in play, Reis came ready to fight winning on the cards, 97–93, 97–92, 96–94, to become the new champion.

In yet another main event to close out the pandemic year, this time in Mexico City, the WBC world super fly titlist Guadalupe Martinez

Guzman (19–9, 6-KOs) faced the ever-professional Lourdes Juarez (30–2, 4-KOs), losing to her by unanimous decision 100–90 on all three cards.

If the year had started with a promise of an unlimited future, the pandemic had certainly tempered the expectations for many fighters. As Heather Hardy summed it up, "When the pandemic hit and boxing kind of shut down, I had to go into survival mode. I abandoned my training, I was working full-time teaching boxing lessons throughout the summertime. I was literally just sitting in the park with a set of mitts and gloves and people would run by and take my cards and so I didn't train for about a year, and I've been out of the sport."[17]

Fighters who had been on a trajectory such as United States–based boxers Tiara Brown, Jamie Mitchell, Ebanie Bridges, and Franchon Crews-Dezurn did not fight once the lockdowns began, mostly because the opportunities just weren't in the lottery of the limited cards being contested in bubbles. In Crews-Dezurn's case, she was to have fought on the Ryan Garcia–Luke Campbell card on December 5, but it was postponed when Campbell came down with COVID-19.

Claressa Shields had also not fought since her bout against Habazin at the beginning of the year. Just prior to that fight, in late 2019, Shields announced that she would be looking to sign a deal to fight in MMA in 2020. Following the MMA strand, and after protracted negotiations with two MMA promoters during the pandemic period, Shields chose to sign a three-year deal with the new powerhouse, Professional Fighter League (PFL), over UFC. The decision was motivated by her desire to develop a long-term relationship in MMA, to include the chance to start off at a novice level to let her grow in the sport. She also required the flexibility to continue boxing—which the PFL was happy to accommodate. In announcing the signing, Shields also addressed the fact that she hadn't boxed since facing off against Habazin.

"I haven't fought since January," she said. "You see all these other guys, small time fighters who aren't world champions fighting but these networks are giving me trouble about me being on the card. Giving me problems and not treating me equally."[18]

Her last fight had been on Showtime. In late July, the network announced a lineup of eight shows between August 1 and December

12. The shows were to be promoted by PBC but did not include female bouts on any of the cards.

Asked about the relationship, Shields manager and former HBO executive Mark Taffet emphasized in an email, "[We] are indebted to Showtime for the opportunities they gave to us by televising a number of Claressa's fights early in her career. When Covid hit, we knew we would have to get in the queue for a fight and wait a while as they navigated their way through that difficult maze. We kept in constant communication with them during Covid, and expected to be one of their first 4 or 5 fights when they decided to return to the ring. . . . We were very, very disappointed that they didn't provide a date for us when they announced a slate of fights dominated by PBC events. . . . So we moved on."[19]

The disruptions to the fighting life of female boxers would in some cases never really come back on track, but they did not take away from the boost other competitors were able to enjoy. The biggest surprises of the 2020 summer and fall pandemic seasons were the first-time main-event bouts. There were new titlists crowned as well, and importantly, the boxing world was able to watch the sport grow in "real time" in the UK, despite the challenges the year had wrought.

Eddie Hearn, speaking to an interviewer about the pandemic summer a few days before the TaylorPersoon2 bout, had said, "Honestly, it's so refreshing in women's boxing where genuinely the best want to fight the best. [There is] a real desire to create a legacy and fight the best. That's always been the case with Katie Taylor . . . purely driven to make her mark on the sport but everybody's following suit . . . trying to unify . . . trying to become undisputed . . . mov[ing] up weight divisions to get the biggest fights possible and I think there's incredible momentum now with women's boxing."

He went on to opine that the pandemic had also opened possibilities for women that might not have been there otherwise, observing, "Mikaela Mayer headlin[ing] a card on ESPN, Terri Harper [at Fight Camp] headlining a card on Sky Sports and DAZN . . . Braekhus and McCaskill [as the main event in Tulsa] and the biggest of them all Taylor against Persoon. So, it's a fantastic run for women's boxing you know [Matchroom is] backing it more than ever."[20]

CHAPTER EIGHT

Two- or Three-Minute Rounds and Other Challenges to the Sport

THE ONGOING DEBATE REGARDING TWO- VERSUS THREE-MINUTE rounds seemed to heat up as the pandemic wore down and more women's boxing appeared on streaming and television broadcasts. As it currently stands, most professional women's boxing is contested using two-minute rounds versus three-minute rounds for male fighters. Women's championship fights consist of 10 two-minute rounds, whereas men's title bouts are fought as 12 three-minute round contests. That is not to say that three-minute round fights don't exist for women, because they do. They are legal in most locales, and only one of the four major sanctioning bodies on WBC has continued to refuse to sanction three-minute rounds. This decision is based on their contention that women are more susceptible to head injuries. There's also the fact that elite amateur boxing bouts are fought for a total of 3 three-minute rounds for men and women, including in the Olympics. Added to this is the contention by many female fighters that they will not fight three-minute rounds without a raise in the purse for such fights. And yet other voices in and around the sport contend it can never be "real" boxing until the fight rounds are the same as men. This debate has added to the complexity of how women's boxing is perceived and how it will be contested in the future. Fighters such as Marlen Esparza and Seniesa Estrada have demonstrated their willingness to contest major title bouts using a three-minute per round clock where allowed, but other fighters are content to continue to contest the sport using the two-minute framework. The promoter Lou DiBella has also been quite vocal in his support for two-minute rounds, claiming that what makes the sport so exciting is the nonstop action that two-minute rounds afford. And while some claim that fighting two-minute rounds means less opportunities for knockouts, Mexico's Zulina Muñoz and the United States' Amanda Serrano might beg to disagree, considering that both have thirty knockdowns a piece.

RULES, RULES, AND MORE RULES

In the United States, MMA is the most popular alternative combat sport to boxing. The lexicon of the sport includes strikes instead of punches, but also allows grappling, kicking, elbow strikes, and a host of other moves generally played out in cage. At its most basic, though, MMA's unified rules as currently practiced boil down to two flavors: a nonchampionship fight scheduled for 3 five-minute rounds and a title fight scheduled for 5 five-minute rounds. Importantly, the Association of Boxing Commissions and Combative Sports (ABC), Unified Rules of Mixed Martial Arts (amended with procedure, August 1, 2019), makes no distinction between male and female contestants except for clothing. Men compete without tops, and women wear a proscribed form-fitting top. The Committee Report on Unified Rules for MMA does include a "Females" provision that reads: "Female competitors should be allowed to compete in five-minute rounds, three rounds for non-title bouts and five rounds for title bouts."

Neither set of rules forbids mixed-gender contests.

The ABC issued their latest amended Unified Rules for Boxing in 2016. Those provisions are even more bare bones, with no distinctions made at all between men and women, including the first unified rule, which reads, "1. Each round shall consist of a three (3) minute duration, with a one (1) minute rest period between rounds."

A further dive into unified boxing rules, however, does show a set of guidelines under the heading "Championship Rules" with the subheading "Female Boxing Guidelines." The first provision of those rules states: "1) All bouts shall be scheduled for no more than ten (10) rounds with each round lasting two (2) minutes. One (1) minute between rounds." Given there is no date for those provisions, and the fact that it is not readily accessible on the ABC website, it is a little unclear as to its place as a governing document.[1]

In addition to these unified rules, the U.S. Congress enacted the "Professional Boxing Safety Act of 1996, Muhammad Ali Boxing Reform Act, to aid in the governance of the sport—with the Act coming into law in May 2000." Its stated purpose is "(1) to improve and expand the system of safety precautions that protects the welfare of professional boxers; and (2) to assist State boxing commissions to provide proper oversight for the professional boxing industry in the United States."[2]

The act failed to put a National Boxing Commission in place, although it did require the ABC to develop and pass certain guidelines by majority vote of its member state boxing commissions on a specific timetable.[3]

In the absence of a true national boxing regulatory organization, boxing governance is managed at the state level by each individual athletic/boxing commission with a head nod to the codified federal stipulations. Such commissions are free to set regulatory requirements on a state-by-state basis. As an example, the New York State Athletic Commission (NYSAC) oversees the New York State Special Rules for Professional Boxing. The rules include a specific provision for the "Duration of rounds" (Section 211.24); as written, they do not make a distinction between male and female contestants when setting the requirements: "Rounds shall be 180 seconds long, unless otherwise directed or authorized by the Commission."

Moreover, other than the occasional use of the words "him or herself" to describe the required actions of a boxer, no specific gender-related provisions are included in the rules except requirements for male ring costumes that "shall include a foul-proof guard of the boxer's own selection . . ." (Section 211.11).[4]

As most states have enacted rules to govern boxing within their borders, the thicket of governing provisions can lead to layers of regulations and increased tensions in sorting through the order of preference. This includes questions and arguments related to the duration of rounds for women, and more recently, the number of rounds that should be contested for a championship bout. Nevada, California, and New York have all had three-minute round female bouts in their jurisdictions within the last ten years, and the State of New Jersey changed its rules to accommodate women's three-minute round bouts in 2017.

In explaining the rationale for the change, the commissioner of the New Jersey State Athletic Control Board (NJSACB) said, "Everyone has done two-minute rounds, but the important consideration here is that we don't know of any definitive reasons why women should be limited to two-minute rounds and men fight three minutes. There is nothing we've seen that showed us that the extra minute is any different."[5]

The California Code of Regulations shows the state does not make mention of round duration in its Professional Boxing Rules. As such, a sanctioned, three-minute, six-round bout between Martha Salazar and Sonya Lamonakis in 2013 met with all regulatory requirements.

Nevada had approved twelve-round, three-minute round championship fights in 2007. Savannah Marshall fought her debut four-round bout with three-minute rounds in 2017. Seniesa Estrada, a proponent of three-minute round bouts, had fought in a ten-round, three-minute round WBA world fly championship bout in Nevada against Marlen Esparza in 2019.

For Estrada's July 2021 WBO world light fly title fight against Tenkai Tsunami, she wanted to fight 10 three-minute rounds. Both the California State Athletic Commission (CSAC) and the WBO had agreed in principle to the change with the proviso that both fighters concur; in this instance, Tsunami said "no." Expressing frustration and noting that some states and boxing organizations don't allow it at all, Estrada said, "You have to first get the organization and the state to agree to it, but if your opponent doesn't agree to it then you can't do it . . . we even offered [Tsunami] five thousand dollars more and then I even said I'll give you another five thousand out of my own purse so it would have been ten thousand dollars more and she still said 'no.' It was really disappointing."[6]

She also made the point that as much as fighters wanted the rule to change, it would be that much more difficult if fighters resist the change, but she did not delve further into what that would look like beyond her desire to fight three-minute round bouts.

For the record, the approval process with the CSAC had not gotten to the stage of a formal request, but commission executive director Andy Foster told ESPN, "If we got that request, I would take it to the commission. And I can tell you my recommendation would be that we allow the three-minute rounds for females unless there's compelling medical evidence against it."[7]

In New York State, professional boxer Susan Reno had posed the question of why the state wasn't authorizing three-minute round bouts as early as 2013.

"In a conversation with NYSAC Executive Director, David Berlin, he wondered out loud 'why don't women fight three-minute rounds?' I jumped on that thought and said, 'I'll do it!' He too, recognized women have the skill, stamina and focus to fight the same amount of time as the men. His response was 'Let's make history!'"[8]

With the approval of NYSAC, Reno was able to compete in the state's first sanctioned three-minute round female bout against Paola Ortiz in May 2015. Reno lost the six-rounder on the cards to Ortiz, but it was her tenacity outside of the ring that had made the change possible.

On top of the boxing regulatory ecosystem across the varying boxing commissions, the four major sanctioning bodies set their own rules for fights sanctioned under the auspices of one or another individual organization, even going so far as to use different terms for specific belts. As an example, the 140 lb. belt is designated as super lightweight by the WBA and WBC, whereas the IBF and WBO designate the title as junior welterweight.

THE AMATEURS

In the United States, there are major differences between amateur and professional boxing. USA Boxing has some fifty-six jurisdictions for local and/or regional boxing organizations. In the case of the amateur world, elite contests also must adhere to international governance requirements for cross-border competition and the rules surrounding Olympic competition under the auspices of the International Olympic Committee (IOC).

In the "hot mess" that is international amateur boxing governance since 2019, there have been multiple issues that have spilled over into the public. These include dueling governance organizations, fiery rhetoric, alleged match-fixing and cheating scandals, and the takeover of Olympic boxing by the IOC for the delayed 2020 Tokyo Games and the upcoming 2024 Paris Games. With so many issues unresolved with respect to the overall governance of elite international amateur boxing, the IOC has withheld approval of the sport for Olympic competition in the 2028 Los Angeles Games (as of this writing), and furthermore, at the end of June 2023, formally suspended the International Boxing Organization (IBA), the successor to AIBA. World Boxing, a new global amateur organization, was created in April 2023. Under the leadership of an interim executive board and with such members as the United States, the United Kingdom, Germany, the Netherlands, and the Philippines, the hope is to become the new voice of boxing within the Olympic movement.

The implications of the continuing uncertainty, however, are staggering for elite women's amateur boxing programs. Having finally won the right to compete in the 2012 London Games, the potential for the sport to be jettisoned due to governance matters would do irreparable harm to women in the sport. Much of what has been built on the professional side has been predicated on women winning gold on Olympic stages—so the removal of the sport from the Games would have enormous consequences.[9]

Despite the recent turmoil, rules changes have also spurred the sport to greater growth. As a case in point, under the AIBA umbrella there had been a concerted effort to create equity for elite male and female competitions. The most far-reaching decision in this regard was to change the duration of elite women's bouts to equal those of their male counterparts beginning in 2017. With the change, women's bouts went from 4 two-minute rounds to 3 three-minute rounds. The only lingering difference is women continue to wear headgear in competition, whereas men do not—although this has come with a lot of controversy on the men's side due to the preponderance of cuts and other facial injuries.

The other change was related to how bouts were to be scored—adapting the professional, ten-point "must" system that encouraged a more professional boxing style as the scoring would take other factors into consideration beyond the punch count.

Implementation of these changes has brought about their own complexities. Boxers entering the professional ranks not only need to continue the practice of shedding any remnants of an amateur boxing style, but adapt to longer fights, and step down to fighting two-minute round bouts after having competed in tournaments where they fought three-minute rounds.

Christina Cruz, who only recently turned pro, began her career in the amateurs in 2007 and became a USA Boxing national champion in 2012 after defeating Jamie Mitchell in the bantam final. Cruz made the adjustment from two-minute to three-minute rounds in the amateurs in 2017 and kept at it with the goal of becoming an Olympian. She had finally qualified for the 2020 Tokyo Games representing Puerto Rico. It all came to a crashing halt a few days before the final qualifiers due to the pandemic. When the delayed Games were rescheduled for late July 2021, however, the qualifying rules were changed to a ranking system, which left her out of the running. After much soul searching, she decided to pivot to the professional side of the sport.

"I told my coach I have been doing this for so many years and I never had any thoughts about turning pro, but he told me to try the pro game out for one year and see if I love it and decide from there. I stepped into the professional ring and loved it."

Cruz has admitted that the adjustment to the quicker speed of two-minute rounds took some time, with a rocky start in her debut bout where she grabbed a mixed-decision win. Even though she had started boxing using two-minute rounds, her boxing style had been perfected with three-minute rounds. She had always fought with more of a pro-style, and as rangy fighter she made full use of the ring to set up traps for her opponents. At 5–0, she has worked hard in the gym to quicken her pace to fight the end-to-end style of the two-minute round format, but it remains a challenge.[10]

For Oshae Jones, who won the second female bronze medal as Team USA's first welterweight Olympian in the delayed 2020 Tokyo Games, the challenge of stepping down to two-minute rounds brought other considerations as she readied to turn pro in 2022.

"I have to slow down my boxing style cause with the amateurs it's only three minutes in three rounds," Jones said. "So, you don't have a lot of time to get your points off, get your punches off, but in the pros, you can fight up to 10 or 12 rounds. So, it's all about throwing down my punches, the accuracy, instead of the amount of punches."[11]

SAFETY FIRST, SAFETY LAST, SAFETY ALWAYS

With the WBA, WBO, and IBF having approved the first twelve-round, three-minute round unification bout for women set for October 27, 2023, the lone holdout remains the WBC. The sanctioning organization has steadfastly insisted they will adhere to the two-minute round rule for women as a matter of safety, a position they have held since their first sanctioned female bout in 2005.

At the World Boxing Council convention held in November 2022 in Acapulco, President Mauricio Sulaimán took the opportunity to reiterate the WBC's commitment to its two-minute round policy:

> We did have that discussion at length in several panels during the convention. The WBC is about safety . . . the modern rules of boxing are basically the WBC Rules. I think it's going to be very difficult for the WBC to create a change. Women have a different physiology [in that] the neck area is different from [men] . . . and we will continue to fund a study at UCLA regarding the effects of dehydration and fatigue with an increasing risk for women in boxing.
>
> At this time, it was decided that no fights will be allowed for three minutes, and it was decided not to approve twelve rounds yet because you will be adding twenty percent more action and that's where the accidents could come into place. It was a unanimous decision not to make any changes at this moment.[12]

In other subsequent interviews, Sulaimán has again articulated the previously voiced concern, that women are more susceptible to concussions. Through WBC's continuing support of UCLA's Brain Injury Research Center (BIRC), the hope is new studies will specifically target gaining a greater understanding of the issue—and through this research spur other traumatic brain injury centers to take up the clarion call to study the effects of combat sports on women.

The fact is, both men and women have suffered the consequences of serious brain trauma in the ring, and in the worst instances have lost their lives. Sadly, in September 2021, an eighteen-year-old Mexican boxer, Jeanette Zacarias Zapata, received repeated blows and fell unconscious in the fourth round of a six-round fight in Montreal, Canada. She was taken to the hospital for immediate treatment but succumbed to her injuries five days later. It was subsequently learned that she had been knocked out four months earlier in a fight in Mexico, but having undergone neurological testing, was cleared to come to Canada to fight. The exact nature of the injury she sustained and whether she was still suffering from lingering effects is unknown, but her tragic loss of life is a cautionary tale in support of the urgent need for further research. Along with Zapata, two male boxers also lost their lives in 2021, one of whom was competing in the AIBA youth world championships as an amateur—the first death reported in the history of the amateur governing body. The root causes of those losses also remain unknown, adding to the conundrum of sanctioning a sport that relishes knockout wins, especially among fighters in the heavier divisions.

Advances in research, diagnosis, treatment, and the public's perspective on brain trauma have certainly evolved—but the notion that boxing, MMA, and other combat sports can cause permanent damage and even loss of life is very real. For women, the question of how much is too much is unanswered and has only recently begun to be examined in a limited way scientifically.

One of the earliest research efforts of the effects of female boxing on the health of its practitioners was an Italian study that collected data on all female boxing competitions in Italy from April 2001 to December 2007. The study collected data on a total of sixty-one amateur female boxers longitudinally. The methodology included an analysis of pre- and post-match medical reports of tests performed including data collected on brain health. The review reported very few head injuries and concluded that "Female boxing seems to be a safe sport with a very low incidence of events requiring hospitalization. No specific diseases in female boxers could be observed, in particular regarding the breast and reproductive systems."[13]

On a more general basis, a consensus statement issued at the 3rd International Conference on Concussion in Sport held in Zurich in November 2008 cited in research notes, "The role of female gender as a possible modifier in the management of concussion was discussed at length by the panel. There was not unanimous agreement that the current published research evidence is conclusive that this should be included as a modifying factor, although it was accepted that sex may be a risk factor for injury and/or influence injury severity."[14]

A 2013 report issued in the American Medical Society for Sports Medicine (AMSSM) Position Statement: Concussion in Sport, was more definitive in affirming the correlation between female athletes and concussion, although it too made note of the need for more research and did not include boxing or other combat sports in its findings:

> Recent data suggests that in sports with similar rules females sustain more concussions than their male counterparts. In addition, females experience or report a higher number and severity of symptoms as well as a longer duration of recovery than males in several studies. Decreased head-neck segment mass of females compared to male athletes may contribute to greater angular acceleration of the head after concussive impact as a mechanism for more severe injury. Estrogen and differential cerebral blood flow may also play a role in influencing concussion severity and outcome. Further study is needed to understand if sex is a risk factor for concussion and what mechanisms may account for it, or if sex is merely a predictor of symptom reporting.[15]

With a growing interest in sport-related concussions (SRCs) in female athletes in high school and NCCA team sports, an American review paper published in 2020 studied SRCs in team sports athletics, concluding "that female athletes may be more susceptible to concussion, have prolonged symptoms after a concussion, and are more likely to report a concussion than their male counterparts."

Whether that is less definitive than the AMSSM position is subject to interpretation with the note that the study also found "Possible factors that put female athletes at a higher risk for concussions include biomechanical differences and hormonal differences," but noted "more research is required to determine when and how such injuries are sustained."

Furthermore, "Despite sex-based differences in the clinical incidence, reporting behavior, and outcomes of SRCs, female athletes remain an understudied population, resulting in lack of sex-specific treatment guidelines for female athletes postinjury."

The data set considered incidents of SCRs among a range of team sports in American high schools and NCAA college programs. As it did not include any studies of boxing or other combat sports, any conclusions would need further study to be truly relevant to the sport.[16]

A review article in 2016 examining sex and gender in concussion research also supported the idea that more information is needed:

> Currently, concussion guidelines, to our knowledge, have not made any recommendations on how to manage sex and gender in clinical settings, which warrants explicit consideration. To ensure greater precision in concussion-related policy and practice, integration of sex and gender diversity into all associated activity is greatly needed. This can be done by investigating how the sex of injured persons relate to their social location/societal position and access to healthcare resources; whether male and female persons hold different lifestyle, occupational and family responsibilities before and after the injury, and make different behavioral choices and attitudes toward activities associated with greater risk of concussion; and reflecting these attitudes and behaviors through the lens of relevant gender relations and sex-linked biology. It is anticipated that research advances in these areas will culminate in the development of tailored policy interventions that will be applied to prevent injuries and improve outcomes of all injured persons, regardless of their gender or sex.[17]

The paucity of scholarship specifically researching SRCs among female boxers and/or other combat sports practitioners certainly limits how best to extrapolate data from team sports. And while certain commonsense preventative strategies could reasonably be applied, mitigation of the risks of head trauma sustained in boxing does require focused research to be effective, as does the issue of susceptibility both in short term, and longitudinal studies of retired female boxers.

Of particular concern requiring consideration are the unregulated aspects of boxing training that can involve multiple sparring sessions per week ahead of a fight. Women wear headgear, and typically spar with heavier and more padded gloves, but the purpose of the sessions are not only to work on specific strategies to deploy during the contest while increasing stamina but to harden the competitor for what awaits her on match day. Women also typically train using a three-minute round clock and may spar as many as twelve rounds. A standard practice is to rotate in three fighters who may well be male and/or female, for four rounds a piece. By the last four rounds of the sparring session and facing a fresh opponent, the fighter may experience higher risks due to the accumulation of fatigue and dehydration.

Another consideration is hydration. Many fighters preparing for a bout are also engaged in "cutting weight," with a focus on sweating out excess fluid during training sessions. The concern is that dehydration may allow for cellular damage to take place independent of the degree of trauma from blows to the head during sparring.

"Repetitive impacts can lead to dehydration within the tissues due to fluid movement accompanying inertial movements during the impact." Additionally, "Dehydration can modify symptoms and alter the ability to effectively and properly diagnose the athlete immediately following trauma, impacting acute treatment and stymieing proper long-term care for the injured athlete."[18]

Certainly, men and women face incredible risks each time they enter the ring, leading to important questions for serious consideration. For one, if gender is a determination in susceptibility to concussions, what must the sport do to help provide guidelines for managing risk? It also begs the overall question, in a sport that relishes knockouts regardless of the sex of the fighter, how can any boxer really be safe? And overall, with the high incidence of subconcussive and concussive injury from repeated blows to the head among men, regardless of susceptibility, perhaps the better conversation to be had is changing men's boxing to two-minute rounds. This is a sentiment offered by Dr. Margaret Goodman, a former ringside physician in Nevada and founder and CEO of VADA, who opined, "Exposure to head blows isn't good for anyone. We know that. The less the better. One minute rounds would do less damage than two minute rounds. With three minute rounds for women, there would be more damage. That's a given. There would be less damage in men's boxing if rounds were cut from three minutes to two."[19]

WHICH CAME FIRST, PAY EQUITY OR THE NUMBER OF MINUTES PER ROUND?

The bottom line when it comes to three-minute rounds in the popular conception is this: If women are relegated to fighting two-minute rounds, they will never be accepted as equal to "real" boxers, meaning men. That sort of thinking finds its way into fight night commentary with reminders of how women "only" fight two-minute rounds. This is generally followed with discussions of how female bouts tend to go the distance because there isn't enough time to set up a knockout—although there are plenty of fighters who have found KO success with two-minute rounds.

Amanda Serrano, long a proponent of three-minute rounds, has made history in that regard. She will fight a game-changing twelve-round, three-minute round bout against her WBO mandatory challenger, Danila Ramos. Serrano's IFB and WBA belts are also on the line. All three sanctioning bodies gave the go-ahead for the bout along with the Florida State Athletic Commission in September 2023. As if to punctate the through thread, the poster for the fight in itself is instructive on whether women's ten by two fights are legitimate. The headline reads "Women's Championship Boxing," with the word *Women's* crossed out in red, with the line below stating: "12 Rounds/3 Min Rounds." That would seem to indicate where Serrano and her team at Most Valuable Promotions stand on the issue.

Asked whether WBC would entertain a twelve-round, three-minute round fight, Mauricio Sulaimán said WBC would not change its stance until "there is clear medical research clearance to do any changes."[20]

Promoter Lou DiBella has been adamant that people stop comparing women's boxing contests to men's and start appreciating them more on their own terms. "The shorter women's fights are incredibly active, and incredibly entertaining and provide immediate gratification. Ultimately, that's what people want in any sport . . . people want entertainment that's right there, fast, right in front of you. And that's women's boxing. The fights are quicker, they're more active and it's actually a better product."

Reflecting on it a bit more, DiBella said, "If people were setting up boxing right now, they wouldn't invent it with three-minute rounds, they'd invent it with shorter rounds, because shorter rounds would be more action and a quicker result."[21]

Alicia Ashley, a former WBC champion and 2022 inductee to the International Boxing Hall of Fame, has been outspoken on the three-minute round issue across her career: "MMA had the foresight to have women on an even footing immediately. [This] is something that powers behind boxing never had," Ashely said, adding, "How can you say women cannot box three-minute rounds when MMA proves that women can fight five-minute rounds? Hopefully MMA will help open the eyes of the boxing world. We as female fighters can only keep pushing for change or at least the option of fighting for three minutes."

She added, "[W]omen can and will fight longer if given the opportunity. It is a step in the right direction to competition and hopefully pay equality."[22]

One need not look any further than the 2017 IBF rules governing female, USBA, intercontinental, and regional championship contests to gain an appreciation of the uphill climb. Section 9B of the rules lays out the minimum amounts for a championship bout based upon four weight ranges. The ranges are abysmal for men and even worse for women, but when one adds in the equivalent male world title minimums, the disparities become all too readily apparent (see table 8.1).[23]

As Heather Hardy put it succinctly in a recent interview, "if you want to get into boxing to be a fighter, be smart and learn how the money is made because that's the only way you're going to get anywhere. It's not for fun. You don't get hit in the head for fun. You don't get knocked out

Table 8.1

Weight Class	IBF Minimum Bid	Regional Minimum Bid	Female Minimum Bid
100–122 lbs	$25,000	$2,500	$1,000
126–147 lbs	$50,000	$5,000	$2,000
150–200 lbs	$100,000	$7,500	$4,000
Heavyweight	$200,000	$10,000	$6,000

for fun. If you love it and you love fighting, be smart. It's not just a sport, it's a business."[24]

The WBO in its female world championship regulations stipulates a minimum purse bid amount of $10,000 for all divisions. The minimum purse bids for male championships, however, begins at $80,000 for the mini-flyweight to flyweight division ranging up to $1,000,000 for heavyweights.[25]

WBA's minimum purse bid amounts for male world title fights is the same as the WBO, with an even higher amount for unified title fights. While the updated rules include a section on female boxing and an appendix that stipulates sanctioning fees for female title bouts, there are no minimum purse bids listed.[26]

A review of the WBC Rules and Regulations did not include the minimum purse bid amounts for male or female world title fights, although it did include a table noting the sanctioning fees. No gender designation was incorporated into that fee structure. The WBC did have a provision that stated, "The WBC reserves the right to refuse any purse offer it determines at its sole discretion to be too low."[27]

None of the sanctioning bodies provide justification for the discrepancies in minimum pay rates. The lamentable reading with respect to title fights does point to the hurdles that many women face as professional boxers with little if any opportunity to earn a living from title fights, never mind six- and eight-rounders without working full-time jobs in other roles.

Pay equity for women's sports is, however, an issue whose time has come across all sports for professional as well as amateur athletics. The United States' women's soccer team members have been particularly outspoken in spelling out the inequities between the men's and women's teams, highlighting the differences male and female team members receive for everything from travel arrangements to bonuses for appearances on the medal stand at competitions.

In response to the voices demanding equity, the U.S. Congress passed the Equal Pay for Team USA Act of 2019 in December 2022, to ensure all athletes who represent the United States in global competition receive equal pay and benefits, regardless of gender. Senator Maria Cantwell (D-Wash.), who co-sponsored the bill, said, "The Equal Pay for Team USA Act erases any ambiguity, setting the standard that—when it comes to pay, medical care, travel arrangements and reimbursement of expenses for players of the same sport—nothing short of equal is acceptable, regardless of gender."

She also expressed her gratitude, to "the group of women athletes who—at the top of their game—raised their voices to demand equal pay for their success . . . sending an unequivocal message to all young women and girls who dream of a future in sports: you deserve equal pay and it will be the law of the land."[28]

For the boxing champions of Team USA, this represents the culmination of a remarkable thirty-year journey back to a time when women were forbidden from competing in amateur boxing.

Sonya Lamonakis recently recalled that early in her amateur career, "The women didn't even stay at the USA Olympic Center" where the competitions were held and where male competitors were housed. "We got our own hotels, we weren't treated the same. We didn't get the uniform, the sneakers, everything the guys get we didn't get."[29]

Claressa Shields had also made note of the fact that in 2014, women's stipends were less than the male counterparts at USA Boxing. With the 2016 Rio Olympics the pay leveled out for female boxers thanks to the women on the team who clamored for equity, including Shields herself, but the passage of the Equal Pay Act will enshrine the equal treatment in a way that will ensure protections for current and future team members.

Speaking to the pejorative nature of how the three-minute round debate is often framed, in February 2021, Claressa Shields remarked, "I wish more people would realize that we did not put those rules in place—the men did. So the men need to change those rules to where every world champion boxer for women can fight three-minute, 12 rounds."

Top Rank's CEO Bob Arum has also remarked, "If I could get three-minute rounds, I would sign a number of women."[30]

Mayweather Promotions CEO Leonard Ellerbe is another promotional executive firmly on the side of three-minute rounds. "That would be one way to increase the popularity with the sport. . . . You're talking about hitting people with body shots, breaking them down slowly so you get to the later rounds, seventh, eighth round, and then you'll see a lot more action and a lot more devastating endings."[31]

Speaking about the issue with DAZN in March 2022, Shields expanded on her position:

> Championship rounds matter. If people say like, "Oh, punching power! Oh, knockouts!" The truth is I have two less rounds, and also [20] minutes compared to 36 minutes the men have to knock somebody out. I'm not the only one they say that about.
>
> "She's 12–0 with 2 knockouts," but nobody is saying that about the men and they have 36 minutes and to me it matters. I'm going to be sparring with the men for three-minute rounds.
>
> It's a level of competition and . . . that's why equal pay is needed. You can't say women's boxing is less than men's boxing if they won't even put us on . . . and let us prove ourselves. Women overwork.
>
> There's going to be more punches, there's going to be more power shots. To see the equalness, they will understand. Stop saying men's boxing and women's boxing, it's boxing.[32]

To Shields's point, practically every broadcast of her fights shows someone opining on her "lack" of "knockout power"—as if she is fighting powderpuffs or doesn't know how to fight, neither of which is true. Her level of skill seems to grow exponentially from fight to fight—and the excitement generated over the twenty minutes of fight time is real and palpable.

Hardy's strong statement that boxing is a business remains at the heart of questions surrounding whether to go forward with three-minute rounds for some women and the related question of fairness in the purse structure.

On the matter of pay equity, given the low purses women often receive, if it really is down to the twenty minutes versus the thirty-six minutes, then prorate the per-minute fee and multiply that by the total number of minutes spent boxing.

The very idea came through in a recent exchange on social media. In answer to a question posed by Women's Fight News on Instagram that read, "Thoughts on 2 or 3 minute rounds?" former WBC world super feather champion Olivia Gerula made just that point in her posted reply: "Honestly, in my opinion it comes down to pay. The majority of women train & Spar 3min rds but if I'm getting paid say $800 for a 2 min rd that has to increase to $1200 per rd to make sense. Make sense?"[33]

Gerula, who has become a potent journeywoman fighter in the latter part of her career, has a record of achievement in the sport that reaches back to the era of Christy Martin. In her last four fights between 2021 and 2023, two were eight-rounders, one was fought at six rounds, and one at four rounds, for a total of twenty-six rounds. Based on the $800 rate she noted in her Instagram post, she would have grossed $20,800—for four fights. At $1,200 per round for a three-minute round bout, she would have been paid $31,200. Minus all the requisite fees to her promoter, her corner, and so on.

With fights in Illinois, Delaware, Rhode Island, and Tennessee, the itinerant nature of the work is further called out—as is the understanding of just how low women's paydays continue to be outside of the limelight.

As thrilling as it is to know that elite professional women are starting to fight for six figures, and even seven figures, the undercards reveal another truth. It is also another layer to the question of whether women "need" to fight three-minute rounds to be accepted as boxers.

The issue itself continues to percolate in the press and in social media. This is due in part to the high level of boxing talent women are exhibiting, and their willingness to fight fighters of equal abilities. The outcomes of those battles are tighter and tighter, even in the six- and eight-round bouts with up-and-coming fighters with strong amateur pedigrees and discernable talent. The result is some of the fights have become almost impossible to score.

Closely contested fights, inevitably, lead to the pundits talking about adding the extra minute—with a constant refrain of "if only the round went another minute, she would have been down."

Claressa Shields's manager, and former HBO executive, Mark Taffet has taken a different path in the discussion:

I think women's boxing just like women in MMA are going to create their own path and are going to create a road map for success, that is going to be different than traditional boxing. [On that basis,] It's not going to take traditional boxing fans for women's boxing to grow. It's going to take sports fans, who see that women are making their mark. That their passion, their hearts, their commitment, their determination, their competitive spirit, is so great that you have to love and respect them.

On the issue of three-minute rounds, Taffet, speaking in 2022, was equally thoughtful:

I think the time is coming over the next year or two for that discussion. I've heard people say it's great because the excitement is better in two-minute [rounds.] Others say, oh, the women physically can't compete for three-minute rounds without putting themselves in jeopardy.

When the timing is right, you get the better, deeper conversation. You get more expertise in the conversation because people are more concerned about the outcome. So, the right discussion is going to take place and we'll make sure we have a lot of leaders from the fields that are part of that discussion.[34]

At the end of the day, boxing is a business, where the fighters are the commodity. The answer to the questions will ultimately rest with the women themselves as they leverage their exceptional talents to redefine boxing on their own terms. Amanda Serrano has certainly shown the truth of that by charting her own way.

CHAPTER NINE

The Era of the Super-Fight and Beyond

PROFESSIONAL WOMEN'S BOXING, AS CONTESTED TODAY, IS SAID TO HAVE started in 1996, when Christy Martin faced off against Deidre Gogarty on the undercard of a Mike Tyson PPV bout. The main-event "super-fight" in the arena at Madison Square Garden, between the undisputed lightweight champion, Katie Taylor, and the seven-weight class champion, Amanda Serrano, was surely the culmination of the promise of what women's boxing could become. Lauded as the fight of the year, male or female, it took well over two years to promote. It also has a storybook ending of a sold-out arena and the highest number of viewers of a female bout in history, according to the DAZN Boxing streaming service—and only topped by the combined number of viewers on Sky Sports and ESPN for the all-female O2 Arena card.

The Taylor–Serrano fight, though, has come to symbolize something else: a promise served, one in which two of the top three most talented female pound-for-pound boxers in the world were able to demonstrate just how brilliant they could be on their own terms. Based upon the success of the Taylor–Serrano battle, the era of super-fights has begun, with the promise of more to come. Whatever happens in the future, there will always have been an epic battle between two champions at the top of the card that set the stage for a new era of elite female boxing. Where this will all lead is subject to the vicissitudes of a sport in flux, but whatever the outcome, women's boxing has been legitimized, and as new skilled fighters join the professional ranks, their excellence in the ring will serve to further solidify that legacy—all in a rush of extraordinary accomplishment.

FACING DOWN THE PITFALLS

With coronavirus vaccines available to folks in many corners of the world and the first prescriptions of the oral antiviral Paxlovid tablets available for particularly at-risk patients, there was at least some modicum of hope that things could get back to normal.

Franchon Crews-Dezurn certainly thought so.

Right out of the box on Saturday, January 2, 2021, Crews-Dezurn (6–1, 2-KOs) won a non-title eight-rounder by unanimous decision against journeywoman Ashleigh Curry on their rescheduled Golden Boy Promotions card.

She was very happy with the chance to fight again, not to mention get the decisive win, after the debacle of her WBC and WBO super middleweight unified title defense the year before against the former WBC world heavyweight champion, Mexico's Alejandra Jimenez (12–0–1, 9-KOs). The pair had fought at the Alamodome in San Antonio, Texas, on January 11, 2020, as the co-feature of a Golden Boy Promotions card on DAZN. Jimenez had been the split-decision winner on all three cards, costing Crews-Dezurn her belts.

As a condition of their WBC title fight, both boxers had agreed to be drug tested under the guidelines of the WBC Clean Boxing Program (WBC CBP)—an integrated protocol developed alongside the Volunteer Anti-Doping Association (VADA). At the time of testing, A and B samples were taken with strict processes in place for the chain of custody in concert with the test laboratory.

Less than two weeks after the bout, the WBC announced that Jimenez's "A" sample test administered a day before the fight tested positive for a banned substance. It was later revealed to be Stanozolol, a synthetic steroid derived from testosterone that had been banned by the IOC in 1974. In the United States it was classified as a Schedule III drug—having been added to the list of prohibited drugs in the Anabolic Steroid Control Act of 2004, and again in the more stringent Designer Anabolic Steroid Control Act of 2014.

In reaction to the news of the failed test, Golden Boy Promotions Chair and CEO Oscar De La Hoya said, "As Franchon's promoter, we are incredibly disappointed for her as she worked incredibly hard to defend her titles. However, our job is to ensure the safety of our fighters both inside and outside of the ring. Thus, we have always insisted and supported testing through the Voluntary Anti-Doping Association for all of our world championship fights. Jimenez's fight against Franchon Crews-Dezurn is no exception.

"Now our job is to find justice for Franchon by working closely with the WBC and the WBO in order to reinstate her as a world champion."[1]

In a Twitter post on that same evening, Jimenez revealed that the test taken on the day of the fight was negative, attaching copies of the test results for January 10 and January 11.

The Texas Department of Licensing and Regulations (TDLR) acted swiftly upon notification of the "A" sample irregularity, changing the split-decision win to a no-decision, and suspending Jimenez from fighting until April 11. The WBC, for its part, intended to follow its protocols to include an in-depth investigation of what may have led to the positive test, as well as to work with Jimenez and her team to select a date to witness the next step in the process.

Jimenez herself was in attendance and observed as the "B" test sample was opened and tested on February 19. By the next day, the test result was revealed; it precisely matched the results of the "A" sample test.

The WBO was the first of the two sanctioning bodies to reinstate Crews-Dezurn's belts. Based on its review of the facts and the failure of Jimenez to present evidence to mitigate the findings, it issued a ten-page resolution. Its final ruling stated, "The WBO World Championship Committee hereby strips Ms. Alejandra Jimenez of her WBO Female Super Middleweight Championship Title and it reinstates WBO Female Participant Ms. Franchon Crews-Dezurn as the official WBO Female Super Middleweight Champion."[2]

With the pandemic starting to impact regular order, the WBC took additional time to perform its own investigation. The process was then completed in June and its findings were made public with the release of an adjudication agreement between the WBC and Jimenez. It detailed the findings along with the terms of her suspension and probation. It also changed the bout results to a no-contest and fully reinstated Crews-Dezurn's WBC world super middleweight title.

The positive finding highlighted the fact that VADA testing was new for female fighters. Olympian and former captain of the U.S. Olympic Team Ginny Fuchs was found to have tested positive from an out-of-competition test she had taken in February 2020, with the results released a month later in March. They showed she was positive for two banned substances, and learning of the results in and around the same time she learned that the 2020 Tokyo Games had been postponed due to the ongoing pandemic came as a big blow to her.

A subsequent investigation by the United States Anti-Doping Agency (USADA) revealed that her "partner had been taking products that included the two banned substances, and the levels of Fuchs' violations were consistent with recent exposure through sexual transmission."[3]

Fully exonerated in June, the near-miss revealed the greater need for education on the many forms banned substances can take—as well as the many routes for transmission to include intimate relations.

The latest women in boxing to be caught up in positive drug tests for banned substances are Hanna Gabriels and Alycia Baumgardner. In Gabriels's case, her team insisted the substance entered her system when she was medicating her dog. She was to have faced Claressa Shields in a rematch in June 2023, but was replaced on the cards with no further information made available on any other actions to be taken against her. Gabriels also remains the WBC world heavyweight and WBA world light heavyweight champion (as of this writing).

Baumgardner's "A" sample taken prior to her rematch with Christina Linardatou in August 2023 was found to have two banned drugs. It was also revealed that like Alejandra Jimenez, her postfight test was clean. Baumgardner has been outspoken since the positive "A" sample test was released, insisting she has never taken drugs and did not use the substances. As of this writing, the test findings are still under investigation, including the results of the "B" sample.

The Whirlwind Rush to Greatness

Pandemic or not, women were ready to contest at the highest levels of the sport—and come back to training in whatever spaces they were able to find.

If there was a difference at all, aside from the obvious with respect to the continuing threat from the coronavirus, it was the breathtaking whirlwind of championship bouts. The four main sanctioning bodies had been bestowing championships for nearly two decades in some cases. The difference was the newest crop of championships were often broadcast in real-time on various boxing media and offered to a broader audience. The perception of women in boxing as skilled and exciting fighters also became more and more obvious—even the downstream fights with new and emerging talent that had been honed in the amateurs and the Olympics.

This was particularly the case in the United Kingdom, which was leading the way in the resurgence of the sport—whether through the increasing dominance of their promotional organizations or through such outlets as DAZN Boxing, which presented Matchroom Boxing and Golden Boy Promotions women's boxing content on an increasing number of cards. It was true that Showtime, through their new exclusive relationship with PBC, was showing few if any women's bouts in 2021 and beyond, but there were notable exceptions. ESPN, through their relationship with Top Rank, was once again showing occasional women's bouts—a circumstance that would grow as Top Rank slowly began to add fighters to their roster. With Sky Sports ending their relationship with DAZN, ESPN became an important outlet for some of their bout cards in the United States, which increasingly featured women's bouts. There were also "one offs," if you will, with other sports broadcasters that televised women's boxing or self-promoted cards on new streaming upstarts including FITE TV. Smaller local market shows and even major promoters were also streaming fights live on YouTube and Facebook, increasing visibility for the sports practitioners and even mainstream network sports groups who were looking at boxing again.

Amanda Serrano's main-event extravaganza on March 25, 2021, in her native Puerto Rico was a case in point. The eight-bout card was broadcast by the NBC Sports Network under their new Ring City USA series—and treated Serrano to fighting the Argentinian world bantam and super bantam champion Daniela Romina Bermúdez (29–3–3, 10-KOs) at the head of the card. The undercard included former world fly champion Arely Muciño competing in an eight-rounder in her first bout in two years.[4] Serrano put on a dazzling performance for the cameras, defending her WBC and WBO feather titles, and adding the vacant IBO hardware for good measure. A left hook to the body thrown with Serrano's usual precision felled Bermúdez, giving Serrano her thirtieth knockout win, two shy of the record set by Christy Martin a generation before.

Only five days before at the Dickies Arena in Fort Worth, Texas, Seniesa Estrada also put on a spectacular performance as the co-feature on the Vergil Ortiz Jr.–Maurice Hooker card broadcast on DAZN Boxing. Fighting Anabel Ortiz, considered the number one fighter in the world at minimum weight and the WBA title holder in her twelfth defense, Estrada landed Ortiz on the deck with a straight right hand to the jaw in the second round and otherwise fought impressively with her footwork, switch hitting, and shots from all angles to capture the title.

The Jessica McCaskill–Cecilia Braekhus rematch was also held in March at the American Airlines Center in Dallas, Texas. On the undercard of the Juan Francisco Estrada–Roman Gonzales card and broadcast on DAZN Boxing, Jessica McCaskill was looking to rewind her extraordinary win and remain undisputed at welterweight. As in her first fight, she came out blazing, delivering a jab and very heavy overhand right that landed and wobbled Braekhus in the first round. Braekhus had been landing herself and roughing up McCaskill but was hurt again by an overhand right in the second round. McCaskill continued her onslaught, delivering an even cleaner performance than in their first faceoff, and was able to acquit herself well in the later rounds as Braekhus bravely fought back. In the end, McCaskill made it clear she was there to stay as the undisputed champion, gaining a unanimous decision 110–89, 99–90, 98–91 on the score cards.

Most spectacular of all for the March 2021 outings was Claressa Shields's return to the ring on March 5, when she was set to box the undefeated Canadian Marie Eve Dicaire (16–0, 1-KO), the IBF world super welter champion. With Dicaire's IBF title, plus Shields's WBC, WBO belts and the vacant WBA belt, the stage was set for unifying all the super welterweight titles. A win for Shields would also give her bragging rights as the first boxer, male or female, to win it in two weight classes in the four-belt era.

The competition had originally been scheduled as a Showtime fight on May 9, 2020. Postponed due to the pandemic, despite attempts by the Shields team to reschedule it, Showtime never put the bout back on the calendar. Moving past the disappointment, the Shields team was determined to find another way, eventually promoting the card themselves under the Salita Promotions banner at the Dort Federal Event Center in Flint, Michigan. With Showtime out of the picture, they broadcast the event as a PPV event on the FITE streaming service—a first since Layla Ali fought Jacqui Frazier-Lyde at the head of a PPV show nearly twenty years before in 2001.

The team also wanted to make "herstory" on their Superwoman card with the Shields–Dicaire main event as the anchor for a night that would feature a total of four women's fights. The roster of fighters included Marlen Esparza and former amateur champion Jamie Mitchell, each fighting in six-rounders, and the relative newcomer to professional boxing Danielle Perkins in an eight-round WBC silver heavy title outing.

"Headlining my first pay-per-view event with this historic women's card, particularly at such an important time in the evolution of women's boxing and around the International Women's Day celebration, is so meaningful to me," Shields said ahead of the fight. "We're going to put on one heck of a show for the world to see."[5]

In coverage of her "herstoric" undisputed win, no less a vaulted publication than the *New York Times* wrote, "With so much at stake, under so much pressure as she tested both her sport and her skills, she needed to succeed. And, in 10 rounds of punches so snappy they looked like blurs, she did."

In their analysis of the fight, the *New York Times* further opined, "Shields, now 11–0 as a professional, won every round on every judge's scorecard, largely by beating Dicaire to the punch and baiting the 34-year-old Canadian into mistakes."[6]

With the successes of the March battles in the rear-view mirror, the April championship roster began on April 10 with British fighter Shannon Courtenay's ten-round unanimous decision win over the always entertaining Ebanie Bridges (who went on to win the IBF world bantam title a year later in March 2022). The fight was the co-feature on the Conor Benn–Samuel Vargas card from the Cooper Box Arena in Hackney Wick, and broadcast on DAZN Boxing and Sky Sports. With the win, Courtenay picked up the vacant WBA world bantam title.

Jumping up from super welter, where she had held the WBA belt, for her first fight in two years, Hanna Gabriels contested for the vacant WBA world light heavy and WBC world heavy at the head of her own card in her hometown of San Jose, Costa Rica, on April 21. Fighting Mexican boxer Martha Patricia Lara Gayton (11–9, 6-KOs), Gabriels peppered her opponent with scoring shots before getting the TKO win after throwing several unanswered punches in quick succession at the end of the second round.

The next evening, April 22, at the United States Military Academy, in the headline bout of the evening broadcast on the Ring City USA series on NBC Sports Network, the longtime WBA world feather champion, Canadian boxer Jelena Mrdjenovich (42–10–2, 19-KOs), faced the southpaw Mexican fighter Erika Cruz for her sixth title defense. The original main event was to have been between Jermaine Franklin and Steven Shaw, but their fight was canceled due to Franklin's positive COVID test. Mrdjenovich and Cruz did not disappoint in their new role as the anchors of the card. The two women threw down hard from the beginning of the first round along with their first of two head clashes. The headbutts became a theme across the fight, as did Cruz's unrelenting array of power punches. Mrdjenovich suffered a deep gash from a headbutt in the sixth; by the seventh round, the referee grew very concerned and stopped the fight early in the round, telling the judges that the fight would be determined on the cards. Ahead 70–63 as determined by all three judges, Cruz became the newest WBO world feather strap holder, defeating Mrdjenovich again by unanimous decision in their rematch in Sonora, Mexico, on September 3, 2022, and broadcast on DAZN Boxing.

Katie Taylor, proving once again she was willing to risk her undisputed status by boxing strong contenders, faced Natasha Jonas at the Manchester Arena on May 1. Jonas executed another beautiful evening of boxing—losing on the cards in a very close fight that gave Taylor the unanimous decision win, 96–95, 96–94, 96–95. The southpaw Jonas began the fight countering in the early rounds before starting to let her hands go with focused intensity. Both fighters put on a classic display between a southpaw and orthodox fighter. Even with the loss, Jonas proved her worth as a fighter, ahead of her switching management to Ben Shalom's new promotional outfit, BOXXER, and jumping up in weight to begin her winning campaign at super welter in February 2022, with her TKO win over Chris Namus for the WBO world super welter title—and eventually contesting twice more in 2022, adding the IBF title to her WBC and WBO hardware. Her phenomenal performances also brought her the extraordinary honor of being the history-making first woman to be chosen as boxer of the year by the BBBC. As an added feat, Claressa Shields was proclaimed the overseas fighter of the year—another first.

Other huge fights and wins in 2021 included Denmark's undefeated Dina Thorslund (15–0, 6-KOs), who captured the WBO world bantam title to become a two-weight champion in her fight against Mexican Jasseth Noriega in the main event in June.

Marlen Esparza also got on the championship boards in July by taking the WBC world fly title from the always exceptional Ibeth Zamora Silva in a close unanimous decision win at the Don Haskins Center in El Paso, Texas.

The fall of 2021 did not disappoint, either. Jamie Mitchell, who had last fought on the undercard of the Shields–Dicaire PPV show, fought as the "B" side fighter against the WBA world bantam champion, Shannon Courtenay. She was fighting in Liverpool for her first defense of the belt on October 9. She had already lost the title on the scales prior to the fight, with Mitchell winning the close contest in the ring by outworking her across the ten rounds and gaining the title by mixed decision on the cards.

Mary McGee, in her first defense of her IBF super lightweight title, fought the WBC titlist Chantelle Cameron in a showdown to unify the belts. The pair were squared off as the main event at London's O2 Arena with an undercard that included future IBF world junior featherweight title holder Ellie Scotney in only her third contest. Perhaps a bit overmatched against Cameron, who displayed exceptional footwork and balance, McGee worked hard to overcome Cameron's sharp punching, but lost on the cards.

In a first for Hannah Rankin, she was the main event contesting for the IBO and WBA vacant super welter titles against Sweden's Maria Lindberg (20–9, 10-KOs). She won on the cards in front of the crowd at the Tottenham Banqueting Hall, and the broadcast audience on the UK's Fightzone streaming service. Rankin went on to be the first woman in Scotland to headline a main-event boxing show in May 2022, defeating Alejandra Ayala by TKO in the tenth round after being on the receiving end of an undefended barrage. Clearly in trouble after the fight, Ayala was rushed to the hospital after being attended to in the ring. Once at the hospital it was discovered that she had suffered a subdural hematoma. She was put in a medically induced coma, and after repeated surgeries gradually improved enough to begin rehabilitation.

In an interview a year later, Ayala, who had been told she could never box again, was continuing to heal from the injuries she sustained, but had moved on with her life. She'd married a few months before and was beaming with pride at being pregnant with a boy. She had to learn to walk and speak again, and in answering a question about the state of her health said, "My head injury continues to cause me problems, in language and sometimes spasms. I still can't fully do things as before, such as working all day."

She went on to say, "I can't have regrets over what happened because it's changed my perspective on life for the better."[7]

Ayala's collapse in the ring was a reminder of the dangers of the sport, and of the need to ensure that fighters have the best tools on hand to mitigate the risks. Rankin was understandably upset to think that she had played a part in the incident and did what she could to support Ayala as she underwent her ordeal.

On the heels of her first WBO super feather title defense win on the cards against Erica Anabella Farias in June 2021, Mikaela Mayer defeated the French knockout queen and IBF title holder, Maiva Hama-douche (22–1,18-KOs), to unify the titles after defeating her on the cards. The November 5 clash contested at the Virgin Hotel in Las Vegas, was broadcast on the ESPN+ streaming service as the main event, the second time Mayer boxed at the head of a card in her career.

The following weekend, Terri Harper faced off against American Alycia Baumgardner (10–1, 6-KOs) with her WBC and IBO super feather titles on the line. Broadcast from the Sheffield Arena in Shef-field, England, Baumgardner's spectacular right hand in the fourth round stunned the announcers calling the fight. The ferocity of the blow was so stunning, in fact, that Harper stood nearly stock still but listing slightly until grabbed by the referee as he waived off the fight with Baumgardner in the background looking to continue the fight.

Harper was able to recover quickly—as Baumgardner celebrated, looking forward to a brighter future in the sport with her newly won belts in hand. A year later Harper followed Jonas, jumping up in weight to super welter to capture the WBA world title in September 2023 by unanimous decision over Hannah Rankin.

FIGHT OF THE YEAR
With three active undisputed fighters, one of whom had captured the undisputed mantle in two weight classes, and a new group of incoming champions who were gaining recognition beyond the borders of the Mexican and Argentinian victors of a decade ago, women's boxing was reaching further than it had ever been before. It was also at a point where great rivalries were being formed again—with none more interesting or exciting than the specter of the girl from Bray, Ireland, who'd pretended to be a boy when she started competing, fighting the girl from Carolina, Puerto Rico, who'd grown up in Bushwick, Brooklyn.

With their chance at destiny seemingly over and done with when Serrano walked away from their pandemic summer showdown, both con-tinued to warily eye each other with the sense that perhaps the moment had not passed. Serrano, though, was also on a quest for an undisputed crown of her own at feather, having started down the path with her strong win against Daniela Romina Bermúdez to capture her second title in the weight class she'd always considered her natural weight. She'd also accomplished what no other female fighter had ever done before, capturing seven championship belts in seven weight classes.

Boxing in general was also going down unique pathways with the rise of so-called influencer boxing—fights between social media "stars" from YouTube and TikTok among other platforms pitted against each or combat sports figures, often on legitimate boxing cards. Two of the most successful in this new genre of boxing were Logan Paul and his brother Jake Paul, with Logan fighting Floyd Mayweather Jr. in June 2021, live on Showtime PPV—and selling over a million buys, something mainstream boxing would have salivated over. Flush with the success of the fight card, Showtime was looking for another opportunity.

Jake Paul had set himself up to call the shots for a PPV bout scheduled for August 29, 2021. Among other things, he wanted to put a women's bout on the card, and as noted by Michael Rothstein in his insightful article on how the Taylor–Serrano fight was made, he quoted Showtime's president, Stephen Espinoza, as saying, "The name we immediately suggested was Amanda and he immediately agreed. It was a short conversation."[8]

Serrano, claiming her payday was the most in her career, fought Mexican super bantam titlist Yamileth Mercado (18–2, 3-KOs), who'd jumped up in weight to take the bout and without risk to her own title. Serrano was able to dominate Mercado throughout with her usual flair, winning on all three score cards. That aside, what was memorable about the outing were two things. The first was the relationship she began to forge with Jake Paul training alongside him in Puerto Rico as they worked to get ready for their respective bouts.

The second was in her postfight interview when she said, "I want that fight with Katie Taylor in the future. First I want to fight the other featherweight champions and become undisputed in my weight class. Then we'll have two undisputed champions against each other when Katie and I fight."[9]

Her next move was to leave her longtime promoter, Lou DiBella, to join Jake Paul's new Most Valuable Promotions (MVP) company, which he'd formed with Nakisa Didarian, the former chief financial officer for the UFC. Speaking of signing with MVP, Serrano said, "They're such a powerful team. I've seen what they've done in the last two years—what Jake has done, what Nakisa has done for Jake. I'm looking forward to what they can do for me."

The signing also marked a turning point in the potential for a fight date with Katie Taylor, with a stated goal of matching Serrano and Taylor and making note that discussions were underway with Taylor's promoter, Eddie Hearn, targeting a "second quarter fight at New York's Madison Square Garden."[10]

With a lot of back and forth, and with Taylor and Serrano both having fights at the end of 2021, the stage was set for the final agreement to meet Serrano's bottom line—a seven-figure payday or nothing.

For Eddie Hearn, it was what he and Taylor had dreamed of all those years ago when they started their journey together: the best fighting the best, headlining on the biggest stages. He'd also been working hard with DAZN to bring them in as the broadcast partner, and with MSG, going all in offering up the main arena, a history-making first for women's boxing.

There were, however, still the naysayers. As Hearn put it, "When we announced this fight there were a lot of people snickering and a lot of laughing about going to the main room at the Garden and when they see what they're going to see on April 30, it's going to feel really sweet because everything we believed in will come true."[11]

Top Rank's Bob Arum was particularly critical, saying, "As good a fight as that is—come on. You know, whatever reason it is, people don't particularly pay attention to the women's fights, . . . I don't want to denigrate fights, I don't want to be accused of being anti-women in sports, but I'm telling you, this is like the Premier League against women's football."[12]

Called out for being a dinosaur by a very vocal Jake Paul, the preparations for the fight continued with the arena being set up to accommodate twenty thousand fans. As fight day came closer, such women's boxing royalty as International Boxing Hall of Fame inductees Christy Martin, Layla Ali, and Marian "Lady Tyger" Trimiar were scheduled to attend.

MSG even went so far as to offer Trimiar seats in a box to accommodate her wheelchair, their way of honoring the 1970s trailblazer.

The fight card itself also added a second unification bout between Franchon Crews-Dezurn (7–1, 2-KOs) and Swedish title holder Elin Cederroos (8–0, 4-KOs), with each putting two championship belts on the line, in a winner-takes-all battle for the undisputed crown at super middle. Both had also been signed by Matchroom Boxing in anticipation of placing their twice-canceled battle due to the pandemic, on the biggest boxing platform of their careers. Asked about the opportunity, Cruz-Dezurn said, "I really don't [want to] talk, I'm just going to bring that action for the main attraction and get everything I deserve. It's about legacy and survival so I appreciate Eddie Hearn, Matchroom, DAZN and [my manager] Peter Kahn for making this happen. It's my time to live up to my own expectations."

Cederroos added, "I have been ready for this fight for a long time now. I am grateful that Matchroom and DAZN has given us the opportunity to make it real. . . . Hopefully I will be able to show my true power. We come from the land of the ice and snow."[13]

A third female bout was added as the opener, a six-rounder between the Australian Olympian Skye Nicolson (2–0), who sported an impressive 107–32 amateur record, versus Shanecqua Paisley Davis (3–1), a virtual boxing novice from Houston, Texas.

The day of the fight on April 30 had been bright, with a high temperature of 65 degrees Fahrenheit—making it a lovely spring day in New York City. Fans didn't mind milling outside on the corner of 30th Street and 8th Avenue waiting to be let into their seats—with some fans dressed to be seen, costumed for the pomp and circumstance of a major fight at the Garden. Inside, the arena started to fill up with cheering fans periodically illuminated by flashing arcs of green light. Fans were sporting Irish and Puerto Rican flags in anticipation of the main event and excited to the point of tears later in the evening as the song "Sweet Caroline" started to play; the crowd swept up with excitement, having learned the girl from Bray and the girl from Carolina had indeed sold out the Mecca of boxing.

Trimiar, watching from her majestic box above as the stands began to fill, said in a wistful tone, "One million dollars for each fighter. I never earned much more than a thousand dollars, and that was for a title fight."[14]

With the preliminaries over, including Crews-Dezurn's win and entry to the undisputed club with her points dominance over Cederroos, all was by turns hushed and frenetic in anticipation of the ring walks of the two women.

The arena was also jolted through with the enchantment that is an event that transcends its time and place. Becoming already immortal. Engrained in the consciousness of those in attendance as something special.

Both women had let their personalities shine through as they exited the tunnel into the arena. Amanda Serrano was full of sass and strength and pride as she bounced from foot to foot, her gloved hands clapping together to the roaring crowd as she entered the ring, but still taking a moment to turn inward and gather herself before her great, beaming aura shone through.

Katie Taylor's entry was more cerebral. She walked slowly, taking her time, gazing out at the crowd as they started to cheer, especially when she pumped the air with her fists. Gently nodding to the right and to the left, her face sweated from her prefight warm-up; she savored the moment, and took a beat or two standing on the apron to nod at the fans before turning and ducking under the ropes to enter the ring.

Across the ten rounds of the battle, each woman brought her whole being into the fight. Each member of the audience rising and falling with each feint, each heart-stopping combination of thudding shots, each buckled knee—their hands and feet a study in quickness and efficiency as they worked to impose their will upon each other.

In a fight-of-the-year battle, they boxed in between the shots, in the clinches, at distance and close in, parrying and thrusting, the pair of them demonstrating they were the best fighting the best, with a crowd so loud the veteran Canadian referee Michael Griffin couldn't hear the bell. A few days later he was to say he'd "never felt that kind of electricity."

At the end of the fight, Taylor emerged victorious, earning a split decision on the cards with scores of 96–93, 97–93, 94–96. There were some cries of robbery among the pundits and the fans, but most believed

Taylor had indeed won it—with the consensus overall that the fight was one of the greatest boxing matches in the history of the sport.

Regardless of outcome, its place at the apex of boxing will always be there, just as the magic of the tender smile that passed between Taylor and Serrano in the moments before they fought spoke to the enormity of what they were about to achieve. They were making history in a main-event prize fight between two of the best boxers in the world—who because they happened to be women meant the special sauce of their well-matched contest was also infused with all the opportunities that had been denied in the past. With fights relegated to the unstreamed portions of fight cards, for little money, and far, far less than equal treatment. Here were two warriors of heart and spirit, meeting their moment of greatness, with power, with fortitude, and with grace. Willing by their presence on boxing's biggest stage that they would pay it forward so that others could achieve an equivalent transcendent magnificence.

GREATNESS AT THE O2 ARENA

Boxing had always been filled with rivalries—real and manufactured. It worked well for business, drumming up interest enough to be able to sell tickets or buys on PPV or money payouts for subscriptions to streaming services. Claressa Shields and Savannah Marshall had been nursing theirs since Marshall handed Shields her only loss as an amateur in the run-up to the 2012 Olympic Games.

To set up for the showdown Shields had signed a two-fight promotion deal that had netted her seven figures with BOXXER, who also sported Marshall on their roster of fighters. Pivoting from MMA, where she had earned a 1–1 record to her first love, boxing, she looked to the UK for what would be her best deal. The two-fights would include a "tune-up" championship bout for each fighter, and presuming they both won, a showdown fight carrying as much weight and heft as could be mustered. With delays due to injuries, Ben Shalom had been looking for how best to feature the pair, seeking out a date in the early fall of 2022.

The solution was yet another push to lionize women in the ring. BOXXER, along with broadcasting partners Sky Sports and ESPN, were determined to put on what would have seemed impossible before the Taylor–Serrano fight at Madison Square Garden: an all-female fight card at London's O2 Arena. Headlined by Claressa Shields and Savannah Marshall, the pair put all the middleweight belts on the line for a chance at undisputed glory—and for Shields, a history-making third time wearing the crown, and second at middleweight. Postponed for a month due to the death of Queen Elizabeth, the eleven-fight card was rescheduled for the night of October 15, 2022, in front of a sold-out house of twenty thousand cheering fans.

The success of the Taylor–Serrano fight, which not only sold out the Garden, but gave DAZN some 1.5 million views over the course of the card, had solidified BOXXER's decision to go all in for the all-female card. Even Bob Arum's Top Rank got involved, adding Mikaela Mayer to the bout sheet to further unify the super feather division battling fellow American Alycia Baumgardner. If nothing else, the old fox of boxing promotion admitted that he'd misread the tea leaves prior to Taylor–Serrano and was all in on the O2 Arena event.

Having registered over 2 million views between Sky Sports and ESPN, on top of the sold-out arena, the fight card was enormously successful. Shields dominated Marshall across the fight with her speed and movement, but acknowledged Marshall's enormous power, as she once again stood crowned in achievement by taking the undisputed mantle at middleweight for the second time.

The stunner of the evening was Mikaela Mayer's unification bout with Alycia Baumgardner, losing on the cards by split decision 95–96, 95–96, 97–93. With Baumgardner having surprised Mayer early on with excellent movement in the ring and a series of hard shots, Mayer switched gears in the middle rounds disarming Baumgardner by coming inside. Unperturbed, Bumgardner was able to adjust in the later rounds using her power to great effect. With her win, Baumgardner made it clear that her focus was to become the undisputed super feather champion, thereby closing the door on a rematch with Mayer.

THREE MORE UNDISPUTED CROWNS

The first of the new crop of undisputed warrior women boxers was Chantelle Cameron. With her own IBF and WBC belts, and the vacant WBA and WBO belts on offer, Cameron was slated to battle in a super-fight against Jessica McCaskill on November 5, 2022, in Abu Dhabi. On the undercard of the Dimitri Bivol–Gilberto Ramirez card, the two women fought ten hard rounds. Cameron's prowess and multidimensional fighting abilities won the day, giving her a unanimous decision win, 96–94, 96–94, 97–93, and her shot at boxing history.

Serrano had finally won her undisputed status with a ten-round all-out war against Erika Cruz for supremacy at featherweight at MSG's Little Theater on February 4, the pair having thrown over 1,900 punches in the twenty minutes it took to contest the fight. Cruz, with an enormous gash on her forehead, fought gallantly with the blood at times blinding her but waving off even her own corner to let her continue, on her own terms. The referee, Ricky Gonzalez, sensing that he was witnessing history, let the women fight, checking on Cruz but assessing that the fight could continue. Serrano did not escape unmarked, as both women continued to pummel each other until the closing bell with Serrano winning on the cards, 98–92, 98–92, 97–93.

The co–main fight featured a second undisputed unification bout, which saw Alycia Baumgardner gain supremacy and the coveted undisputed status at super feather over the French fighter, Elhem Mekhaled, who had last battled with Delfine Persoon the previous May in Abu Dhabi.

At the end of the Serrano fight, Katie Taylor came on stage and together with Serrano announced a May 20 rematch in Ireland—a homecoming for Taylor and the first time in her career as a professional that she would have the opportunity to fight at home.[15]

With Serrano postponing her appearance in the fight due to an undisclosed injury at the end of February, Taylor switched gears and entered a conversation with Chantelle Cameron on Twitter, who'd offered herself up as an opponent. Agreeing to fight, the terms called for them to fight for Cameron's belts at super light, where she'd end up being the "B" side even though they'd agreed to fight for her belts. Taylor's homecoming was the culmination of a dream for the people of Ireland. Cameron understood the magnitude and trained away from the fray before their battle commenced. Fighting with heart and skill in their contest, she was able to overpower Taylor, gaining a mixed-decision win that handed Taylor her first defeat as a professional.

It was a shocking loss for Taylor, but as with all things, she took it in stride, admitting to the hurt, but with her abiding faith and sense of purpose as an ambassador for women in the ring. She was gracious in defeat—and agreed to terms for a rematch in the fall. Perhaps an era had ended and begun, but her place in the sport remains undeniable.

SISTERS IN BOXING

In the parallel universe that lives outside of the business of boxing, fighters will sit side by side, feeling genuine affection and gratitude for the opportunity to share the battlefield of the ring. As a sign of mutual respect that went back through their years of their boxing sisterhood, Amanda Serrano and Heather Hardy crossed to the center of the squared circle to face each other one last time on August 5, 2023. Ten rounds later, the bloody, puffy eyelids of Heather Hardy as she bowed to and embraced her victor revealed a truth at the heart of why women box.

Hardy had begun a renaissance of sorts. She'd lost her eight-round lightweight comeback fight in the middle of nowhere, Tennessee, that Lou DiBella had gotten for her in May 2021 even though she'd put her opponent, Jessica Camara, down on the deck in the first round. Hardy admits she was unprepared mentally and physically, having come off her awful pandemic year. She'd spent it hustling for training gigs to keep food on the table for her and her daughter, and by the time she'd gotten the call about the fight, boxing seemed as shrouded in the mist as a foreign country.

Following that loss, it was her closeness to her old trainer, Hector Roca, that started to bring her back. A fixture at Gleason's Gym, Hardy had grown close to the man she called "Papa." She had him work her corner of her winning comeback six-rounder in October at the Sony Theater in New York, promoted by Larry Goldberg in his first outing with his new promotion company, Boxing Insider.

Roca became ill not too long after she won the bout, and though hospitalized and fighting off serious illness, Hardy brightened his days with her visits. He also relished giving her boxing lessons as he sat in a chair in his red-and-black checked robe putting up his hands for Hardy to shadowbox.

Two days before his death, Hardy sat with him in his hospital room. She recalled he said, "Everyone thinks you passed your prime, but I don't think you hit it yet. And I think 2023 is going to be your year."

Speaking about the experience further, she said, "And it just sat with me. So after he passed away, [promoter] Larry [Goldberg] called me and I said, 'I'm going to do the show.' I felt like a second wind, so to speak. Yeah, this can be my year if I make it my year. So here I am."[16]

Hardy went on to win an eight-rounder by majority decision in February 2023, but felt more determined than ever to heed the feeling of grace that came with Roca's words. And so she put it out there. The sense that she had it in her. The chance for one more shot at the brass ring—and then, bold as you please, put out the word that she wanted a rematch with her old friend Amanda Serrano.

And why not? Why not give Hardy the shot? It was, after all, Serrano's undisputed crown, and with the Taylor rematch off until she'd had her rematch with Cameron, and no mandatories banging on her door, it was her fight to offer.

More than the offer to fight, Serrano was offering Hardy something else: the first six-figure paycheck of her life. The kind of thing one Brooklyn girl would do for another. The one from Bushwick and the other from Gerritsen Beach, but having each other's back all through the days of no money fights. Passing the hat of opportunity back and forth. Hardy was the little sister to Amanda and Cindy Serrano who'd started out earlier in the fight game but gave Hardy the chance to spar and learn something. It was Hardy who made the introduction of Serrano to Lou DiBella when magic began to happen at Brooklyn's Barclay's Center, when they could sell tickets in the tens of thousands of dollars for very little money in return, but still got to box and delight their fans.

With the WBO belt firmly in her hand, Hardy had given Serrano the shot to fight her. Serrano was the better fighter, but Hardy had heart in every sinew of her being and was willing to face the loss for a shot at greatness—whether it was for her or her boxing sister. The brass ring, then, was a shot at Katie Taylor, reason enough to put it all on the table.

Loss, pandemic, comeback had been Hardy's path, while Serrano began to find her way to a promised land that had taken all those years of bloody battles for no money.

With the fight signed for and three months of camp, Hardy went to work to get down to featherweight, something she hadn't done since they fought in 2019. The grace kept following her as she shed the pounds and sparred ceaseless rounds with southpaw guys who could mimic Serrano's power in the ring.

The next bit of grace came in the form of comedian Louis CK. He'd known Hardy and, learning that she had to keep working during camp, Hardy recalled he looked at her and said, "Tell me how much to write your check for, I don't want you to work for this last month."[17]

That was in June, which meant for all of July, Hardy could just train. No side hustles. No 6:00 a.m. walks to the gym to meet a client. Just train.

Fight night was the hardest of a lifetime—the alpha and omega moment. Forty-one years of age. Probably in the best shape she'd been for years. Refreshed in mind and spirit, but facing off against a boxing machine, whom she'd promised she'd bang with in the center of the ring—a promise she was honor-bound to keep.

What they both found was a kind of truth.

Serrano was lifting Hardy up to join her on the adventure, which was boxing on the top of the mountain, while Hardy boxed her heart out through pain and a desire to win that pushed her through all the doubts she'd ever had in her life. Losing on the cards, the output in their twenty minutes of war showed she alone had thrown 557 punches to Serrano's 739.

Speaking of Serrano after the fight, Hardy said,

To have her grab my hand and say, "Come on Heat, let me help you, because I know what you went through." It just means everything. I gave everything I had today. I gave everything, for three months. Everything, I have no excuses, that was everything.

As tears stung Hardy's eyes, Serrano leaned in and said, "It shows, it shows. This is why we need to come together, as female boxers that work together. Don't degrade each other, let's work together, and make this beautiful sport of women's boxing, grow together."[18]

Promises Made

Back in 2011, Kaliesha West gave Ava Knight the paycheck in their WBO world bantam match. West was facing the problem of fighting for the title or returning it, but in that moment, she was also lifting Knight up. Giving her a shot at becoming a champion.

That was the moment between Serrano and Hardy. The West and Knight story paid forward. The same way Mary Magee and Claressa Shields had put on cards and made certain that their boxing sisters were a part of it. The way Katie Taylor had embraced Chantelle Cameron as her homecoming partner.

Or perhaps it is in the moments of a Blanca Gutiérrez Beautiful Brawlers show when retired boxers Martha Salazar and Elena Olsen guide their young fighters to live out their dreams of Olympic gold. Or when Sue Fox embraces pioneer boxers who shared the ring with her in the 1970s, giving these remarkable women the recognition they deserve.

What's clear is that the women of boxing have persevered. Bringing each other along through the camaraderie of the gym, and the willingness to push the boundaries of the sport to make it better for the next woman who stands for a moment on the apron of a ring before entering the field of combat. That spirit endures, through hardships and disappointments, but most assuredly as the moments of grace that shine through to make it all seem new again.

NOTES

INTRODUCTION

1. Pierce Egan, *Boxiana: or, Sketches of Ancient and Modern Pugilism*, Vol. 1, 1830 (Reprint London: Elibron Classics), 2005, 300.

2. Christopher Thrasher, "Disappearance: How Shifting Gendered Boundaries Motivated the Removal of Eighteenth Century Boxing Champion Elizabeth Wilkinson from Historical Memory," *Past Imperfect* 12, (2012): 53–68.

3. Malissa Smith, *A History Of Women's Boxing* (Lanham, MD: Rowman & Littlefield, 2014), 35.

4. *New York Clipper*, October 17, 1874, 230, quoted in Smith, *A History of Women's Boxing*, 35.

5. *New York Sun*, February 6, 1876, 1, quoted in Smith, *A History of Women's Boxing*, 36.

6. "Female Boxers," *New York Herald*, March 17, 1876, 3.

7. See "A Female Boxing Match. A Novel and Nonsensical Exhibition at Harry Hill's," *New York Times*, March 17, 1876.

8. It would take until the 2012 Games in London before the sport was seen again in the Olympics and women's boxing was not fully legalized as an amateur sport in the United States until the 1990s.

9. "Myrtle Knocks Out Poor Mabel," *The Evening Standard,"* April 27, 1912, p. 2.

10. "France Has New Champion," *The Washington Herald*, March 6, 1914, p. 4 (Library of Congress).

11. *El Paso Herald*, April 18, 1914, p. 26.

12. *The Aberdeen Evening Express.* November 26, 1918, p. 1 (The British Newspaper Archive).

13. T. S. Andrews, "Prize Fighting Becoming a Favorite Pastime for Women," *El Paso Herald*, July 28, 1914, p. 6 (Library of Congress).

14. Elizabeth Tucker. "Woman Manager Says Boxing Is Best Training," *The Tacoma Times*, October 16, 1917, p. 6 (Library of Congress).

15. Edith E. Moriarity. "As a Woman Thinks," *Tulsa Daily World*, July 31, 1920, p. 6 (Library of Congress). The author further wrote that Dempsey believed women in the future would go to the gym a few times a week to work out. In the opinion of the author, while women might take up "golf, swimming, tennis, basketball, bowling or skating," they would never "go in strong for boxing."

16. Cathy Van Inglin, "Seeing What Frames Our Seeing: Seeking Histories on Early Black Female Boxers," *Journal of Sport History*, Spring 1913, p. 105. See also, "Wields Wicket Left," *The Pittsburg Courier*, October 29, 1928, p. 16; "Emma Maitland in Mexico," *California Eagle*, November 2, 1928, p. 8. While Maitland and Wheeldin were a dancing and boxing act on the Vaudeville circuit, the point of distinction was not only their skill levels, but for Mailtand in particular, what was seemingly her opportunities to participate in real fights during her travels.

17. Cecilia Rassmussen, "1st Woman Boxing Referee Rolled With Punches," *Los Angeles Times*, May 21, 2006, p. B2.

18. A panel in Wonder Woman, Issue #2, states, "But Wonder Woman, moving faster than the eye can follow, knocks the pistol aside and lands a right uppercut on the German's jaw." He goes on to decry, "Awk—Don't hit me! Wait—Ouch!" William Moulton Marston and H. G. Peter, *Wonder Woman*, No. 2, Fall 1942, DC Comics.

19. *Dixie Dugan*, #1, Story by J. P. McEvoy. McNaught. 1942. Cover.

20. Smith, *A History of Women's Boxing*, 82.

21. "Girl Boxer Banned from Public Ring," *Gloucestershire Echo*, January 11, 1949, p. 3, quoted in Smith, *A History of Women's Boxing*, 89.

22. *San Antonio Light*, October 9, 1957, p. 39, quoted in Smith, *A History of Women's Boxing*, 109.

23. "'Boxing' Fem Rasslers Shine," *Abliene Reporter News*, October 5, 1965, p. 11.

24. "On Lawsuits for Licenses: The Fight for Women's Wrestling in New York (long-form)," *Finding Aid*, September 5, 2016. Website. See also, President Lyndon B. Johnson, Executive Order 11375—Amending Executive Order No. 11246, Relating to Equal Employment Opportunity, issued on October 13, 1967.

25. "On Lawsuits for Licenses: The Fight for Women's Wrestling in New York (long-form)," *Finding Aid*, September 5, 2016. Website. See also, President Lyndon B. Johnson, Executive Order 11375—Amending Executive Order No. 11246, Relating to Equal Employment Opportunity, issued on October 13, 1967.

26. Smith, *A History of Women's Boxing*, 128.

27. Jack Newfield, "The Great White Hype," *The Village Voice*, October 9, 1978, pp. 1, 15–16.

28. Lacy J. Banks, "Lady Tyger's Fast Didn't Help Cause," *Chicago Sun Times*, July 27, 1987, p. 114, quoted in Smith, *A History of Women's Boxing*, 190.

29. Smith, *A History of Women's Boxing*, 197–198.

30. Malachy Clerkin, "Deirdre Gogary, a Trailblazer Who Fought Her Corner," *The Irish Times*, March 3, 2016.

31. Christy Martin with Ron Borges, *Fighting for Survival* (Lanham, MD: Rowman & Littlefield, 2022), 113.

32. Mark Sachs, "My Favorite Weekend: Laila Ali," *Los Angeles Times*, August 3, 2006, p. 89.

33. Laila Ali with David Rita, *Reach! Finding Strength, Spirit, and Personal Power* (Hyperion, 2002, She Be Stingin' Inc. Updated 2017), 178.

34. Robert Cassidy, "Ali–Frazier IV a Good Rumble," *Newsday*, June 10, 2001, p. 73.

35. Statistics for the AIBA World Women's Championship events, as available, can be found on the IBA.sport website (as of June 2023).

36. "Female Boxing Denied 08 Olympics," *Boxing Ontario*, November 5, 2005.

37. Smith, *A History of Women's Boxing*, 252.

38. Christopher Clarey, "Women's Boxing Added for 2012 Olympics," *New York Times*, August 13, 2009.

39. Ben Dirs, "Nicola Adams Wins Historic Boxing Gold for Great Britain," BBC, December 5, 2012. Quoted in Smith, *A History of Women's Boxing*, 260.

CHAPTER ONE

1. "Beautiful Brawlers All Female Show," Womensboxing.com (WBAN), August 30, 2012.

2. *The Colbert Report*, Season 8, Episode 158, September 25, 2012.

3. Eric Woodyard, "Claressa Shields' Inaugural Boxing Clinic at Atwood Stadium Draws Small, but Enthusiastic Group," mLIVE, September 15, 2012.

4. Ron Fonger, "Flint's Claressa Shields Joins in Honoring Muhammad Ali with Liberty Medal," mLive, updated September 14, 2012.

5. Kathy Matheson (Associated Press), "Muhammad Ali Receives Liberty Medal in Philly," *The Spokesman-Review*, September 13, 2012.

6. Associated Press, "Off to College, Olympic Boxing Champ Defies Odds," *Deseret News*, August 8, 2013.

7. Franchon Crews currently fights as Franchon Crews-Dezurn and is married to professional boxer, Glenn Dezurn. He has also acted as her coach.

8. "Claressa Shields Leads Junior and Youth Women in to World Championships," *USA Boxing*, September 10, 2013.

9. Alexis L. Loinaz, "Knockout! Olympic Boxer Marlen Esparza To Launch Fashion And Beauty Line," *Enews* (Online), August 15, 2012.

10. Edith Manzanares, "Influential Houston Hispanics: Marlen Esparza, Boxer Turned Scholar," *The Venture*, March 7, 2013.

11. "Order of the British Empire (Civil Division)," *The London Gazette*, Supplement 1, Dec. 29, 2012, p. N24.

12. "Order of the British Empire (Civil Division)," *The London Gazette*, Supplement 1, June 16, 2007, p. B15.

13. "Katie Taylor Wins First Olympic Gold for Ireland," *BBC News*, August 9, 2012.

14. Jim Allen, "Dr. Pepper Aside, Mayer Has a Thirst for Boxing," *The Spokane-Review*, March 22, 2013.

15. Aimee Berg, "Long Road from London to Memphis for Claressa Shields and Marlen Esparza," *ESPN*, October 28, 2015.

16. Ava Wallace, "Marlen Esparza Returns to U.S. Olympic Boxing Trials on a Mission," *USA Today*, October 25, 2015.

17. Greg Beacham, "Army Boxer Naomi Graham Fights Her Way to Olympics for US," Associated Press, Miltary.com, July 7, 2021.

18. Sarah Deming, "Meet the US Women's Boxing Olympic Trials Champions," Stiffjab.com, November 7, 2015.

19. Julie Goldsticker, "Virginia Fuchs, Mikaela Mayer and Claressa Shields Clinch Berths in the Championship Round at the Olympic Trials for Women's Boxing," Womensboxing.com, October 29, 2015.

20. Sarah Deming, "Meet the US Women's Boxing Olympic Trials Champions," Stiffjab.com, November 7, 2015.

21. Karen Rosen, "Claressa Shields Wins Second Olympic Trials; Virginia Fuchs Knocks Off Olympic Medalist Marlen Esparza," TeamUSA.org, October 31, 2015.

22. Sarah Deming, "Meet the US Women's Boxing Olympic Trials Champions," Stiffjab.com, November 7, 2015.

23. Karen Rosen, "Mikaela Mayer Surges Back to Win Olympic Boxing Trials," TeamUSA.org, November 1, 2015.

24. Michael O'Neill, "AMBC Review of Semis and Preview of Finals in Buenos Aires and Yaounde," Womensboxing.com, March 18, 2016.

25. "Mikaela Mayer Qualifies for the Olympic Games on a Gold Medal Day For Team USA," TeamUSA.org, March 19, 2016.

26. Jeff Seidel, "The 'Raw Truth' behind Olympic Boxing Champ Claressa Shields," *Detroit Free Press,* March 26, 2016.

27. David Barron, "Houston's Ginny Fuchs Falls at AIBA Boxing World Championships," Chron.com, May 21, 2016.

28. Andrew Binner, "Ginny Fuchs: Boxing Saved Me from My OCD," Olympics.com, May 13, 2021. Ginny Fuchs has spoken out about her OCD symptoms, which are related to keeping her body clean. This has been particularly challenging for her in the environment of boxing gyms and associated boxing venues.

29. Lynn Rutherford, "Top 4 U.S. Storylines at the Women's World Boxing Championships," TeamUSA.org, May 18, 2016.

30. "From Childhood Abuse to Absolute War with Billy Walsh, Claressa Shields Has Earned This the Hard Way," The42.ie, April 13, 2019.

31. Greg Beracham/Associated Press, "Coach–boxer Conflicts Build Ties," *Press of the Atlantic,* July 28, 2016, p. 22.

32. "From Childhood Abuse to Absolute War with Billy Walsh, Claressa Shields Has Earned This the Hard Way," The42.ie, April 13, 2019.

33. "From Childhood Abuse to Absolute War with Billy Walsh, Claressa Shields Has Earned This the Hard Way," The42.ie, April 13, 2019.

34. "Olympic Boxing: Men to Stop Wearing Protective Headguards," *BBC*, March 1, 2016.

35. Dev Trehan, "Top WBC Boxers Face Two-year Ban If They Fight at Olympics," Sky Sports, June 3, 2016.

36. Jake Hughes, "IBF Joins WBC, Will Punish Professional Boxers If They Compete at the Olympics," *VICE,* June 21, 2016.

37. Owen Gibson, "Rio 2016: Olympic Boxing Tournament Hit by Corruption Allegations," *The Guardian,* August 1, 2016.

38. "Introducing USA Boxing's Captain Virginia Fuchs," TeamUSA.com, July 11, 2016.

39. Greg Becham, The Associated Press, "Mikaela Mayer Found Life Direction in the Ring," *Holland Sentinel,* July 16, 2016.

40. In an investigation into AIBA and allegations of a bribery and fight fixing at the 2016 Rio Games, Professor Bill McLaren issued a report that labeled Katie Taylor's loss to Mira Potkonen as having benefited from the three out of five judge score sheets being considered: "When analysed against the bout sheets of all five judges, [the fight] would have returned a different winner had all five scores had been considered." See *McClaren Independent AIBA Investigation*, September 30, 2021, 101.

41. Alan Baldwin, "Boxing: U.S. Coach Angered by Judging after Mayer Defeat," *Reuters*, August 15, 2016.

42. Kevin Baxter, "Women Winning Fight for Equality in the Olympic Boxing Ring," *Los Angeles Times*, August 15, 2016.

43. Alan Baldwin, "Boxing: U.S. Coach Angered by Judging after Mayer Defeat," *Reuters*, August 15, 2016.

44. Laura Wagner, "Laura Wagner, U.S. Boxer Claressa Shields Is a Gold Medalist Again. Will Her Dominance Ever Pay Off?" Slate.com, August 22, 2016.

45. Zac Cheny-Rice, "Olympic Boxer Claressa Shields Proves Greatness Knows No Gender," mic.com, August 22, 2016.

46. Owen Gibson, "Top Boxing Executive 'Reassigned' after Judging Controversy," *The Guardian*, August 1, 2016.

47. Alan Baldwin, "AIBA Drops Some Referees, Judges after Scoring Controversy," *Reuters*, August 17, 2016.

CHAPTER TWO

1. "Female Slugger," *Jet Magazine*, September 19, 1974, p. 48.

2. Kevin McRae, "Single Mom Heather Hardy Fighting for a Place In Harsh World of Women's Boxing," *Bleacher Report*, May 25, 2015.

3. Lou DiBella, interview with the author, September 16, 2022.

4. *Boxing World Weekly*, "Heather Hardy vs. Mikayla Nebel/Full Fight/Boxing World Weekly," August 2, 2012, Boxing World Weekly, YouTube video, May 4, 2022.

5. "Heather Hardy Interview ahead of Her January 23rd Fight at BB Kings!" Girlboxing.org, January 18, 2013.

6. "An Interview with Shelito Vincent, to Fight on 1/19/2013!" Girlboxing.org, January 15, 2013.

7. Brent Brookhouse, "Shane Mosley: 'Embarrassment' That UFC Shows More Respect to Women than Boxing." *USA Today*, August 18, 2015.

8. "Maureen Shea to Host Female Boxing Reality Show 'Todas Contra Mexico' in Mexico," East Side Boxing, boxing247.com, March 1, 2011.

9. Alex Williams, "Smile When You Call Her a Diva," *New York Times*, March 23, 2011, NP.

10. Jelena Mrdjenovich vs. Melissa Hernandez II (WBC Women's World Feather Title Bout), Forum de Boxe de Montreal, Dailymotion, September 9, 2014.

11. Jose Santiago, "Inside Punch: Melissa Hernandez vs. Nicole Woods," YouTube video, March 19, 2015.

12. "Jelena Mrdjenovich vs. Melissa Hernandez III [WBC Women's World Feather Title Bout], Diana Kate," YouTube video, May 31, 2013.

13. Thomas Gerbasi, "The Unseen Trilogy of Layla McCarter and Melissa Hernandez," *The Ring*, November 18, 2014.
14. David A. Avila, "Layla McCarter vs Melissa Hernandez in Alabama," *The Sweet Science*, July 15, 2016.
15. "Cecelia Braekhus to Fight Ivana Habazin for Four Major World Titles," Womensboxing.com (WBAN), August 13, 2014.
16. Nadarajah Sethurupan, "Norway Ends 33-year Ban on Professional Boxing," *Norway News*, May 15, 2016.
17. International Boxing Hall of Fame, Induction Requirement, IWBHF.com.
18. Sue Fox, interview with Malissa Smith, April 23, 2023.
19. It should be noted, the author is a member of the IWBHF Board and acts in the capacity of historian/public speaker.
20. "IWBHF Event July 10, 2014," Talkinboxing, YouTube video.
21. "Christy Martin International Womens Boxing Hall of Fame Induction 7/10/2014," BillyCBoxing, YouTube video.
22. Sue Fox, interview with Malissa Smith, April 23, 2023.

Chapter Three

1. Michael Rosenthal, "Martinez Comes from a Rich Boxing Tradition in Argentina," ringtv.com, April 14, 2023.
2. Cesar R. Torres, "Sporting Violence in Argentina during the Interwar Years: The Cases of Boxing and Fencing," *Estudios Interdiscipilinarios de America Latina y el Caribe* 31, no. 2 (July 2020), 17.
3. Diego Morilla, interview with Malissa Smith, May 19, 2023.
4. Irene Deserti and Yesica Palmetta, interview with Malissa Smith, May 5, 2023.
5. Diego Morilla, interview with Malissa Smith, May 19, 2023.
6. "Mazatlán's Famous Feminist: La Maya," VidaMaz.com, May 4, 2018.
7. Marjolein Van Bavel, "The Commission Knocked Out Cold: Laura Serrano and the End of the Mexico City Prohibition of Women's Boxing in the 1990s," *Gender & History*, May 2022, pp. 1–18.
8. *El Proceso*, May 8, 1995, pp. 61–63, quoted in, Marjolein Van Bavel, "The Commission Knocked Out Cold: Laura Serrano and the End of the Mexico City Prohibition of Women's Boxing in the 1990s," *Gender & History*, May 2022, pp. 1–18. (Translation provided by Marjolein Van Bavel.)
9. Laura Serrano García, La Poeta Del Ring, in *9 Estampas de Mujeres Mexicanas*, Mexico City, DEMAC, 2009, 484–485, quoted in Marjolein Van Bavel, "The Commission Knocked Out Cold: Laura Serrano and the End of the Mexico City Prohibition of Women's Boxing in the 1990s," *Gender & History*, May 2022, pp. 1–18. (Translation provided by Marjolein Van Bavel.)
10. AP, "Ban on Female Fights Is Lifted," *New York Times*," April 16, 1998, p. C7.
11. Hortensia Moreno, "Women Boxers and Nationalism in Mexico," en Héctor Fernández L'Hoeste, Robert McKee Irwin y Juan Poblete, Sports and Nationalism in Latin/o America, 2015: Palgrave Macmillan, New Directions in Latino American Culture, pp. 181–200.

12. Yuriko Miyata, interview with Malissa Smith, May 19, 2023.

13. "Olympic Boxing Champ Irie to Pursue Passion for Frogs in Grad School," *Kyodo News*, September 2, 2022.

14. James Hadfield, "Shô Miyake's 'Small, Slow but Steady' Brings Audiences into a Silent Ring," *The Japan Times*, December 9, 2022.

CHAPTER FOUR

1. Dan Rafael, "Claressa Shields to Face Franchon Crews in First Pro Fight," *ESPN*, November 3, 2016.

2. Detroit Brawl, "Claressa Shields versus Franchon Crews Full Fight [11/19/2016]," Detroit Brawl, YouTube video, March 29, 2022.

3. Bryan Armen Graham, "Olympic Boxing Champion Claressa Shields Wins Her Professional Debut," *The Guardian*, November 20, 2016.

4. Claudia Trejos, Claressa Shields versus Franchon Crews post-fight commentary, *ESPN*, November 19, 2016.

5. Bryan Armen Graham, "Olympic Boxing Champion Claressa Shields Wins Her Professional Debut," *The Guardian*, November 20, 2016.

6. "Katie Taylor Signs with Matchroom Boxing," *Boxingnews24.com*, October 27, 2023.

7. Johnny Watterson, "Katie Taylor Ready to 'Break Down Barriers' ahead of Pro Debut," *The Irish Times*, November 23, 2016.

8. "Katie Taylor Documentary Undisputed a Fighter's Tale," Just4Fun, YouTube video, August 12, 2019.

9. The Archive, "Katie Taylor vs. Karina Kopinska (Pro Debut—Full Fight) [November 23, 2016]," Matchroom Boxing, YouTube video, July 26, 2019.

10. Marlen Esparza [@Marlen112Boxing], "I am going pro. We will be announcing soon" [Tweet], Twitter.

11. "Golden Boy Promotions Signs Olympic Gold Medalist Marlen Esparza to Multiyear Deal," Roundbyroundboxing.com, December 14, 2016.

12. "Esparza Launches Pro Career with Multi-Year Golden Boy Promotions Deal," Hispanicallyyours.com, December 15, 2016.

13. Gabriel Montoya, "Olympian Marlen Esparza on Her March 23 Pro Debut w/ Golden Boy, Virgil Hunter & More," The Ring Digital, YouTube video, March 21, 2017.

14. Tom Hopkinson, "Nicola Adams out to Rule Boxing Like Her Hero Muhammad Ali as She Prepares for Pro Debut," *Mirror*, March 5, 2017, updated, March 15, 2017.

15. Gabriel Montoya, "Olympian Marlen Esparza on Her March 23 Pro Debut w/ Golden Boy, Virgil Hunter & More," The Ring Digital, YouTube video, March 21, 2017.

16. Frank Warren, "Frank Warren Column: It Is Nicola Adams' Time to Shine for Women's Boxing," *The Star*, April 8, 2017.

17. Nick Parkinson, "Nicola Adams Cruises to Victory over Virginia Carcamo on Pro Debut," *ESPN*, April 8, 2017.

18. "Natasha Jonas: 'Katie Was the Reason I Could Turn Pro. When I Said Goodbye to the Amateurs, I Was Saying Goodbye Forever,'" Fightpost.co.uk., April 10, 2022.

19. Sonny Donnelly, "Natasha Jonas on Why She's Turning Professional, Talking Joe Gallagher / Steve Goodwin & Katie Taylor," IFL TV, YouTube video, April 12, 2017.

20. PA Sport, "London 2012 Olympic Boxer Natasha Jonas Turns Professional," *ESPN*, June 20, 2017.

21. AP, "US Olympic Boxer Mikaela Mayer Turns Pro with Top Rank," *USA Today*, July 14, 2017.

22. AP, "US Olympic Boxer Mikaela Mayer Dominates Her Pro Debut," *USA Today*, August 5, 2017.

23. Kugan Cassius, "Savannah Marshall on Why She Turned Pro with Floyd Mayweather / & Relishes a Claressa Shields Clash," IFL TV, YouTube video, May 18, 2017.

24. Luke Brown, "Savanah Marshall Kicks Off the Floyd Mayweather vs Conor McGregor Undercard with Debut Win," Independent.co.uk, August 27, 2017.

25. Kal Saljad, "WBO Champion Savannah Marshall on Why Trainer Peter Fury Has Been So Instrumental to Her Success," *BBC*, April 1, 2022.

26. Gabriel Montoya, "Olympian Marlen Esparza on Her March 23 Pro Debut w/ Golden Boy, Virgil Hunter & More," The Ring Digital, YouTube video, March 21, 2017.

27. "Amanda Serrano v. Yazmin Rivas—Official Weigh In & Face Off Video (From Brooklyn New York)," IFL TV, YouTube video, January 13, 2017.

28. Katie Richcreek, "Amanda Serrano's Win Marks Return of Nationally Televised Women's Boxing," *ESPN*, January 14, 2017.

29. Dan Rafael, "Amanda Serrano Makes History, Earns Title in 5th Weight Division," *ESPN*, April 22, 2017.

30. Michael Woods, "Heather Hardy Wins Broadway Boxing Main Event, Heads to MMA," NYFights.com, May 19, 2017.

31. "Heather Hardy on Why She Went to MMA Over Pay Frustration—MMA Fighting," MMA Fighting on SBN, YouTube video, June 21, 2017.

32. Helen Yee, "Boxing Champ Layla McCarter Shocked by Rousey: Amanda Nunes and Holly Holm Made the Point for Me," Helen Yee Sports, YouTube video, January 4, 2017.

33. Ted Kulfan, "Claressa Shields KOs Nikki Adler, Wins Two Title Belts," *The Detroit News*, August 5, 2017.

CHAPTER FIVE

1. Kurt Streeter, "A Surprise in the Ring," *Los Angeles Times*, July 10, 2005.

2. Kurt Streeter, "I Gave Up on Boxing, Not on This Boxer," *New York Times*, August 3, 2023.

3. Round By Round Boxing, "Seniesa Estrada Signs with Golden Boy Promotions," Roundbyroundboxing.com, January 12, 2018.

4. Michele Chong, "Future 'Golden Girl' Seniesa Estrada," Myboxingfans.com, November 22, 2010.

5. WBN, "Seniesa Estrada Headline Golden Boy's March 16 LA Fight Club," Worldboxingnews.com, February 15, 2018.

6. Jorge Castillo, "'Look Where She's at Now.' How Boxer Seniesa Estrada Became the Role Model She Never Had," *Los Angeles Times*, March 23, 2023.

7. Alex Solano, "Women's Boxing Is Part of Gennady Golovkin's Forum Card," *Los Angeles Times*, April 22, 2016.

8. Eric Ramos, "Seniesa Estrada Wins Her Golden Boy Debut," Roundbyroundboxing.com, March 17, 2018.

9. Marlen Esparza [@Marlen112Boxing], "Finally!!! Everyone, I will be fighting 3min rounds no more 2min!! . . ." [Tweet] Twitter, April 28, 2017.

10. Marlen Esparza [@Marlen112Boxing], "Finally!!! ITS TIME! Im excited and ready to announce Ill be fightin 3min rounds like the men! . . ." [Tweet] Twitter, April 28, 2017.

11. Bob Velin, "Marlen Esparza, Fighting 3-minute Rounds, Wins Decision vs. Samantha Salazar," *USA Today*, May 6, 2017.

12. Marlen Esparza [@Marlen112Boxing], "I got the W tonight boxing 6*3 min rounds . . ." [Tweet] Twitter, September 16, 2017.

13. As stated in code section 18720 of the SCAC Laws and Regulations Manual, "(a) No boxing contest or match shall be more than 12 rounds of not more than three minutes each in length. . . ." The statute does not reference gender. It should also be noted that prior to Esparza's December 2017 bout, heavyweights Martha Salazar and Sonya Lamonakis fought in a main-event six-round, three-minute-per-round contest at the Lions Gate Convention Center in Sacramento, California, on April 13, 2018. See *Laws & Regulations: Guidelines and Policies for Officials, CSAC Laws and Regulations Manual,* DCA.CA.gov/CSAC/Stats_regs, September 2018, 10.

14. Kevin Iole, "Cecilia Braekhus Putting Belts on the Line in HBOs First Women's Boxing Match," *Yahoo News*, May 1, 2018.

15. Katie Barnes, "Cecilia Braekhus on HBO Fight: 'We Want to Put on a Big Show,'" *ESPN*, May 3, 2018.

16. Dan Rafael, "Welterweight Champion Cecilia Braekhus Will be Part of First Women's Bout Televised on HBO," *ESPN*, April 26, 2018.

17. Kieran Mulvaney, "One-on-One: Cecilia Braekhus," HBOBoxing, YouTube video, May 3, 2018.

18. "Cecilia Braekhus Makes History as the BWAA's First Female Fighter of the Year," *Boxing Writers Association of America*, bwaa.org.

19. "Cecilia Braekhus Wins Female Fighter of Year," ESNEWS, *YouTube video*, May 12, 2018.

20. Heather Hardy, interview with Malissa Smith, September 30, 2022.

21. "Shelly Vincent: Fighting for the Positive," Girlboxing.org, October 25, 2018.

22. Heather Hardy, interview with Malissa Smith, September 30, 2022.

23. Mike Coppinger, "HBO Close Curtain on Boxing with Uninspired Show Topped by Cecilia Braekhus' Win," *The Ring*, ringtv.com, December 8, 2018.

24. Greg Beacham, "Wave of the Future: Women's Boxing Headlines HBO's Last Show," apnews.com, December 7, 2018.

25. "Estrada, Shields, Braekhus Post-fight Comments," fightnews.com, December 10, 2018.

26. Ryan Songalia, "Katie Taylor Shuts Out Eva Wahlström in Garden Debut, Retains Lightweight Belts," *The Ring*, ringtv.com, December 15, 2018.

CHAPTER SIX

1. Jake Chaney, "All That Glitters Is Not Gold. Why Cecilia Braekhus Must Beat Layla McCarter to Be the True Lineal Champion at 147lbs," Linealboxingchampion.com, June 8, 2019.

2. Michael Woods, "A Deeper Look Into Christina Hammer," *The Ring*, ringtv.com, May 14, 2018.

3. Kevin Iole, "Claressa Shields, Christina Hammer to Battle for Undisputed Middleweight Title on April 13," Yahoo News, YahooFebruary 12, 2019.

4. Doug Fischer, "Ratings Update: Inaugural Ring Women's Title on the Line in Shields–Hammer Showdown," *The Ring*, ringtv.com, February 22, 2019.

5. Brian Campbell, "Claressa Shields vs. Christina Hammer Fight Prediction, Fight Time, Odds, Watch Showtime Boxing, Live Stream," CBS Sports, April 13, 2019.

6. Dan Rafael, "Shields Beats Up Hammer, Wins Undisputed Title," *ESPN*, April 13, 2019.

7. Brayn Armen Graham, "Katie Taylor Unifies Lightweight Titles with Ninth-round TKO of Rose Volante—as It Happened," *The Guardian*, May 16, 2019.

8. Luke Reddy, "Katie Taylor v. Delfine Persoon: 'This Might Just Be the Women's Boxing Match We Have Waited For,'" *BBC Sport*, BBCMay 31, 2019.

9. Lance Pugmire, "Women's Lightweight Champion Will Return to Police after Title Fight against Katie Taylor," *Los Angeles Times*, May 29, 2019.

10. Brayn Armen Graham, "Katie Taylor Becomes Undisputed Champion in Epic Scrap with Define Persoon," *The Guardian*, June 2, 2019.

11. Michael Rosenthal, "Heather Hardy Tests Positive for Banned Diuretic: Report," *Boxing Junkie*, October 3, 2019.

12. Hans Themistode, "Heather Hardy Clears Her Name in Failed Drug Test Allegations," *Boxing Insider*, December 17, 2019.

13. Lance Pugmire, "Former Boxer Mia St. John Admits Using PEDs in Wake of Alvarez–Golovkin Controversy," *Los Angeles Times*, August 11, 2018.

14. Michael Woods, "Mia St. John Discusses Controversial PEDs Tweet, Drug Use in Boxing," *SB Nation Bad Left Hook*, August 15, 2018.

15. Greg Levinsky, "Claressa Shields to Fight for Another World Championship in August in Flint," *Detroit Free Press*, June 11, 2019.

16. Brendan Savage, "Claressa Shields, Scoffs at Claim Ivana Habazin Will KO Her Oct. 5 in Flint," mLIVE, September 20, 2019.

17. Brendan Savage, "Claressa Shields–Ivana Habazin Weigh-ins Erupt in Melee, Trainer Leaves in Smbulance," mLIVE, October 4, 2019, updated February 12, 2020.

18. Michael Benson [@MichaelBensonn], "Claressa Shields gives her side of the story after opponent Ivana Habazin's coach was sucker-punched at their weigh-in today. Shields still wants the fight to go ahead: 'Her name is Ivana "No Excuses," so I'm hoping we don't have none.'" [Tweet] Twitter, October 4, 2019. The tweet included a copy of live video of Claressa Shields addressing her fans on Twitter.

19. Noah Trister, AP, "Claressa Shields Issues Statement on Incident That Canceled Her Title Fight in Flint," *Yahoo*, October 5, 2019.
20. News from Ivana Habazin, October 5, 2018, "With deep regret my trainer James Ali Bashir was punched in the back of his neck by someone in Shields entourage," Facebook.
21. Roberto Acosta, "Police Seek Arrest Warrant for Assault at Claressa Shields' Weigh-in," mLIVE, October 7, 2019; updated October 8, 2019.
22. Press release, "Claressa Shields vs. Ivana Habazin Rescheduled," *Frontproof Media*, November 17, 2019.
23. Dan Rafael, "Claressa Shields Beats Ivan Habazin for Junior Middleweight Title," *ESPN*, January 11, 2020.
24. Ed Brophy, interview with Malissa Smith, September 12, 2023.
25. Amendments to Voting Process, Adopted by IBHOF Board of Directors—April 2019, *International Boxing Hall of Fame*, ibhof.com. As a point of full disclosure, I am a founding member of the screening committee and a voter for the two women's category. As a screening committee member, I am charged with reviewing the eligibility of fighters for inclusion on the list of candidates for the annual election cycle.
26. Ed Brophy, interview with Malissa Smith, September 12, 2023.

CHAPTER SEVEN

1. "Mary McGee vs. Deanha Hobbs/Linardatou vs. Vicot Presser Quotes," Boxing-news24.com, February 6, 2020.
2. Felipe Leon, "Brian Cohen and Female Prizefighting Champions," *The Prizefighters*, tpf.ib.tv, February 23, 2023.
3. In early 2009, it was alleged that Roger Mayweather, the famed uncle and trainer of boxer Floyd Mayweather, struck St. Vil several times in the ribs before choking her nearly to death. The incident was said to have taken place in the apartment she rented from him along with another fighter. St. Vil had come to the Mayweather gym in Las Vegas to train and had been out there for eight months or so. He was eventually charged with two felony battery charges in 2011. Shortly before a scheduled court date, Mayweather struck a deal with the prosecutor allowing him to plea "no contest" to two misdemeanor counts of battery, payment of a small fine, and community service. St. Vil was plagued for some time afterwards as "the Mayweather girl" before she was finally able to step past it.
4. Boxing Insider, "Melissa Hernandez Says Fight Against Mikaela Mayer on March 17 Will Be a Good Win," boxinginsider.com, YouTube video, March 4, 2020.
5. Julia Hollingsworth et al., "March 4 Coronavirus News," *CNN*, March 4, 2020.
6. Johnny Stapleton, "Michael Conlan's St Patrick's Day Fight Card Cancelled," Irish-boxing.com, March 13, 2020.
7. Michael Rothstein, "How a 'Bubble' in Las Vegas Became the Solution for Top Rank and Boxing's Return," *ESPN*, June 8, 2020.
8. Matt Traub, "Case Study: How Top Rank Created a Boxing Bubble," *Sports Travel Magazine*, July 13, 2020.
9. Rothstein, "How a 'Bubble' in Las Vegas Became the Solution for Top Rank and Boxing's Return," *ESPN*, June 8, 2020.

10. Michael Rothstein, "Mikaela Mayer Won't Fight in Top Rank Card after Positive Coronavirus Test," *ESPN*, June 7, 2020.

11. "Helen Joseph, the Iron Lady—Getting Ready to Rumble," Girlboxing.org, October 27, 2019.

12. Jake Donavan, "Abel Sanchez: Been a Pleasure Working with Braekhus This Camp, She Is Really Special," Boxingscene.com, August 12, 2020.

13. Scott Christ, "McCaskill Wins Debatable Decision, Ends Cecilia Braekhus' 11-year Ttle Reign," *badlefthook.com*, August 16, 2020.

14. Seconds Out, "Katie Taylor Admits: Amanda Serrano the BIGGER PROFILE, but Persoon Rematch a HARDER FIGHT," Seconds Out, YouTube video, August 19, 2020.

15. Mark Lelinwalla, "Katie Taylor vs. Delfine Persoon 2 Results: Taylor Grinds Out Unanimous Decision," Dazn.com, August 22, 2020.

16. Matchroom Boxing, "AND STILL! Katie Taylor Reacts to Fight Camp Win over Delfine Persoon," Matchroom Boxing, YouTube video, August 22, 2020.

17. Peter Hoffman, "The Fight Fan with Pete Hoffman: Heather Hardy," WFAN Sports Radio, Radio.com Sports, Peter Hoffman, YouTube video, February 5, 2021.

18. Damon Martin, "Claressa Shields Explains Why She Joined PFL over UFC and Her Frustrations with the Current State of Boxing," *MMA Fighting*, December 15, 2020.

19. Mark Taffet, interview with author, August 30, 2023.

20. Seconds Out, "Katie Taylor Admits: Amanda Serrano the BIGGER PROFILE, but Persoon Rematch a HARDER FIGHT," Seconds Out, YouTube video, August 19, 2020.

CHAPTER EIGHT

1. See the Association of Boxing Commissions and Combative Sports website, abc-boxing.com. Note that under the Unified Rules tab, several updated rules are listed with hyperlinks to the documentation. The Unified Rules tab does not, however, include links to any rules for female boxing. That could only be found using the Google search engine with the key words, "female unified rules of boxing." This pointed me to the Association of Boxing Commissions, Female Rules hyperlink, but as noted, the rules do not include a date of adoption, nor do they include an amendment date.

2. See 15 USC Ch. 89, Professional Boxing Safety from Title 15—Commerce and Trade, uscode.house.gov.

3. In 2017, Representative Markwayne Mullen (R-Okla.) introduced the Muhammad Ali Expansion Act, to incorporate Mixed Martial Arts and other combat sports into the rules. It also called on the ABC to establish minimum contract guidelines, and guidelines for "objective and consistent" ratings. One of the focuses of the expanded rules was the addition of conflict of interest provisions to create a greater financial firewall between promoters and managers to better protect the fighters. The bill met with resistance from the MMA industry and was not passed.

4. See New York Codes, Rules and Regulations, Title 19, Chapter VII, Part 211—Special Rules for Professional Boxing, dos.ny.gov.

Notes

5. Dan Rafael, "New Jersey Board Gives Option of 3-minute Rounds to Women," *ESPN*, April 17, 2017.

6. Inside *The Ring* with Rebecca Ruber, "SENIESA SUPERBAD ESTRADA WANTS 3 MINUTE ROUNDS! TENKAI TSUNAMI DECLINES 3 MIN ROUND OFFER," Inside *The Ring* with Rebecca Ruber, YouTube video, July 7, 2021.

7. Michael Rothstein, "More Time, More Opportunity: Are Three-minute Rounds Coming to Women's Boxing?" *The Ring*, ringtv.com, July 8, 2021.

8. "Three Minute Rounds for Female Boxing in New York State," Girlboxing.org, May 10, 2015.

9. As of June 22, 2023, the International Olympic Commission withdrew recognition of the International Boxing Association (IBA—formally known as AIBA) in accordance with Rule 3.7 of the Olympic Charter (OC). The IOC Executive Committee based its decision on the ICO Comprehensive Report issued earlier in June. The twenty-four-page report examined long-standing issues with respect to governance and other matters including what it perceived as the lack of progress of AIBA's successor organization, IBA, in meeting its obligations, and the lifting of the suspension of the organization to run the Olympic qualifying events and competitions at the 2024 Paris Games. What this portends for the future is unknown, as the IOC stated that "As an additional consequence of the above decision, the IOC Session has decided that the IBA will not organize the Olympic Games LA28 boxing tournament." See "IOC Session Withdraws Recognition of International Boxing Association," June 22, 2023, olympics.com. The link to the IOC Comprehensive Report on the Situation of the International Boxing Association (IBA—formerly known as AIBA) is included in the IOC statement.

10. "Christina Cruz: 'I Walked into the Gym That First Time and Immediately Fell in Love with the Sport,'" Fight Post: Boxing and MMA News, fightpost.co.uk, January 10, 2023.

11. Amanda Levine, "After Olympic Success, Oshae Jones Turning Sight to Pro Boxing Ranks," The Blade, toledoblade.com, May 22, 2022.

12. Boxing News, "WBC Convention Review/Mauricio Suláiman & Rob Tebbutt in Acapulco," Boxing News, YouTube video, November 14, 2022.

13. M. Bianco, N. Sanna, S. Bucari, C. Fabiano, V. Palmieri, and P. Zeppilli, "Female Boxing in Italy: 2002–2007 Report," *British Journal of Sports Medicine* 45, no. 7 (June 2011): 563–570.

14. P. McCrory et al. (2009), "Consensus Statement on Concussion in Sport: The 3rd International Conference on Concussion in Sport Held in Zurich, November 2008," *Journal of Athletic Training* 44, no. 4 (2008): 434–448.

15. Kimberly G. Harmon, MD, et al., "American Medical Society for Sports Medicine Position Statement: Concussion in Sport," *Clinical Journal of Sports Medicine* 23 (2013): 1–18.

16. N. K. McGroarty et al., "Sport-Related Concussion in Female Athletes: A Systematic Review," *Orthopaedic Journal of Sports Medicine*, Vol. 8, Issue 7, July 2020, NP.

17. T. Mollayeva, G. El-Khechen-Richandi, and A. Colantonio, "Sex & Gender Considerations in Concussion Research," *Concussion* 3, no. 1, March 2018, NP.

18. James E. Clark and Emily Sirois, "The Possible Role of Hydration in Concussions and Long-term Symptoms of Concussion for Athletes. A Review of the Evidence," *Journal of Concussion* 4: 1–15.

19. E. Magraken, "Sexism or Science? WBC Championship Rules," combatsportslaw.com, May 2, 2021.

20. Michael Rothstein, "Serrano–Ramos Women's Title Bout Set for 12 three-minute Rounds," *ABC News*, September 6, 2023.

21. Lou DiBella, interview with author, September 16, 2022.

22. "Three Minute Rounds for Female Boxing in New York State," Girlboxing.org, May 10, 2015.

23. "IBF Rules Governing Female, USBA, Intercontinental and Regional Championship Contests, Posted and Effective: April 19, 2017," International Boxing Federation, www.ibf-usba-boxing.com.

24. Chrissy Chaos, "Heather Hardy Talks about the Corruption of Combat Sports," chrisdcomedy, YouTube video, July 31, 2023.

25. See "WBO Female Regulations of World Championship Contests" and "WBO Regulations of World Championship Contest," wboboxing.com.

26. See "Rules of World Boxing Association (Asociacion Mundial de Boxeo), Last Amendments made on December 12, 2022," wbaboxing.com.

27. See "Rules & Regulations of the World Boxing Council (as Amended Per Approval of the WBC Board of Governors, May 15, 2019)," wbcboxing.com.

28. "Historic Win for Women's Equality in Sports/Equal Pay for Equal Work Coming to Team USA as Cantwell–Capito Bill Heads to President's Desk," U.S. Senate Committee on Commerce, Science, & Transportation, commerce.senate.gov, December 21, 2022.

29. Ryan Songalia, "New Yorkers Sonya Lamonakis, Bruce Silverglade Get Their Spot in Women's Hall," *The Ring*, ringtv.com, August 30, 2023.

30. Michael Rothstein, "Serrano–Ramos Women's Title Bout Set for 12 three-minute Rounds," *ABC News*, September 6, 2023.

31. Michael Rothstein, "More Time, More Opportunity: Are Three-minute Rounds Coming to Women's Boxing?" *The Ring*, ringtv.com, July 8, 2021.

32. Alexander Netherton, "Should Women Fight 12 Three-minute Rounds like Men?" Dazn.com, March 12, 2022.

33. @olivia_thepredator_gerula, "Honestly, in my opinion it comes down to pay. The majority of women train & Spar 3min rds . . ." Reply to, @WomensFightNews1, "Thoughts on 2 or 3 minute rounds?" instagram.com, September 3, 2023.

34. Mark Taffet, interview with author, September 21, 2022.

CHAPTER NINE

1. Steve Kim, "Alejandra Jimenez Fails Drug Test, Putting Super Middleweight Titles in Doubt," *ESPN*, January 24, 2020.

2. "WBO World Championship Committee Resolution Regarding WBO Female Participant Alejandra Jimenez," wboboxing.com, March 17, 2020.

3. Greg Beacham, "American Olympian Boxer Ginny Fuchs Cleared of Doping Violation Caused by Sex," The Associated Press, cba.ca, June 13, 2020.

4. Arley Muciño had been stripped of her WBO title in July 2019 when she was unable to mount a defense due to an injury sustained in a car accident. She regained her champion status in October 2022 when she defeated Leonela Paola Yudica to gain the IBF world fly title.

5. Salita Promotions, "Claressa Shields vs Marie Dicaire on March 5, Live PPV Stream!" *Boxing News 24/7*, February 28, 2021.

6. "How Claressa Shields Beat Marie-Eve Dicaire for the 154-Pound Championship," *New York Times*, March 5, 2021. See also, "Analysis: Shields Had an Answer for Dicaire's Every Move."

7. Jenny Morrison and Chiara Pollock, "Boxer Who 'Touched Death' after Glasgow Match to Become a Mum," GlasgowLive, glasgowlive.co.uk, May 12, 2023. See also, Crail Scott, "Alejandra Ayala Is Awake: Now What," Boxing Social, May 27, 2022. In the article, writer Crail Scott discussed an MRI finding in 2018 following Ayala's fight with Marshall that was alleged to show a 3mm brain tumor. A Mexican outlet had contended the British Boxing Board of Control contacted the Federation of Professional Boxing Commissions of the Mexican Republic. The story remains unconfirmed.

8. Michael Rothstein, "How Katie Taylor vs. Amanda Serrano Fight Was Made and What It Means for Boxing," *ESPN*, April 12, 2022.

9. Damon Martin, "Paul vs. Woodley Results: Amanda Serrano Outclasses Yamileth Mercado to Win Lopsided Decision in Co-main," MMA Fighing, August 29, 2021.

10. Michael Rothstein, "Amanda Serrano Signs with Jake Paul's Most Valuable Promotions," *ESPN*, April 30, 2021.

11. Michael Rothstein, "How Katie Taylor vs. Amanda Serrano Fight Was Made and What It Means for Boxing," *ESPN*, April 12, 2022.

12. iFLTV, "Bob Arum Reacts to Fury v Whyte $41M Pursde Bid Win!/& Squashes Hearn's 'Untrue' Claims about Fury," iFLTV, YouTube video, January 29, 2022.

13. Daniel Yanofsky, "Matchroom Secures Future of Women's Boxing with Franchon Crews-Dezurn, Elin Ceederoos Match Up, Signings," *The Sporting News*, January 6, 2022.

14. "Katie, Amanda, Lady Tyger, and Me," Girlboxing.org, May 6, 2022.

15. In 2015, a major feud broke out in Dublin, Ireland, between the Kinahan and Hutch criminal organizations. With four deaths credited to the feud in 2015, a shooting at the Regency Hotel in Whitehall, Dublin, escalated the already rising tensions. Armed with AK-47s, several assailants stormed the area where the Kavanaugh–Berto weigh-in was underway for their European lightweight bout, resulting in one death and two injuries. With the fight canceled, professional boxing came to a halt as the two gangs continued their bloody feud and trail of murder victims. After years of investigation, the Kinahan crime organization's leadership, including boxing figure Daniel Kinahan, were sanctioned by the Irish Criminal Assets Bureau, and the United States Office of Foreign Assets Control, among others. It was judged that with appropriate security in place, it would be safe for Katie Taylor to have her homecoming fight in Ireland—a first for her professional career.

16. Thomas Gerbasi, "Heather Hardy: I Believe I Deserve a Shot at One of Those World Titles," Boxingscene.com, February 15, 2023.

17. Chrissy Chaos, "Heather Hardy Talks about the Corruption of Combat Sports," chrisdcomedy, YouTube video, July 31, 2023.

18. MVP, Most Valuable Promotions, "An Emotional Moment between Amanda Serrano and Heather Hardy. Heather's a Warrior," @Most_Valuable_Promotions, YouTube video, August 3, 2023.

Index

ABOUT THE AUTHOR

Malissa Smith is the author of *A History of Women's Boxing*, the first comprehensive narrative of the sport that *The Ring* magazine dubbed "The Bible of Women's Boxing." Smith maintains positions in boxing as a founding board member of the International Women's Boxing Hall of Fame, is on the women's boxing screening committee for the International Boxing Hall of Fame, and serves on *The Ring*'s women's ratings panel. Smith also speaks and writes frequently about the sport. Maintaining her own wellness, she trains at the world-renowned Gleason's Gym in Brooklyn, New York.

Milton Keynes UK
Ingram Content Group UK Ltd.
UKHW020647210724
445703UK00002B/24